CLASSIC WALKS IN
Scotland

by Cameron McNeish & Roger Smith

The Oxford Illustrated Press

© 1988, Cameron McNeish, Roger Smith and Peter Evans
as credited

ISBN 0 946609 51 9

Published by:
The Oxford Illustrated Press Limited, Haynes Publishing
Group, Sparkford, Nr Yeovil, Somerset BA22 7JJ, England.
Haynes Publications Inc., 861 Lawrence Drive, Newbury
Park, California 91320, USA.

Printed in England by:
J.H. Haynes & Co Limited, Sparkford, Nr Yeovil,
Somerset.

British Library Cataloguing in Publication Data
McNeish, Cameron
Classic walks in Scotland.— (Classic
walks series).
1. Scotland – Walkers' guides
I. Title   II. Smith, Roger, *1938–*
914.11'04858
ISBN 0-946609-51-9

Library of Congress Catalog Card Number
88-081063

CONTENTS

INTRODUCTION

For all its vast land area, Scotland has only ten per cent of the population of Britain, and as most of those are crowded into the central belt between Edinburgh and Glasgow it takes little imagination to realise the extent of the hill and loch country beyond.

One lifetime is scarcely sufficient to even begin scratching the surface of what Scotland has to offer the walker. One can spend many years exploring the same range of hills, climbing them from different directions, at different times of the year, and in different weather conditions and still find a different type of pleasure and satisfaction on every walk.

Our aim in producing this book has been to introduce what we believe to be the classic Scottish walking routes, both low and high-level. Many of the walks described are very popular, others less so, and we have tried for a good variety of strenuous and easy ones to suit a wide range of ability and experience.

Each walk includes a map but neither these nor the walk descriptions are intended to do more than give the reader an outline of the possibilities. You should always have the appropriate Ordnance Survey (OS) map with you. Knowing how to read a map and how to use a compass are vital skills and will add immeasurably to your scope and enjoyment.

Please note that the walks described are for summer conditions, unless it specifically says otherwise. Many of the walks described become serious mountaineering expeditions in winter conditions, and should only be undertaken by those with the appropriate experience.

Wherever you are in Scotland, you are not far from good walking country, and whether your taste is for coasts, lochs, glens or the high tops, you will find something to interest you here.

The Scottish Tradition

People have walked the hills of Scotland since time immemorial. Most of the roads we take for granted nowadays were laid down less than 200 years ago. Before that it was tracks or nothing. Shepherds, drovers and lairds alike walked if they needed to travel, or at best rode hardy ponies.

The remembrance of this long tradition of pedestrianism persists strongly today, and is one reason perhaps why the parallel tradition of free access to the hills is jealously guarded, and why many Scottish mountaineers feel that the waymarked path and the cairned trail are very much out of keeping with tradition.

After the roads came the surveyors and the scientists, and among them we can number the first of the great hill walkers: men like James Robertson, an Edinburgh botanist who covered many of the major hill ranges in the 1770s.

Despite the efforts of Robertson and his ilk, and of the early ordnance surveyors, no mean walkers themselves, the topography of Scotland was a mystery to most people and up to the end of the nineteenth century the general belief was that there were at the most 50 mountains higher than 3000ft (914m). The man who put an end to that misconception was Sir Hugh Munro of Lindertis, founder member and third President of the Scottish Mountaineering Club.

In 1891 he brought out his *Tables of Heights over 3000 Feet'*, listing not 50 but close to 300 mountains, some perhaps never ascended. The list appeared in the second edition of the SMC Journal and it has been available and argued about in some form ever since. The first fully metric version appeared in 1981.

The man gave his name to the hills he loved and listed, and the 276 3000-footers have been known as Munros ever since. He never succeeded in climbing them all himself; he left Carn Cloich Mhuilin in the Cairngorms to last, as it was an easy hill and ponies could carry the celebratory food and drink, but the Inaccessible Pinnacle, a rocky spire in the Cuillin of Skye, defeated him several times.

The first Munroist was the Rev. A.E. Robertson in 1901. The list now numbers over 500 and several walkers have completed all the Munros in one single expedition, even in winter conditions.

Munro-bagging can be anything from a lifetime's incidental pastime to a fierce passion, but in its purest form it is a reflection of the joy of visiting unknown country and being granted the privilege of free access to magnificent hill country. It isn't necessary to ascend a single Munro to gain great pleasure from walking in Scotland but it is, we would suggest, necessary to appreciate how fortunate we are to have this

A party of well-equipped backpackers on the Moine Mhor, The Great Moss, en route to Braeriach. (Photo: Cameron McNeish)

splendour of 'the land of the mountain and the flood' to wander in, and to respect those few restrictions which may apply at certain times of the year and which are detailed later in this introduction.

Rights of Way and Access

The situation regarding rights of way is not the same in Scotland as it is in England and Wales. For most practical purposes we believe it is better, and the visiting walker should at least be aware of the differences.

A right of way in Scotland can be defined as a route between places of public resort for which use over a continuous period of 20 years can be proved. After that the right stays until disuse over a similar period can be shown, when the right is deemed to have lapsed. Partly because there is less purely agricultural land, there are no definitive maps showing rights of way for each region or administrative district as there are in England and Wales. The nearest to such maps is the set kept within the offices of the Scottish Rights of Way Society, a body which has kept a close eye on rights of way and has defended them for well over 100 years. You are bound to come across their distinctive metal signposts if you walk in Scotland for any period of time. Some District Councils also keep sets of maps showing rights of way.

The Society has published maps showing rights of way in some areas, and the two-volume work by D.G. Moir, *Scottish Hill Tracks,* is also useful. Basically if a clear track exists from one place to another, it can be taken to be a right of way, though there has been some dispute as to whether mountain summits can be defined as places of public resort! Certainly on fine weekends many of them are!

There have been battles over classic rights of way in Scotland just as there have been elsewhere. One of the most famous was the battle of Glen Tilt in 1847 when the Duke of Atholl tried to prevent Professor John Balfour and a party from Edinburgh using this great through route. After a considerable scandal the Duke lost the court case, and this superb route from Blair Atholl to Aviemore is open to this day.

You'll find many walks along rights of way described in this book of classic walks; others are easy to work out using the appropriate OS map.

Off the rights of way in open country, there is, generally speaking, little restriction to access. As we have said there is a great tradition of free wandering or stravaiging in Scotland and this is generally maintained today. In the lambing season, from March to

May, and while stalking is in progress, from August to October, some areas may be closed to access. Information should be sought locally at these times and the restriction respected, particularly for stalking which is a prime source of income in many Highland estates. The police and estate factors will generally be able to offer you advice or recommend alternative routes that you can take.

Quite large areas of Scotland are under the aegis of the National Trust for Scotland, the Nature Conservancy Council and the Forestry Commission. Access is again given freely and added interest can be gained from calling at the visitors' or information centres to be found at some of these places.

We couldn't finish this section without mentioning Scotland's abundance of drove roads and military roads. In the second half of the eighteenth century English ordnance surveyors, notably General Wade and his successor Caulfeild, planned and had made the first network of roads in the Highlands; primarily to ease the task of the army in keeping the rebellious clans in order.

Many of these old roads are now hill tracks and offer splendid walking on good surfaces, and you can find them marked as old military roads or 'General Wade Roads' on maps. The Corrieyairack Pass from Laggan to Fort Augustus is a good example.

Drove roads are less often marked as such but their route can be traced with the aid of books and some are described here, a notable example being the route from Peebles to Craig Douglas in the Borders. The Glen Tilt right of way was also a drover's road.

Climate and Weather

It has often been said that we in Britain don't have a climate, only weather. In Scotland the saying is if anything even more true. We have known still December days when it was possible to bask in the sun at summit cairns, and June days when it snowed a blizzard. Winter often comes early and stays late, and summer occasionally brings fierce heat. Only one thing is certain. You can't predict with any accuracy what the weather is likely to be, so you must always be prepared for change.

The best, or at least the most settled weather is usually to be found in the spring; April, May and June can bring long sunny periods and magnificent walking conditions with perhaps the last traces of winter snow on the tops and the trees bursting with new life in the glens. This is a great time for exploring, for wildlife, for simply being outside.

In some years spring is a very relative term, and there seems to be hardly any transition period between winter and summer, but May is probably our favourite month in Scotland, another distinct advantage being that the midge has not yet appeared on the scene.

The summer months from June to August are blessed with very long hours of daylight, and in the far north it hardly gets dark at all at midsummer. This gives the walker the chance to capture two magic times of the day with a very early start or a late finish; sunrises and sunsets, perhaps especially on the west coast and among the islands, are unparalleled.

Around June the midge does emerge and this little pest bites happily away until the autumn chill chases him away again. He can be, to say the least, an absolute nuisance, but he is just something that has to be put up with; don't let him spoil your holiday. Insect repellent will help, and a mosquito net on your tent door is vital.

Overall the summer months show a rather changeable pattern with long settled periods the exception rather than the rule but this very aspect of the weather brings its own rewards in sunshine after rain, hills glimpsed through shower clouds, rainbows and the feeling of being granted something very special when you do get a good spell.

Autumn is an incredible time. The magic is different from the magic of spring, because the days are growing shorter rather than longer, but it's a season to make the most of; crisp clear days with perhaps a dusting of snow on the mountains and all the glory of the flaming bracken and autumn colouring on the trees lower down. When you have the two together, snowy tops and golden glens, the effect is indescribably beautiful and makes all the effort of reaching your chosen viewpoint so worthwhile. Even if you don't aim high, the vistas are still there and in the glens you will be bombarded by the primeval sound of rutting stags.

Autumn days end differently from spring ones; they close down with a suddenness and a finality that makes a homecoming to a fire and a dram or two all the more welcome. This is a time when most of the visitors have gone, a time ideally suited to the walker.

Right up to November there can be days when the warmth lingers, when the air is clear and the views enormous. Eventually, in recent years sooner rather than later, the last vestige of the warmer season goes and, perhaps with the ending of summer time, we are into a different type of walking altogether.

For five months the days are short and ambitions have to be tempered accordingly. This is really a time for only the experienced to attempt the longer or harder walks. Winter has

its own rewards, of course, and facing the elements and meeting the challenge is hugely satisfying. Those establishments that do remain open are usually wise to the ways of the winter walker, and know how to deal with us, our appetites, and our wet gear!

Each season has its blessings and its drawbacks; know that and plan accordingly and you will get the most from your walking in Scotland.

Gear and Safety

Comparison of the seasons and their delights lead us naturally to consider the equipment necessary for walking in Scotland, particularly in the hills.

The climate in Scotland is fickle and severe conditions can be met at any time of the year, especially at higher altitudes. For the reader who only intends walking the shorter low-level routes all that is really needed is a pair of reliable lightweight walking boots and reasonable protection from wind and rain.

There are many brands of lightweight boots on the market nowadays, most of them requiring very little effort to break in. Many walkers too are quite happy just to wear a pair of good trainers on low-level walks and we believe it is fair to say that a good pair of trainers are superior to the cheaper walking boots in terms of comfort and support.

Socks are, if anything, just as important as boots. Ill-fitting or worn socks can be agonising and ruin a walking holiday on the first day. Wool socks are probably best.

In rainwear you only get what you pay for. Better quality jackets and overtrousers will offer good wind resistance, a vital point for those who intend walking the higher-level routes. There is little doubt that Gore-Tex laminated suits are still the best for water resistance combined with breathability. There have been many other attempts to match the quality of Gore-Tex but no one has even come near it yet.

Remember too that the extremities, heads and hands, lose heat more rapidly than other parts of the body. Even in the summer it is unwise to go into the hills without a woolly hat of some description and a pair of mitts. They weigh very little and can offer tremendous comfort if you become chilly.

Mountain Safety

The safety aspect really only presents itself on higher-level excursions. If you are confining your walking to the straths and glens and stick to the tracks you are less likely to get into serious difficulties.

So much well-meaning advice is thrown at

A less experienced walker, attempting a serious mountain walk such as this one over Aonach Beag, should take a companion and be well versed in navigation techniques. (Photo: Hamish Brown)

us walkers in the name of safety that we often wonder if it is safe to go out at all! The hills should, of course, be respected at all times, and it's as well to know the guidelines for safe walking, and what to do if things go wrong, before you venture onto high ground.

What may seem a balmy day in the glen can turn out rather differently on the tops. Temperature decreases rapidly with height as a rule, and winds increase. Never be afraid to turn back if you don't feel happy. There's always another day, and the hills will still be there.

The item in the Mountain Code that perhaps causes most problems is the one that says 'never go alone'. Many people are of the opinion that solo wandering is the best kind, and in many ways the only way to gain real mountain experience, but for the less experienced walker it does make sense to go with a companion, perhaps someone a bit more experienced than yourself.

If you are going alone into the mountains, try to leave word of your route and likely time of return with someone, your family, your accommodation, or if necessary the police, so that if you are seriously delayed the alarm will be raised. This may sound rather dramatic but it is surely better than getting into difficulties without anyone knowing where you might be.

Scotland is blessed with a most willing and efficient mountain rescue service, made up largely of volunteers. We hope you'll never have to call on their skill, but if they are needed simply ring 999 and ask for the police. Tell them you need the mountain rescue team, and give them as many details as you possibly can about the person in difficulty, where he or she is if you know that or where the most likely area to search is if you don't know the exact location, and anything else that could be considered as helpful—what colour of clothes he or she is wearing for example.

One of the most important aspects of safe travel in the mountains is the ability to use a map and compass. If you don't know how to use them—learn, it could save your life. If you don't have this simple skill, and you take off on a high-level walk and experience low cloud or mist, then you will probably become lost.

We sincerely hope that the possibilities outlined in this book will enable you to enjoy the best of walking in Scotland according to your needs and experience, and to increase that experience by coming back time and time again. Do it gradually and you'll be more likely to do it safely.

Long Distance Paths

Long distance paths in Scotland divide into two categories; those officially designated and grant-aided by the Countryside Commission and those established by other bodies such as local authorities, clubs and individuals.

There are at least 100 such routes in England and Wales of which about 15 are official. The enthusiasm for such routes has never been felt in Scotland, the tradition here being much more of the wanderer working out his or her route and adapting it to circumstances and whim as he or she proceeds. However, the Countryside Commission for Scotland has designated three long distance paths in Scotland; the West Highland Way from Glasgow to Fort William, the Southern Upland Way from Portpatrick in Galloway to St. Abbs Head in Berwickshire and the Speyside Way from Speymouth in Morayshire to Glenmore in Inverness-shire.

Of these three routes only the West Highland Way could be described as anything approaching a 'classic' walk, but it is so severely eroded due to the tremendous numbers of walkers that we find it hard to recommend. The official long distance footpath concept has never been fully accepted by a great number of Scottish walkers and it is hoped that the Countryside Commission for Scotland won't plan any more.

Transport

Scotland is well served by public transport, except in the most remote areas, and has well-made roads. The roads have improved considerably in the past twenty years or so—surfaces are better, some of the worst bends and gradients have been eased and the motorway network in central Scotland is complete, allowing rapid passage to the gateways to the Highlands at Stirling and Perth.

Further north and west, even A-class roads may be single track with passing places, but they are generally well maintained and provided you accept the slower pace they invite you to take will open up the whole country to you.

For the non-motorist or for those who prefer to leave their cars behind, there is still a good rail network. The best of both worlds can perhaps be gained by taking the motorail to Perth, Stirling or Inverness before starting your driving, or by travelling by plane and hiring a car in Scotland for the duration of your holidays.

Rail lines penetrate to the west coast at Mallaig, Fort William and Kyle of Lochalsh— all rather special journeys well worth taking in their own right. The West Highland Line has a strong and proud tradition and taking the train to one of those great wee stations like

Lochailort, Corrour, Morar or Lairg gets any walking holiday off to a great start. The journey up the east coast to Aberdeen is also a fine one and the one furthest north of all, to Wick, has a quite unique flavour.

Air travel is also well developed. There are regular flights from the south to Glasgow, Edinburgh, Aberdeen and Inverness and a complex network within Scotland and to all the principal islands.

Most people going to the islands however, prefer to use the more traditional means of travel, the ferry boats, and the name of Caledonian MacBrayne, the principal operators, is familiar everywhere. Ferries operate throughout the year on many routes with extra services in the summer linking with the rail lines, so that you can travel by train to Oban or Mallaig and thence by steamer to the Hebrides. Many of the ferries—to Arran, Mull and Skye for example—take cars.

The bus network still survives in reasonably good shape both locally and long distance. You can travel from Glasgow or Edinburgh to Inverness, Aberdeen or Fort William by bus, and at a very local level, the postbus has become an accepted part of the transport system.

Indeed postbuses operate to the most unlikely places, Cape Wrath for one! A timetable is issued and details of how to obtain it are available from most post offices.

Accommodation

Scotland is well served by the tourist industry so accommodation is rarely a problem, from the five star Gleneagles variety to simple bothy accommodation. Prior planning will pay dividends.

The tradition of Scottish hospitality is very much alive and all the Scottish hotels and guest-houses, especially in the remoter areas, are keen to offer *ceud mile failte,* a hundred thousand welcomes.

Towns and larger villages offer a range of accommodation to suit all pockets and the many tourist information centres open throughout the summer operate a very useful bed booking service; they know what is available and will do their best to find something to suit your needs. Self-catering accommodation in cottages, chalets and caravans is also widespread and the relevant Scottish Tourist Board publications give all the details you will need.

There are perhaps fewer well-equipped camp sites in Scotland than one would like, but it is not an ideal world, and if an organised site is not available, an informal pitch on a farm can often be found. There is generally very little restriction on wild camping except during the lambing and stalking seasons, which is only sensible.

The Scottish Youth Hostels Association has a chain of eighty hostels throughout Scotland and the islands, and for a modest membership fee you can avail yourself of their facilities. They make ideal bases for walking holidays.

Sources of Information

Scottish Tourist Board, 23 Ravelston Terrace, Edinburgh, EH4 3EU (031 332 2433). London Office 5/6 Pall Mall East, SW1 (01 930 8661/2/3).

The STB publish a wide range of brochures and timetables including *Where to Stay in Scotland, Self Catering Accommodation in Scotland,* and *Scotland for Hillwalking.* A publication list and order form are available on request.

Regional tourist bodies are worth contacting in advance of your visit, as they can often supply more detailed information on a particular area:

Borders Regional Council, Tourism Dept, Newtown St. Boswells, Roxburghshire (083 52 3301)

Dumfries and Galloway Tourist Association, Douglas House, Newton Stewart, Kirkudbrightshire (0671 2549).

Lothian Regional Council, Dept of Recreation and Tourism, 40 Torphichen Street, Edinburgh EH3 8JJ (031 229 9292).

Strathclyde Regional Council, Dept. of Leisure and Recreation, Viceroy House, India Street, Glasgow (041 204 2900)

Fife Tourist Authority, Fife House, North Street, Glenrothes, Fife (0592 75441).

Central Regional Council, Tourism Department, Viewforth, Stirling (0786 3111).

Tayside Regional Council, Dept of Recreation and Tourism, Tayside House, 26/28 Crichton Street, Dundee DD1 3RD (0382 23281).

Grampian Regional Council, Tourism Department, Woodmill House, Ashgrove Road West, Aberdeen AB9 2LU (0224 682222).

Highlands and Islands Development Board, Bridge House, 27 Bank Street, Inverness IV1 1QR (0463 34171).

Transport Enquiries

Getting Around the Highlands and Islands published and updated annually by the Highlands and Islands Development Board (address above) is invaluable to the traveller in Scotland; it lists all routes by rail, by sea, by air

A bothy such as Culra Lodge bothy on the Dalwhinnie to Fort William walk, is a welcome sight at the end of a hard day's walking. (Photo: Cameron McNeish)

and by bus. For other information contact one of the offices below.

British Airways, 85, Buchanan Street, Glasgow G1 3HQ (041 332 9666).

British Caledonian Airways, 127 Buchanan Street, Glasgow G1 2JA (041 332 1681).

Loganair, St. Andrews Drive, Glasgow Airport, Abbotsinch, Glasgow (041 889 3181).

British Rail, Buchanan House, 58 Port Dundas Road, Glasgow G4 0HG (041 221 3223); or any main line station.

Scottish Omnibuses, Bus Station, St. Andrews Square, Edinburgh (031 556 8231).

Scottish Postal Board, Operations Division (Postbuses), West Port House, 102, West Port, Edinburgh EH3 9HS.

Caledonian MacBrayne, The Pier, Gourock, Renfrewshire PA19 1QP (0475 33755).

Western Ferries, Kennacraig, West Lock Tarbert, Argyll PA 29 6XS (088 073 271/2).

P & O Ferries, Jamieson's Quay, Aberdeen (0224 572615) (for services to the Orkneys and Shetlands).

Gaelic Names

Most of Scotland's mountains—and lochs, castles and villages— have very beautiful descriptive and evocative Gaelic names. It is a difficult language to come to grips with, but the effort is well worth making, at least to learn some of the basic root words, if only so that you know why there are so many Ben Mores about!

Many of the mountain names are given in the text of the book with their Gaelic names beside them and the brief key listed here will hopefully help you decipher some of the others. This isn't an exhaustive list by any means, but it should help a little with the more common names.

Aber: River mouth
Abhain: river (pronounced *aven*)
Allt: stream
Aonach: ridge
Ard: height, promontory
Ban: white
Bealach: pass
Beg or **beag:** small
Ben, bheinn, beinn: mountain, hill
Breac, vrackie: speckled
Cairn, carn: hill
Creag: crag, rock
Dearg: red (pronounced *jerak*)
Druim, drum: high land
Dubh: dark or black (pronounced *doo*)
Eilein: island (pronounced *ellan*)
Fionne; fionn, fyne: white or shining (pronounced *feen*)

Garbh: rough (pronounced, *garve*)
Inver: mouth
Knoc: knoll, hillock
Lairig: pass
Liath: grey
Linn or **Linnhe:** pool
Meall or **mheall:** round hill
Mor, mhor, more: big
Na, nam an: the, of, of the
Ru, rhu, rua: point
Sgurr: peak
Stob: peak
Strath: a broad valley
Tarbet or tarbert: isthmus, neck
Uaine: green (pronounced *ooina*)
Uamh: cave (pronounced *ooav*)

The Mountain Code

1. Respect private property and keep to paths when going through estates and farmland. Avoid climbing walls or fences, and close any gate you have to open. Leave no litter.

2. In the lambing season (March—May) and the stalking season (mid-August to late October) enquire from local keepers, farmers or estate factors (or the police) before going onto the hills.

3. In forests keep to paths. Do not smoke or light fires. Avoid damaging young trees.

4. Plan your route with care, taking into account the experience and fitness of all the members of the party, and both prevailing and likely weather conditions. Allow plenty of time.

5. Be properly equipped for the season, and take adequate food.

6. Leave a note with a responsible person, giving your route and likely time of return, names of the party, etc.

7. Don't be afraid to turn back if conditions deteriorate or you find your expedition over-stretching you. There is always another day.

8. Be particularly careful on descents, especially if the route is unfamiliar to you. If it is easier to do so, go down by your route of ascent.

9. In the event of an accident requiring a rescue team, one person should stay with the injured walker or climber while one or two go for help. If there are only two in the party, the injured person should be left with all spare clothing and food while the other goes for help. To reach mountain rescue teams, dial 999 and ask for the police.

PEEBLES TO MOFFAT (Borders Region)
by Roger Smith

Distance: 35 miles (56 km).
Ascent: 6200ft (1890m).
Start/Finish: Start in Peebles. Finish in Moffat.
Maps: OS 1:50,000 Sheets 73, 78 and 79.
Summary: Hill paths, minor roads, some open hill. Generally reasonable going on grass, some peaty ground. Main ascents come at the start of each day, with nothing too severe. Some forest walking involved.
Points of Interest: Long traverse of historic Border country with fine old towns at start and finish. Superb empty hills to walk through and over. A very satisfying walk.

Looking from Peat Hill to Loch of the Lowes and St Mary's Loch. (Photo: K. Andrews)

I had the pleasure of living in Peebles for a time when I first moved up to Scotland, and I revelled in the joy of discovering the magnificent hill country around the town. The area to the south, a vast upland expanse stretching for many miles down towards the Border, is particularly fine, and it is a part of this country that this walk explores.

It does not, perhaps, take the more usual and more direct route from Peebles to Moffat, a south-westerly traverse by Broad Law, Loch Skeen and Hart Fell. Instead it takes a slightly more circuitous route starting on a southerly line and swinging west on the second day. This is a walk that will occupy two full and happy days, and give the option of a fine camp in the hills or a stay at a historic inn.

The walk has the additional advantage of starting and finishing in splendid and historic Border towns. Although Peebles is a considerable way from the actual England–Scotland march, it has a definite Border feel to it, perhaps because it stands on the Tweed, the most truly Border river of them all. Certainly there is an authentic fortification at Neidpath, a mile or so west of the town, which should be on every visitor's agenda. On a crag high above the Tweed is a fifteenth century stronghold with walls 12ft thick. It was adapted to serve as a dwelling house in the seventeenth century and is very well preserved. The castle is open to visitors from Easter to October.

Peebles itself has been beautifully described by Nigel Tranter as 'the comfortable, sonsy and still good-looking matron of the Borderland'. The main street is broad and characterful and modern housing development has been largely confined to the area across the Tweed to the south. It is in this direction that our walk starts, over the fine bridge and along the road leading to Glen Sax.

Day One

At the road end do not take the lane going right towards Glen Sax but go straight on along a sometimes muddy track through what is known locally as the fairy glen. A footbridge leads over a burn and up a steep bank, whereupon the scene opens out remarkably. It is also remarkable to consider that you are on part of an old droving route, along which vast herds of cattle were driven on their way to the markets of the south.

A little higher up the hill the drystone dykes delineating the former width of the drove can both be seen: they are a considerable way apart. Pause here and think of the effort involved in getting beasts the long distances to market. Although Peebles had an excellent bridge over the Tweed, it had a toll on it and about half a mile to its west, in what is now Hay Lodge Park, is the Cow Ford through which the beasts could be crossed without fee.

The clear path ascends steadily to Kailzie Hill, where the west and highest edge of the extensive Cardrona Forest is met. The hill views are beginning to open up now, and you can rejoice at the thought of the long miles of pleasure ahead. Below is lovely Glen Sax, a fine walk in its own right.

Keep on the highest ground all the way over Birkscairn Hill and Stake Law. I once had a very strange encounter up here. I had pulled up from Glen Sax—a tough enough climb for

The Drove Road, Kailzie Hill. The walls show the width of the road. (Photo: Roger Smith)

anyone—and as I puffed over the final few feet ready to rest by the old dyke I saw an owl flying just above me. I thought it was a little unusual to find an owl at this level, but maybe it had come out of the forest below.

However, I soon began to wonder if the bird had either a nest or young nearby, for it would not leave me alone. It flew round me at a distance of no more than ten feet from my head, making several circles—in complete silence, which added to the strangeness of the encounter. I was clearly unwelcome, so I did the decent thing and left, upon which the bird flew off down the slope toward Glenshiel to the south-east. Its mastery of the air was total and I felt very humbled by the experience.

The next short rise after Stake Law leads you to Dun Rig, at 2435ft (742m) the high point of the day. It's worth a pause for that alone, but the view, which I sincerely hope you will get to the full, would stop anyone. It seems the whole Border country is spread out before you. Away to the east the triple tops of the Eildon Hills are unmistakable. It is said that these were originally one hill, and were cloven in three by a wizard.

To the south-west can be seen the radio station on the summit of Broad Law, at 2723ft (830m) the highest of this group of hills. Northward is the valley of the Tweed and beyond it yet more hills, declining in height as they run out towards Edinburgh and the plain of the Forth Estuary. It is a great panorama and a reminder that by no means all the finest hills are north of the Highland Line.

Most of the day's climbing is now done. It is always good to get the tough part done first, and be able to enjoy the afternoon and evening with the knowledge that you have the main ascents behind you. A big climb late in the day when you have a heavy pack can assume a significance far beyond its actual effort and can have a psychological effect on you for hours, marring the enjoyment of what is actually around you. It is very difficult to dismiss such thoughts, especially when you are out on your own.

From the trig pillar on Dun Rig an old boundary marches south-west down a clear ridge. Take this route until flatter ground is reached. On the left you will see the trees surrounding the former steading at Glenshiel Banks—a beautiful spot and an ideal campsite, though reached much too early for our purposes. It was in fact used as the overnight camp on the Karrimor International Mountain Marathon in 1978. The camp was quite a sight with dozens of small tents and people busy sorting out their gear and making plans for the second day of the competition.

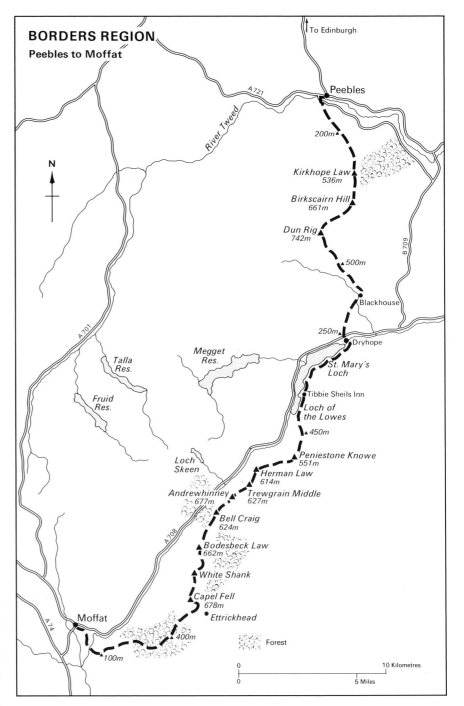

Go over Whiteknowe Head and drop down into the small glen between Bught Rig and Brakehope Rig, where a path leads on to meet the track by Douglas Burn. Turn left and follow this track for half a mile or so to Blackhouse, with its tower. This was formerly a well-populated area, one of the homes of the Douglas family, the hereditary Keepers of the Ettrick Forest, where the Kings of Scotland came for hunting.

Those were turbulent times, as is evidenced

Map to show the 35-mile walk from Peebles to Moffat—a long traverse in historic border country with fine old towns at the start and finish. Superb empty hills to walk through and over.

by the number of fortified towers around: there are at least six within a very few miles, almost one to every glen. Blackhouse Tower is the setting for the tale known as the Douglas Tragedy. The fair daughter of the house, Margaret, had fallen in love with a handsome young man named only as Lord William. It is clear that he was from a different family and was unacceptable to the Douglases as a suitor.

Margaret and William were left with no option but to elope, and that they did, pursued by her father and no fewer than seven Douglas brothers. The fight that ensued must have been worth seeing, for according to the story William slew all eight Douglas men: there are reputed to be seven stones on the hillside marking the spot where the brothers fell, their father apparently not getting such a memorial.

William and Margaret rode off to St Mary's Loch where they rested, and the lady became aware that her lover was sore wounded. He tried to make light of it saying, 'tis nothing but the shadows of my scarlet cloak, that shines on the water sae plain.' They carried on to his home where he succumbed to his wounds and she, broken-hearted, died beside him. They were buried at the chapel of St Mary that gives the loch its name.

That loch is our next target. To reach it do not carry on down the Douglas Burn but cross the burn and strike over the hill to the south-west. This is now part of the Southern Upland Way footpath and is waymarked accordingly. After about a mile and a half the path joins the track coming down the Dryhope Burn to Dryhope itself, where there is another tower.

Cross the A708 and carry on over the bridge spanning the Yarrow Water, the outflow from lovely St Mary's Loch. Follow the track along the south side of the loch (still on the Southern Upland Way) past the farmstead of Bower-hope. The loch is one of the largest in the Border country and its beauty is renowned far beyond Scotland. It is normally photographed in serene mood reflecting the shapes of the surrounding hills but has quite another face on a wild winter day when the wind whips up the waves into 'white horses' and keeps the sailing enthusiasts confined to their clubhouse at the loch's western end.

The walk along the loch is four miles of beauty all the way, with the never-failing interest of the water scene and its associated birdlife, and the added pleasure of knowing that the end of the day is near. At the west end of the loch is the Tibbie Shiels Inn, which has been giving comfort to travellers for over two centuries. The inn is named after a shepherd's wife, Tibbie Shiels, who ran it very autocrati-

cally in the nineteenth century. Walter Scott was a frequent visitor. Tibbie died in 1878 at the age of 95 years. Near the inn is a café where refreshments can also be obtained, and a monument to James Hogg, the noted local poet known as the Ettrick Shepherd.

The Ettrick Valley is very long—a full 25 miles (40km) from Ettrickhead to Selkirk—and very beautiful. You will walk above its upper reaches on the second day of the present journey, but it is worth saying a few words here about perhaps its most famous son.

James Hogg was born in Ettrick in 1770. He received no formal education but he had a great gift for writing both prose and verse. He rose to considerable fame in the Edinburgh of the Golden Age and achieved great success—a prose work with the unmemorable title *An Essay on Sheep* earned him £300, a very princely sum, and one of his volumes of poetry sold 10,000 copies in the USA alone. He was a great traveller and as befits a man brought up as a shepherd, not afraid to use his legs to get around. He knew all this Border country intimately.

One of my favourite Hogg stories concerns Sir Walter Scott, whose firm friend he became. Hogg called the great man Wattie, the common country name for Walter, which outraged Scott's society friends—but the man himself took no offence. On a visit to Scott's house in Edinburgh, at a stage when he lacked society manners but desired to acquire some, Hogg noticed that Scott's wife (who was, in fact, unwell) was reclining on a sofa. Thinking this was the done thing, Hogg did likewise—without removing his sheep-stained coat or his muddy boots!

Hogg's work is very much worth reading. As well as his poetry and his writings about the Borderlands, another favourite of mine is his book *A Tour in the Highlands,* an account of a long journey he took in 1803. It is marvellously vivid and he is not afraid to make fun of himself and his rude manners. At one point he admires the view around him (from a hill above Loch Lomond) in disbelief, explaining his feelings by saying, 'I had drunk some whisky the preceding evening, and had a very indistinct recollection of our approach to that place, and it was actually a good while ere I was persuaded that everything I saw was real.' I know walkers today who suffer from the same problem!

The overnight stop on the way to Moffat can be taken either at the Tibbie Shiels Inn or by camping nearby—enquiry will reveal any number of possible sites. The latter would be my chosen course in anything approaching fine weather.

Capel Fell and Craignichen Scar. (Photo: K. Andrew)

Day Two

The second day starts by continuing on the Southern Upland Way as it slants uphill above the east side of Loch of the Lowes. This little stretch of water was once conjoined to St Mary's Loch but gradually became separated from it through the deposition of material brought down from the hills by the Thirlestane and Crosscleuch Burns on the east and the Oxcleuch Burn on the west.

The path goes on south through the hills to the Ettrick Valley but you should leave it on the flat expanse of Pikestone Rig and head a little south of west up to Peniestone Knowe. At the south-west end of that hill a careful bit of navigation is needed to switch ridges and gain the slopes of Herman Law. It is not easy in mist but in clear conditions there should be no problem, though the temptation is to continue over Carse Hill and thus down to Ettrick.

Don't do that—it would deprive you of the finest section of the walk. The Southern Upland Way misses it out, in favour of a road walk, which is curious, but that does mean that the discerning walker can have it all to him or herself. Indeed, you are unlikely to see other walkers anywhere except in the area around St Mary's Loch. That for me is another great attraction of the rolling Border hills.

Rolling they are, and well grassed, and from Herman Law they roll away south-west for a six-mile promenade at high level which is glorious in every respect. The height varies only between 1800 and 2200ft (550 and 670m) all the way, and it is a traverse to be savoured. I only hope my eulogy does not lead to it becoming too popular!

The names along the way are splendid too: after Herman Law you cross Trowgrain Middle, Mid Rig, Andrewhinney Hill, Bell Craig and Bodesbeck Law. To the south-east the hills slope gently down to the upper Ettrick Valley, Hogg's country, but to the north-west is an abrupt fall of 1500ft (450m) to the Moffat Water.

A stop on Andrewhinney is obligatory. It is, at 2221ft (677m), the high point of the ridge, but what will draw your eye more is across the valley to the north-west. Here at 1700ft (520m) sits a perfect gem—Loch Skeen, a classic example of a corrie loch in a hanging valley, scooped out by the action of the ice some 12,000 years ago.

Loch Skeen is visited by relatively few people, in contrast to the ground immediately below it. The reason for this is that when the loch was formed, its outflow took the easiest route of escape, creating the Tail Burn and its major feature, the waterfall known as the Grey Mare's Tail. This much-visited spot has been in

the care of the National Trust for Scotland since 1962 and considerable work has been necessary recently on the path leading up beside the fall: it is very steep and had become dangerously eroded. How much nicer to view the fall from across the valley on the quiet summit of Andrewhinney—and you get a more complete view of it together with its loch from here.

To the south and east are the vast forests of Craik and Eskdalemuir, the timber-producing factories of the twenty-first century from which our paper for newspapers, magazines and books will come.

Leave Andrewhinney when you are ready and saunter on along the ridge to Bodesbeck Law with its prominent cairn. To keep to the highest ground you now need to head south-*east* to the clear col below, and then cut back north-west to gain the northern end of White Shank. The slopes down to the Moffat Water have eased now and the valley below is starting to become more wooded and pastoral in nature.

Continue along the ridge to Capel Fell, which overtops Andrewhinney by just two feet and overlooks Ettrickhead, the start of that long and lovely valley running all the way up to Selkirk. You are now into the final stages of the walk, with about seven or eight miles to go before Moffat is gained.

Follow the line of the old boundary south-east of Capel Fell and at Ettrickhead turn right on the old path leading over to Moffat. This route—now incorporated into the Southern Upland Way—is taken to avoid the substantial crags at the south end of Capel Fell—an unusual feature in the Borders. At the junction of glens below these crags, go left and enter the forest below Croft Head, where there are more crags soaring above. In another mile or so a sharp rightward swing is needed to pick up the track leading through the forests of Gateshaw Rig. Be sure again to get on the right route here, otherwise you will find yourself marching down the delightfully-named Big Strushel Burn to the valley of the Esk—a fine spot but not where you want to be! The turn off should be marked with Southern Upland Way signposts.

For the next three miles (5km) or so, you follow the track roughly with the Cornal Burn, through forestry all the way. The trend is generally downhill, though at one point the track takes an uphill slant almost as if to tease us when we had thought the hard work was over. Walking through forests has its own pleasures: trees in themselves are objects of great beauty and there is usually good wildlife in forests, especially birds. I have to confess

Top: **Moffat Water Valley and Saddle Yoke (left) from Forest road to Carnel Burn Valley.**
(Photo: K. Andrew)

Above: **St Mary's Loch**. (Photo: Robin Williams)

however that I am no great lover of the massed ranks of limited species conifers that are cloaking so many of Scotland's hillsides these days.

These new forests seem to me gloomy places, an impression heightened by the close planting of the trees (good economics but pretty uninspiring to the eye) and the similarity of such forests all the way through. Mostly they are sitka spruce and lodgepole pine, with perhaps a leavening of larch to give some variety. As they mature, these forests will become more attractive, but many of them are young at present and their potential for recreational enjoyment is very limited.

On leaving the main plantation, the track swings left by a belt of more mature trees (at the foot of which is yet another fortified tower), crosses two minor burns and reaches a junction. The quicker way into Moffat is to turn right here, but that involves a couple of miles on the main road—not recommended. I therefore encourage you to turn left to Craigbeck. Once out on the lane, it's left again and then first right across the Moffat Water on a fine bridge.

A mile or so downstream the river joins, and loses its identity into, Annan Water. Annan means 'the quiet water' but the history of Annandale is anything but quiet. Even in the turbulent Border story it stands out for bloodletting and feuding, with families such as the Maxwells, Bruces and Johnstones warring amongst themselves at every opportunity, it seems. The Johnstones, in medieval times, marked their victims with slashes to the face, a practice known as the Lockerbie Lick.

Fortunately it is a good deal more peaceful these days with the only arguments likely to be on the price of livestock or timber, and the visitor is warmly and hospitably welcomed everywhere. This is certainly true in Moffat, which awaits you a mile and a bit up the road you are on, through Nethermiln and Holmend to the A708 and left into the town centre.

Moffat still has something of the character of a Border town, far from the actual line though it may be. In its centre is a very handsome square, which you can easily imagine filled with horse-drawn carriages instead of today's noisier and more intrusive transport. And in the centre of the square is Moffat's famous ram, atop the Colvin Fountain. There could not be a clearer indication of the importance of sheep to the local economy.

Mineral springs were discovered here in the mid-eighteenth century and as with many similarly blessed places, Moffat became fashionable as a place for 'taking the waters', though never attaining the fame of some other spas. Modern visitors, especially those like us, are likely to be looking for something more substantial than mineral water, and there is no shortage of places to supply it, whether it be tea or good ale you seek.

The country you have passed through—or at least the latter part of it—was once known simply as the Forest. It was indeed well wooded, with principally Scots pine, oak, birch and hazel: would that that cover could be restored. It would be worth any price. But the forest of the title was a hunting-place above all, the royal hunting forest of Scotland.

It was empty land then and it is empty land today. Those traversing it centuries ago were likely to be outlaws, fugitives, men intent on taking or avenging. One can only surmise at whether they admired the landscape or cursed it. The link we have with them is that, now as then, the foot traveller gets the best of this country, seeing all of it and appreciating it to the full at the best pace. We are fortunate indeed to have such lovely wild country to wander through. It asks nothing of us save one thing and in return it gives us refreshment of body and spirit that is priceless in a world of too much noise and hurry.

The one thing the land asks is that we care for it, act as responsible stewards, and pass it on in good condition to the next generation so that they too can take essential refreshment. I often wonder whether as a nation we do anything like enough to care for and conserve our wonderful landscapes and the creatures that inhabit them. Perhaps that is a fitting thought on which to conclude this walk, for we should not take such pleasures as being forever granted. They are a privilege that we must earn.

PENTLAND HILLS AND LOCHS
(Lothian Region) by Roger Smith

Distance: 12 miles (19 km).
Ascent: 2600ft (800m).
Start/Finish: Car park at Flotterstone.
Maps: OS 1:50,000 Sheets 66 and 65.
Summary: Hill paths and minor lanes. Nearly all the climbing is in the first part of the walk: once off West Kip the going is much gentler.

Points of Interest: Traverse of main Pentland ridge and ascent of highest point, Scald Law. Ancient right of way then leads to reservoirs with fine birdlife before an old hill pass returns the walker to the start point.

Facing page: **The main Pentlands range from West Kip.** (Photo: Roger Smith)

Far finer writers than I have extolled the beauties of the Pentlands, Edinburgh's own hills. You can hardly get further removed from these hills than Samoa in the Pacific Ocean, yet it was from that distant tropical archipelago than Robert Louis Stevenson looked back on his childhood at the foot of the Pentlands and called them 'the hills of home'. To millions of Edinburgh folk that is exactly what they always will be.

Sir Walter Scott, Borderer though he was, knew their worth too:

'I never saw anything more beautiful than the ridge of Carnethy against a clear frosty sky, with its peaks and varied slopes. The hills glowed like purple amethyst; the sky glowed topaz and vermilion. I never saw a finer screen than Pentland, considering it is neither rocky nor highly elevated.'

The peaks and varied slopes are explored in this walk, which also takes in the lochs to the north-west of the main Portland range before returning through a fine pass to its starting point. As Scott said, the hills are not 'highly elevated': the highest point, Scald Law, is just over 1900ft (580m). But you'll know you've been on a hill walk if you do the full ridge from Turnhouse to West Kip: there is plenty of up and down to exercise the legs!

The walk starts and ends at Flotterstone on the A702, where there is a car park (beyond the inn) and a small visitor centre which has very good literature on the area. The inn is open all day for the refreshment of travellers: if you can resist the temptation, it may be better to wait to the end of the walk before stepping inside or you may never step out again!

The whole Pentlands area was designated a regional park recently. I have little to say about this designation except to offer the fervent hope that it does not alter the essential character of the hills. The aim is supposedly to provide a unified management system. Only time will tell if this has been achieved. I have

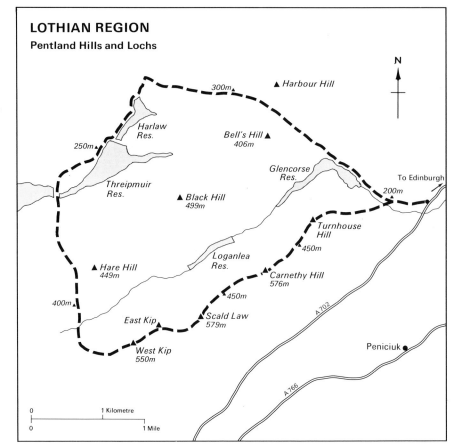

LOTHIAN REGION
Pentland Hills and Lochs

N

▲ Harbour Hill
300m
Harlaw Res.
Bell's Hill ▲ 406m
250m
Glencorse Res.
To Edinburgh
Threipmuir Res.
200m
▲ Black Hill 499m
Turnhouse Hill
450m
Loganlea Res.
▲ Hare Hill 449m
Carnethy Hill 576m
400m
450m
A 702
East Kip
Scald Law 579m
Peniciuk ●
West Kip 550m
A 766

0 ___ 1 Kilometre
0 ___ 1 Mile

Map showing the 12-mile circular walk from Flotterstone, along the main Pentland ridge, and over Turnhouse Hill, Carnethy Hill, Scald Law and West Kip before an ancient right of way takes you past reservoirs and back to Flotterstone.

my doubts. Most of the 'management' will probably be concentrated on the northern flank of the hills, which contains two country parks at Hillend and Bonaly, the former including as its main feature the longest artificial ski slope in Britain.

But back to the walk. The first objective is Turnhouse Hill, gained by taking the track heading west from the car park, branching left after about 400 yards and getting on to the clear ridge leading up to the hill. On the slopes to your left was fought the Battle of Rullion

Above: **The top of Maiden's Cleuch Pass in the Pentlands.** (Photo: Roger Smith)

stocking rate of approximately one ewe to two acres is quite high for Scotland. Birdlife is likely to include skylarks and meadow pipits, and lapwings in the spring to autumn months.

From the summit of Turnhouse a fine panorama opens up. To the west is the subsidiary ridge of Bell's Hill and Black Hill—the latter now unfortunately disfigured by a crudely bulldozed track—while below nestle the reservoirs of Glencorse and Loganlea. There are thirteen reservoirs in the Pentlands in all, between them contributing a total of around four million gallons of water a day to the Edinburgh area. That may sound a lot—and it is—but it represents only ten per cent of the total needed by the city each and every day.

Inevitably, your eye will be drawn to the continuation of the ridge you have now gained. It stretches south-west for about four miles (6km) in a clear line—which this walk follows—to the sharply pointed top of West Kip. Each of the hills between is quite distinct, which means a fair descent and ascent for each one, but it is worth the effort every time.

After a short flat ridge section, the path

Green, on 28 November 1666. It is commemorated by a small plaque.

It is, as we say, a 'fair pech' up onto Turnhouse Hill, the path taking a pretty direct line until the gradient eases near the ridge. On all these hills you are likely to see blackface sheep, the predominant type worked here. The

descends from Turnhouse Hill to a col before climbing quite steeply onto Carnethy Hill. This is a Celtic name found also (as Carneddau) in North Wales. It may refer to a name, Edda, not infrequently used for tribal leaders. Carnethy was certainly a significant place in ancient times, being crowned by the remains of a hilltop cairn or perhaps even a small fortlet, possibly used in ceremonies connected with sun worship at key times of the year.

Carnethy has a longer ridge than Turnhouse and a fine wee walk it is too, before an abrupt drop brings you to the col below Scald Law. Through here runs a very well-used path linking Penicuik and Balerno. It is also part of the route of the race which each year starts off the hill running season in Scotland, the 'Carnethy 5'. Held in February, conditions can be interesting, to say the least, with snow cover a distinct possibility. The race starts and finishes in Penicuik and always attracts an entry of several hundred hardy enthusiasts.

Our pace is somewhat more sedate, especially on the grind up Scald Law, which has little to commend it except its objective, the trig pillar marking the Pentlands' highest point. A pause here will certainly be in order, both to enjoy the views and to recover your breath. You may have noticed that the glens in the Pentlands are generally smooth-sided and regular in form. This is the result of erosive action during and at the end of the last period of major glaciation, about 60,000 years ago.

The Pentlands lay at the edge of the main glaciated area, and thus the effects of the ice are less dramatic here than they are further north in the Highlands. As well as the ice, water liberated as the ice melted had an effect on the landscape, removing considerable amounts of material and carrying it out to sea or depositing it on the land. The sand and gravel of the Old Pentlands area was dumped in this way all those aeons ago.

Much more recently, man's hand is evident in the virtual elimination of the natural woodland and scrub cover and its replacement by moorland grasses. The introduction of sheep accelerated and continued this process. Experiments near West Linton have shown that with enough encouragement and protection from grazing animals, natural woodland will reform. There is no reason why coppice woodland should not provide a viable timber crop, and I would like to see much more of it in the hills.

You may reflect on some of these things as you make your way off Scald Law. Take care to turn west from the ridge—there is an understandable tendency to follow the main ridge south. After descending from Scald Law,

the minor top of East Kip is soon crossed and the last real climb of the walk takes you on to the sharp little summit of West Kip.

As with the other hills in such situations, being at the end of a ridge it commands fine views out across the West Lothian countryside. To the south-west is an extensive area of hill and moorland, well worth exploring if you have more time to spare on another day. To the south, the extensive flats of Hare Moss and Auchencorth Moss lie between the Pentlands and the higher hills of Upper Tweeddale.

This walk however continues by dropping down from West Kip, steeply again, to gain the path (a right of way) running first west then north over to Balerno. Shortly after the path takes its distinct northward turn, a neat little bridge over the Logan Burn makes a fine stopping place for a look back at the ridge you have just traversed.

From the bridge, a gentle upslope leads across the west side of Hare Hill to cross the district boundary and start the descent towards the next stage of the walk, the reservoirs. The path enters a small wood by using a gate. On reaching a lane, turn right for about 100 yards and then left to walk down a fine avenue of trees with glimpses of Threipmuir Reservoir over to the right.

A bridge leads over a narrow part of the reservoir, and it is worth pausing here to check the birdlife. Threipmuir is 220 acres in extent and as well as its open water it has excellent marshland areas much used for nesting and breeding by waterfowl. If you are lucky you may see great crested grebe here diving for fish. There are always coot, moorhen, and various ducks including mallard, and often mute swans as well.

A winter walk to Threipmuir will yield further prizes, for at that time of year the avian population is boosted by teal, wigeon, goldeneye, and whooper swans. The whole area is designated as a Class I Site of Special Scientific Interest, indicating that it is of national importance in conservation terms.

After crossing the bridge, the walk briefly leaves the waterside to continue along the lane for about 400 yards, before turning right along a track (small car park on the left). To the west is the Red Moss Nature Reserve, which is managed by the Scottish Wildlife Trust and is another important area for birds. In a short while the track becomes a rough road; where this goes right to Bavelaw Farm, carry on to rejoin the reservoir and walk along its edge for about half a mile.

Threipmuir is not only important for birds—around its shores nearly 80 different species of plant have been identified. Although

Turnhouse, Scald Law and Carnethy Hill seen from Maiden's Cleuch. (Photo: Roger Smith)

the whole area is well used for recreation, particularly walking and angling, it is managed in such a way as to ensure that conservation comes first. This must not change whatever the pressure of visitors.

At the corner of the reservoir, turn right briefly and then, *before* the small stream, left on the clear path by Harlaw Reservoir. A screen of trees partly hides the water, but you are very likely to see duck and other waterfowl here too, as well as many people enjoying a stroll.

On reaching the northern end of Harlaw Reservoir, turn right to cross the dam and pass in front of a neat cottage. Turn left as signposted by the wall and right along the road, with a wood on your left. It appears you are heading away from the hills, but it is only a short diversion. When the road bends left (car parking), turn right onto the path with the hills and all the later part of this fine walk in front of you.

You now have approximately four miles to go. The first mile or so is not especially interesting, and underfoot it can be very boggy. The first important point is to ensure you take the left fork 200 yards (180m) or so after leaving the road. This path leads up a gentle slope towards the clear pass between Harbour Hill and Bell's Hill. Away on the right is the isolated and now disused cottage of Craigentarrie. It must have been a fine lonely place to live, but tough in the winter, I should think.

At the top of the pass the district boundary is recrossed and the scene changes—you are now clearly back in the hills. Plantations are passed on left and right as you descend to meet the road at the angle of Glencorse Reservoir. This road leads all the way back to Flotterstone.

It is a pleasant enough walk, with the attraction of the water for the first half of the way. Up on the left are the slopes of Castlelaw Hill, which is used for military training purposes and contains a firing range. On its lower slopes, on the subsidiary summit of Castle Knowe, is an Iron Age hill-fort which can be viewed. It consists of two concentric bank and ditch systems, one of them with a 'souterrain' or earth-house. The site is believed to have been occupied up to the second century AD, by which times the Romans were marching across the Pentlands on their forays north.

A final easy mile leads back to the car park at Flotterstone and the end of the walk. It has encompassed a fine hill range, old rights of way, watersheets with splendid birdlife, and aspects of history from many periods. A very rewarding day and a good taste of what this area has to offer. I am sure you will be back for more.

CENTRAL REGION

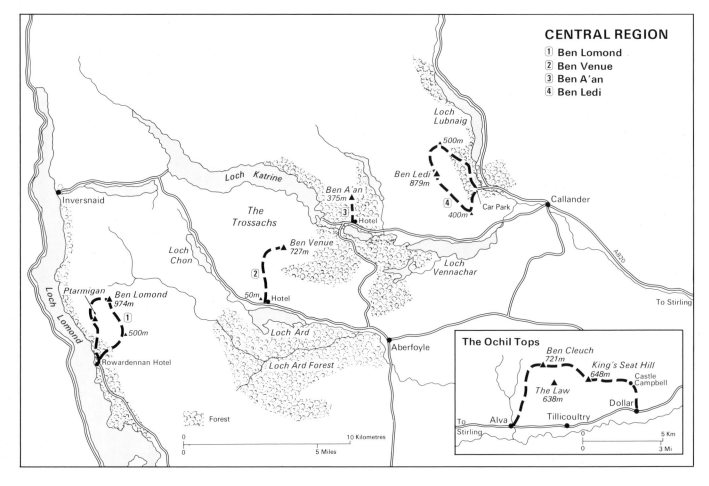

CENTRAL REGION
1 Ben Lomond
2 Ben Venue
3 Ben A'an
4 Ben Ledi

Loch Lubnaig

500m

Ben Ledi 879m ▲

4 *Car Park* Callander

400m ▲

Loch Katrine

Ben A'an 375m ▲

3 ▲ *Hotel*

Inversnaid

The Trossachs

Ben Venue 727m

2

Loch Chon

50m ▲ *Hotel*

Loch Vennachar

A820

To Stirling

Ptarmigan

Ben Lomond 974m

1

▲ *500m*

Loch Lomond

Rowardennan Hotel

Loch Ard

Loch Ard Forest

Aberfoyle

Forest

0   10 Kilometres

0   5 Miles

The Ochil Tops

Ben Cleuch 721m ▲

King's Seat Hill 648m ▲ *Castle Campbell*

The Law 638m ▲

To Stirling   Alva   Tillicoultry   Dollar

0   5 Km

0   3 Mi

Map showing the following walks: The Ochil Tops (p21), Ben Lomond (p25), Ben Venue (p28), Ben A'an (p31) and Ben Ledi (p34).

The 10-mile walk over the Ochil Tops offers fine walking mainly on good tracks, with no severe gradients.

The 7-mile walk to Ben Lomond climbs 3000 ft. It offers an easy and straightforward walk.

The 4 1/2 mile walk to the summit of Ben Venue is a straightforward hill walk, but if you traverse the mountain and go on to the Trossachs, this will add a further 2 1/2 miles and includes a steep descent.

The 4-mile walk to Ben A'an in the Trossachs is ideal for any walker of reasonable fitness; it is a short and easy hill walk.

The 7 miles over Ben Ledi includes some steep ground but nothing too severe.

THE OCHILS TOPS (Central Region)
by Roger Smith

Above, left: **Dollar Glen with Castle Campbell in the distance.**

Above right: **The sections of wooden duckboarding in Dollar Glen need care in winter when they can be slippery.**
(Photos: Roger Smith)

Distance: 10 miles (16 km).
Ascent: 3000ft (900m).
Start/Finish: Start at Clock tower, Dollar. Finish in Stirling Street, Alva.
Maps: OS 1:50,000 Sheet 58.
Transport: Bus 23 (Stirling-St Andrews) runs from Alva to Dollar every two hours, Sundays included.

Summary: Start and finish on good tracks, main part of walk on hill paths or rough ground. No severe gradients.
Points of Interest: Castle Campbell (Fifteenth century stronghold); King's Seat Hill (views); Ben Cleuch (highest point in the Ochil Hills).

I was fortunate enough to live in Alva, at the foot of the Ochil Hills, for six years. During those years I became very familiar with these fine hills, in every mood and in all seasons. Despite the abruptness of the magnificent southern escarpment—a fault line often featured in school geography exams!—they are friendly hills with few difficulties for the walker.

From the south, from the strange flat lands of the carse around the intricate windings of the River Forth, the Ochils present a stern face to the viewer. But once you are up on their grassy heights you can walk for miles with never a steep or rough gradient to bother you. The choice of route is infinite and as with all hill ranges, once you get to know them there are exquisite corners where you can sit at peace and be virtually certain of having that peace all to yourself for as long as you wish.

These are not tremendously high hills. The highest point, on Ben Cleuch, is well under 2500ft (750m), and in all there are perhaps a dozen tops above 2000ft (600m). There is very little bare rock, but there are, particularly on the southern side, dramatically fine glens which over the aeons have formed splendid gorges. The walk described here starts with one such gorge.

This is a classic walk in several senses. It takes in the highest point of a range of hills, one of its most impressive glens, a venerable castle, commands glorious views (in the right conditions) and will occupy you very satisfactorily for most of a day. Its two ends are linked by bus and its lack of severity means that it can be tackled by any able-bodied walker. In mist a little care in navigation would be needed, but there are plenty of 'handrails'. In past years when I was much fitter than I am now I regularly *ran* up here in winter. Traditionally clad walkers were surprised to see this figure in tracksuit and light studded shoes pounding past through the January snow or rain, but I knew that if need be I could be off and to safety in ten or fifteen minutes.

So I have no hesitation in recommending a day on the Ochils to any reader of this book. The vast majority of committed walkers pass this range by, to east or west, in search of bigger game further north and west. So be it: I would not like to see the Ochils become too popular.

The walk starts in Dollar, for several reasons. It is a pleasant town in itself: it provides a relatively easy way up into the hills, with no dreadfully severe gradients: and you can leave your car in Alva, where the walk finishes, and travel by bus to Dollar on the regular 23 (St Andrews) service. Dollar also

starts the walk with a bang, from which the effort of climbing King's Seat will enable you to recover!

From the centre of Dollar, by the clock tower, walk up beside the burn towards the hills. By the first bridge is a plaque to the memory of Andrew Mylne, the first rector (headmaster) of Dollar Academy, the secondary school founded here in 1818. Opposite Academy Place is a rare *working* drinking fountain erected 'with the surplus funds of an industrial exhibition held in Dollar, August 1890'. The purpose of the exhibition is not divulged, but no doubt it seemed a good idea at the time.

Cross a road and enter the lower part of Dollar Glen. It is now in the care of the National Trust for Scotland, having been gifted to them by the late Mr J.E. Kerr, CBE in 1950. Mr Kerr was the master of Harviestoun, an estate west of the town which has considerable associations with the great Scots poet Robert Burns, who visited it several times and wrote a poem in praise of the River Devon, which flows across the plain south of the Ochils to join the Forth near Alloa.

Across the burn you may see golfers starting a round on Dollar Golf Course. The first hole is somewhat daunting: its direction from the tee is indicated by a marker at the top of a vertical bank, the green itself being quite invisible! A plaque nearby records a visit by HRH the Princess Royal in 1979 to mark the 'Facelift' project undertaken by local organisations to clean up the green area here. An information board gives details of the glen proper, which you now enter.

The path climbs steeply and there are several sections of wooden duckboarding, which can demand care in wet or icy conditions. I well remember coming down this way after a winter traverse of the hills — it was the only place where full winter mountaineering skills were needed! In summer there are of course no such problems. As you go up the glen the surrounds become ever more dramatic. A left turn at the Long Bridge leads to the very narrow passage called Windy Edge from where the Glencairn Bridge takes you up a dramatic cleft, with water thundering down on your left, to more open ground beyond.

At the top of this slope is Castle Campbell, a scheduled Ancient Monument and well worth a visit. It is open every day (afternoons only on Sundays). The castle was originally built towards the end of the fifteenth century by the then Earl of Argyll, and was popularly known as 'Castle Gloom'. Even on today's maps you will see that the two burns feeding Dollar Glen are called the Burn of Gloom and the Burn of

The summit of Ben Cleuch, at 2330ft, the highest point in the Ochil hills. (Photo: Roger Smith)

Sorrow. The castle was badly damaged by fire when sacked by Cromwell's troops in the mid-seventeenth century but there is still plenty to be seen, and its setting, looking over the floodplain of the Forth, is quite magnificent.

To continue the walk, face away from the castle and take the path leading around the left side of the knoll ahead of you. This path goes up the Burn of Sorrow. Walk up beside the burn for about a quarter of a mile to the first main feeder burn on the left, then head left up a clear spur to King's Seat. The ascent is toilsome rather than spectacular but is nowhere difficult. Partway up you will note a rather odd erosion effect to the left, almost like a battlement.

In spring and early summer the birdlife here is very fine. You will almost certainly hear skylarks, curlews and cuckoos, and down by the burn dippers and wagtails will be in evidence. The smooth slopes of the hill lead to its being used by cross-country skiers in winter when conditions are right.

The summit is inevitably at the far end of the hill (aren't they always) and is unmistakable with its large cairn. To the right (north) is the long Whitewisp—Tarmangie ridge and to the west much of the rest of the walk is clear, with Andrew Gannell, Ben Cleuch, the Law and Wood Hill standing out. Turning to look back east reveals, on a good day, the Kingdom of Fife and the broad sweep of the Forth estuary. In exceptionally clear conditions I have seen Bass Rock to the east and Arrochar to the west from here—virtually right across Scotland.

To continue the walk, head north-west following a clear path. Leave the path after about 400 yards to head left (west) towards the fence clearly seen crossing Andrew Gannell Hill, and descend steeply to the col at the head of the Gannell Burn. On this col you cross the old right of way once used by traders in both directions—weavers from Tillicoultry and cobblers from Blackford.

Head up Andrew Gannell Hill. If you feel like a pause there is a convenient spring about halfway up. The hill is not named after a person but is a corruption of Gaelic words meaning 'a sandy-bottomed burn'. From near the summit of Andrew Gannell, a fence leads across to the shallow col between the Law on the left and Ben Cleuch on the right. This is all very easy walking and you can stride out or stroll along as you please. At a fence junction, turn right for the final easy-angled ascent to the summit of Ben Cleuch.

Near the top there used to be a rather unsightly radio mast, but it was removed a couple of years ago after persistent campaigning by local conservationists (it had been disused for many years). It was a landmark of a sort, I suppose, but it hardly added to the beauty of the scene and I am glad it has been taken away. The way is clear enough with a well-worn path and a fence to its right.

Ben Cleuch summit, the highest point of the Ochils at 2330ft (720m), is one of the few places on this walk where you will almost certainly meet others. It is undistinguished as a summit—the name means a long, sloping ridge and that is what it is. Nonetheless, the views, particularly to the north, can be outstanding. A rather battered indicator names the peaks visible. Outstanding among them are Ben Vorlich and its neighbour Stuc a'Chroin, Ben Ledi, Ben More and Stobinian.

I reflected as I stood here that I had climbed all those hills and was profoundly glad: not out of any sense of achievement, but out of gratitude for the health and strength that enabled me to take my recreation in such magnificent country. It was feeling like that which led me to my long involvement with the voluntary conservation movement in Scotland: I hope it is a feeling I shall never lose.

A clear path leaves Ben Cleuch to the north-west, soon aligning itself with the fence that comes down from Ben Buck (another 2000ft (600m) plus top easily bagged by a short diversion). The descent is steep but not uncomfortably so. At a fence junction, cross by a stile and turn half left to climb Ben Ever (also just over 2000ft). From here the rest of the route is plain and the panorama across the Forth is fine indeed.

It is all downhill now, but before leaving the Ochil tops take a look around at this fine quiet range of hills. I never tire of them, however many times I return, and there are other tops not covered in this walk which are worthy of a visit if you have time to spare in the area. Blairdenon perhaps, with its memorial to an airman killed in a crash on the hill; Craig Leith and Colsnaur; Whitewisp and Tarmangie. Hills do not have to be exceptionally high or steep to be worth climbing, and the inner peace I have derived from my many excursions into the Ochils has been a marvellous reward for the effort expended.

Leave Ben Ever heading pretty well due south. When you reach the flatter ground be sure to pass to the *right* of a small pool of brackish water, otherwise you will likely end up on Wood Hill! Go on down the hill to join the clear broad track on the slopes of the Nebit. To the left of the track is the Silver Glen, so named because silver was indeed mined here during the 18th and early 19th centuries. The vein is long since worked out.

After passing through a gate do not follow the track as it zig-zags downhill but keep on the small path by the fence on your left. This is the older way up the hill and makes for a much more pleasant descent, through a small rocky gully and down past a large dead tree to rejoin the newer track at a sharp bend. The town of Alva, the end of the walk, is spread out below.

At the next bend in the track, leave it again to take the path on the right down through gorse bushes—a marvellous shock of brilliant colour in late spring and early summer—to reach a small gate beside the intake wall of Rhodders Farm. Go through the gate and pass either side of a Water Board building to go under a large pipe (it used to carry the town's water supply down from the hills) and into the lower part of Alva Glen.

The glen is a very popular short walk and is worth the diversion, at least in part, for the path is cut into the hillside above a quite outstanding gorge. One can only marvel at the power of water needed to carve such a deep gash in the rock, but walk this way as I often have on a wild November day and you can see how it can happen over thousands of years. The water thunders down the gorge, dark brown and boiling in its haste to spill out across the plain below.

A short walk from Alva Glen leads you into the town centre and to your car or the bus back to Dollar, according to which way you have planned the walk. Before leaving the glen, look up left at the imposing building there. This is Strude Mill, the most impressive by far of all the remaining mill buildings in these Hillfoot towns, as they are known.

The mill was built in about 1820 at the time when the weaving industry was becoming mechanised. The clock and bell at the top were installed to signal to the workers the start of their long day. In the mid-nineteenth century a quarter of all the woollen mills in Scotland were based in this small area of country.

The walk has traversed some of the finest scenery of Clackmannanshire, the smallest county in Scotland. Its motto is 'Look Aboot Ye', which is very appropriate for an excursion into its hills. Thus encouraged, many people return time and again to look anew. I have certainly been very happy to do so and to savour the particular pleasures of the Ochils tops.

BEN LOMOND (Central Region)
by Cameron McNeish

Distance: 7 miles (11km).
Ascent: 3000ft (900m).
Start/Finish: Rowardennan Hotel, near Balmaha, Loch Lomondside.
Maps: OS 1:50,000 Sheet 56, OS 1:63,360 Tourist Map—Loch Lomond and the Trossachs.
Summary: A straightforward and easy mountain walk. No real navigation difficulties as a path is followed virtually all the way. Extra care should be taken in winter though when condi-tions can become Arctic. Tends to be very muddy underfoot even in high summer.
Points of Interest: Superb views of Loch Lomond and the archipelago of islands at the south end of the loch. Look out for wild goats, deer, golden eagle, and ptarmigan. Ben Lomond is just north of the Highland Line so offers contrasting views to the south and to the higher mountains of the north.

Bonny Ben Lomond, the Beacon Hill, was well and truly doused. Her summit pyramid was hidden by a swathe of dark grey cloud and her burns and streams coursed down her flanks with urgency and impatience.

On the lochside the wind whipped through the trees, the grand oaks and the contemporary larches and spruces, and the surface of Loch Lomond was boiling with spray and fume. Not the greatest of days for a walk but I hadn't been out for a couple of weeks and the proverbial bear wanted free from his cage, at least for a few hours.

It was over ten years since I'd been on Ben Lomond and in that time the whole Loch Lomond area had come under public scrutiny as various bodies had thrown down plans to institute a national park scheme. Bulldozed tracks had raped the northern slopes of the Ben, and in an attempt to safeguard the rest of the mountain for the nation, the National Trust for Scotland (NTS) had taken the mountain into its collection of mountain properties, pretty gardens, old houses and castles. Interestingly the first indication you get that the NTS is now in charge is a sign that warns you to keep your dog on a lead.

Isn't it strange how these conservation bodies like to stick signs up. There's a nasty undercurrent of possessiveness about it. Perhaps the worst perpetrators after the NTS are the Nature Conservancy Council. Their massive signposts at Creag Meagaidh are both intrusive and unnecessary. Do they have to tell the public at large that this is Creag Meagaidh? If the idea is nature conservation then why dress the place up and invite the public in to see the show?

Despite the foibles, for basically that's all they are, of our conservation agencies, it's good to see and recognise the good work that is done, and the NTS have done some stalwart work on the tourist footpath that runs from Rowardennan up onto the broad whaleback of the Ben. On a track that as far as I can remember was always prone to becoming very wet, the path builders have drained and rebuilt, stoned and fashioned a path that is not entirely out of keeping with the immediate area. I believe that under the circumstances of very heavy traffic (Ben Lomond is one of the most popular hills in Scotland for visitors), the job has been done extremely well.

This footpath to the summit of Ben Lomond begins opposite the Rowardennan Hotel. It carries you quickly up over the lower slopes past birch and oak woods and through dense thickets of bracken. Away to your left, provided it isn't misty, you'll see the summit of the mountain sitting squatly above its broad shoulders. This summit is in fact a curved ridge about half a mile in length from which cliffs fall to the north and east.

Soon the view will be opening up behind you, over the forestry plantations of larch and spruce and down to the waters of Loch Lomond, the biggest sheet of inland water in the country and arguably the most beautiful. The beauty of Loch Lomond I believe is in the fact that it combines water, mountain and woodland in a way that is almost unique. The trees are largely broad-leaved, mainly oak, birch, chestnut and beech, and for the time being at least most of the slopes surrounding the loch are not over-forested.

Loch Lomond lies with her foot in the Lowlands and her head firmly choked off by Highland mountains. Look south from the broad shoulder of the Ben and the view is lowland in character; low volcanic hills rolling into the industrial haze of Clydeside. On clear days the views will carry your eyes on over Clydeside and away to sea, beyond the isle of Arran and her mountainous profile and to-

Ben Lomond is now owned by The National Trust for Scotland. (Photo: Cameron McNeish)

Above left: **Ben Lomond from the north, looking across the waters of Loch Lomond.**

Above: **Feral goats roam the lower slopes of Ben Lomond and thrive on the rich undergrowth of the birch and oak woods.**
(Photos: Cameron McNeish)

wards the Ailsa Craig, said to be halfway between Scotland and Ireland.

Soon the footpath begins to turn northwards and you'll begin climbing rather more steeply onto the long whaleback ridge which leads to the summit pyramid. Across to your right now the hills of the Trossachs will be coming into view, Ben Venue and below it the long stretch of water that is Loch Ard. Leftwards and beyond the rounded Luss hills lie the hills of the Arrochar Alps, the Cobbler, Ben Narnain, Ben Vane and Ben Vorlich.

The easy flattish walking of the ridge doesn't last long before you have to exert yourself again, up a couple of zigzags and onto the summit ridge, a well-worn footpath carrying you around the rim of the northern corries which fall away at your feet towards Comer and the silvery burn which is the infant River Forth.

In winter time this rim becomes heavily corniced and care should be taken as you make your way round towards the summit point. Winter climbers often find good sport in these northern corries with over 300ft (90m) of vegetated cliff to play on, good conditions for snow and ice men when the temperatures are low and the turf is frozen solid.

On the walk I mentioned earlier it was really good to reach the summit, complete with slushy snow, dank cloud and gale-force winds and drop down towards the Ptarmigan Ridge of Ben Lomond for the return journey to Rowardennan.

Here is the true heart of the mountain; the rocky slopes that stretch down to the magic seclusion of the Cailness corrie, the haunt of red deer, wild goats and eagle. And no footpaths.

With the advent of the popular West Highland Way, the east bank of Loch Lomond has lost much of its isolation. There was a time when you could walk the rough path north from Rowardennan towards Inversnaid and come across very few people indeed. You were far more likely to run up against a herd of smelly wild goats than you were people. The east bank of the loch had a special atmosphere in those days, an atmosphere which has been destroyed by the West Highland Way. In many ways it's a shame to suggest this as the way offers thousands of people the opportunity to walk a long distance footpath, people who otherwise probably wouldn't bother walking in an area like this at all. But for any benefits that the West Highland Way may have, something special has been lost.

Handrails have been built on sections of the old footpath that once straggled its way through birch and oak. Bridges have been built on wee burns that you could almost jump across. Sections of the path that were once carpeted with the leaves of decades are now churned up into muddy morasses. If the West Highland Way had never been formally promoted by the Countryside Commission for Scotland I bet you this stretch of lochside walking would still be much as it was twenty years ago.

Cailness too has suffered with a bulldozed

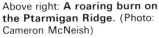
Above right: **A roaring burn on the Ptarmigan Ridge.** (Photo: Cameron McNeish)

track running up from John Groome's old cottage. John was one of the finest ornithologists in the area and a great friend of walkers and climbers. There was a time when you couldn't pass his lochside cottage without hearing a hearty welcome, and the little signposts that he made and left along the path kept many walkers smiling all the way along to Inversnaid. Sadly a new owner bought much of this land and John was made to leave the cottage that he had made a very fine home. At the time of writing John Groome lives in nearby Gartocharn, and the new owner has made himself very unpopular with conservationists and walkers.

As I came below the cloud level the grey outline of Loch Lomond stretched northwards. This east bank looks really wild and lonely from here, a stark contrast to the busy A82 road on the west bank. A ridge of hinds stopped me in my tracks, the greyness exaggerating their size. There was a mystical quality in the atmosphere; the half light melted the foreground and the deer almost looked as though they were floating on cloud. And then they were gone, with a flick of the head and a gallop.

The walk down the ridge was a treat. The archipelago of islands at the south end of the loch lit up in turn as beams of sunlight burst through the heavy cloud, the 'God beams' as my children used to call them, floodlighting the waters into burnished gold. And despite the greyness of the day there was still colour aplenty. Muted in November dress perhaps, but the blonde of the deer grass was still vivid, as were the red and gold of the dead bracken, the ochre and bronze of the still leaf-laden oak trees. Only the birches were devoid of leaf, but their skeletal copper tinge added the final touch to the scene.

I stopped and admired the waterfalls which crashed down the ridge alongside me, the waters of the wet months being discharged at a furious rate. This route down the Ben is in many ways far preferable to the 'tourist' route up the hill. But keep it as a descent route, for making a circular walk up and down one of the most 'classic' mountain routes in Scotland.

Soon the ridge eases off, you'll go through a gate and past some cottages and you'll be on the Rowardennan road near the youth hostel. A short walk and you'll soon be back at your car near the Rowardennan Hotel; no doubt ready for a cool drink or as I was on that damp and dank November day, a cup of tea and a bowl of hot soup.

BEN VENUE, TROSSACHS (Central Region)
by Cameron McNeish

Distance: 9 miles (14km) if going to the summit and back. The through route from Ledard to the Trossachs via the summit is 7 miles (11km).

Start/Finish: Ledard Farm on the B.829 Aberfoyle to Inversnaid road, or finish at the Loch Achray Hotel in the Trossachs.

Maps: OS 1:50,000 Second Series Sheet 57.

Summary: A straightforward hill walk to the summit of Ben Venue. A good footpath goes all the way to the summit trig point. If you decide to traverse the mountain to the Trossachs, take care on the descent as the slopes are very steep in places and the footpath is not as obvious as on the Ledard side.

Points of Interest: The whole area of the Trossachs has strong associations with Sir Walter Scott and his book *Rob Roy*. The lengthy poem 'The Lady of the Lake' is also set in this area. For a small hill, Ben Venue offers spectacular views, particularly towards its bigger neighbours in the north.

The track from Ledard climbs gently over a long distance.
(Photo: Cameron McNeish)

'I want to go climb a hill where there is a good view, some good legends, and which isn't a mountaineering expedition.' So said my friend Peter, home in Scotland for Christmas and with a surfeit of energy. Years of soft living in the States had given him that identifiable pear shape, so I guessed it would have to be a fairly easy hill. I picked Ben Venue in the Trossachs.

Ben Venue, hill of the caves, is one of the finest 'wee hills' in the southern Highlands. With its twin tops, its western outliers and its rugged countenance, it lords over the craggy landscape of the Trossachs, and yet is an easy enough hill to climb. At an altitude of 2,393ft (729m) above sea level Ben Venue isn't a big hill but it is big in character, so much more than many of the Munros of over 3000ft. The slopes which tumble down towards the shores of Loch Katrine contain the Bealach nam Bo (the pass of the cattle) a trade route in past centuries for cattle going to the Falkirk tryst and a back door for beasts stolen by the Clan MacGregor.

Close by is Coire na Urisgean (the corrie of the goblins) mentioned in the Ben A'an walk. Sir Walter Scott, who roamed this area and found inspiration for many of his works, depicted the Goblin's Corrie as a retreat for Ellen Douglas and her father after they had withdrawn from Roderick Dhu's stronghold on an island on Loch Katrine. This episode from 'The Lady of the Lake' is only one scene which can be recognised by wandering the Trossachs area with something of a knowledge of the works of Sir Walter Scott.

Rather than tackle the hill head-on, over and up its craggy bluffs from the east-facing Trossachs side, we drove over the Dukes Pass to Aberfoyle, along Loch Ardside, and parked the car near Ledard. A footpath sign points the way, proclaiming that it is seven miles to the Trossachs via the summit of Ben Venue.

This is a good route up the hill. The ascent is longer in terms of distance but conveniently climbs at an easy and steady gradient, just the thing for my overweight friend. This route can be treated as a 'there and back' as we did on this occasion, reaching the summit and then returning back to the car via the same route, but parties with another car are well advised to leave one near the Loch Achray Hotel at the foot of Ben Venue on the Trossachs side and carry on over the summit into the Goblin's Corrie and down to the pier at Loch Katrine. This traverse of the mountain gives a much better idea of its topography and indeed its character as the two sides of the hill are very different indeed, one side being fairly smooth and open, the other wooded, craggy and full of bracken-filled hollows.

We left the car and took the track which leads past the Ledard Farm, nowadays farming cashmere goats. Some of the goats wandered about the farmyard, tin bells clanking as they moved. In many ways the sound reminded me of the cashmere goats in the Cevennes mountains of southern France. I wonder what Scott would have thought of it. He stayed at this very building, working on his notes for *Rob Roy* and *Waverley*. Indeed, behind the farm and close by the footpath is a very fine waterfall and pool where Scott apparently worked when the weather was fine. It's easy to imagine him sitting there in the south-facing niche, perhaps enjoying the sun as he dreamt of an earlier era when the people, and indeed the country, were considerably wilder.

The path takes an obvious line alongside the Ledard Burn and eventually carries you high onto the eastern slopes of one of Venue's outliers, Beinn Bhreac. If you had plenty of time it would be fine to wander up onto the ridge of Beinn Bhreac and follow it around to the bealach between its northern slopes and Ben Venue. Otherwise you merely have to follow the well-worn path which leaves the woodlands and takes to an open corrie which curves up towards this same bealach. It's a pleasant walk, descending here and there into deep chasms where the hill burns clatter down from above. The footpath climbs steadily and unobtrusively and before you know where you are you will have arrived at the wide bealach which takes you onto the craggy slopes of Ben Venue and the first views of the day start to impress.

Away to the west Loch Katrine stretches, one of its ancient arms cut off now by the strip of land at Stronachlachar. Loch Arklet forms that old arm, running in a transverse line towards the deep trench that holds Loch Lomond. To the north, the Crianlarich hills bow their heads to the higher tops of Stobinian and Ben More, and further east the Ben Lawers range all but dwarf their neighbouring Tarmachans. Tremendous scenery in all directions.

By the time we reached the summit ridge Peter was beginning to tire, but heartily agreed that the walk was hardly a mountaineering expedition. He was delighted with the views which now stretched as far as the eye could see. There were mountains everywhere, but they paled into insignificance compared to the beauty of the countryside closer at hand. The long lochs of the Trossachs were like elongated pools of quicksilver in the afternoon light, and below us the rusty hue of the birchwoods and the emerald forest wove a delightful tapestry

Ledard Farm at the start of the Ben Venue track, is one of Scotland's few cashmere goat farms. (Photo: Cameron McNeish)

against a background of snow-tinged hills.

The walk was good, the views were fine; I now only needed some legend to keep my part of the bargain. As we sat by the summit cairn eating our piece and drinking our coffee I took out of my pack a well-thumbed copy of Scott's 'Lady of the Lake'. I read aloud the verses about the end of the stag chase at the foot of Ben Venue. It is late in the day and the sun is sinking beyond the western horizon. The knight is left alone. His horse, exhausted from the chase, dies quietly and the hounds are recalled. When the echoes of the horn fade away, the beauties of the hollows, the woods and the hills are magnificently described. Brilliant, evocative writing. I paused for effect, and glanced up quickly to see if Peter was enjoying it. He had fallen asleep, his great pear-shaped body wedged up against the summit cairn, head on chest, oblivious to the romantic brilliance of one of Scotland's greatest bards. You can't win them all.

Above: **Approaching the summit slopes of Ben Venue from the south.**

Left: **On the summit ridge of Ben Venue looking down on the Trossachs, Loch Achray and Loch Vennachar.**
(Photos: Cameron McNeish)

BEN A'AN, TROSSACHS (Central Region)
by Cameron McNeish

Above: **The fine summit cone of Ben A'an from the top of the forest track.** (Photo: Cameron McNeish)

Distance: 4 miles (6¹/₂km).
Ascent: 1200ft (370m).
Start/Finish: Forestry Commisson car park near the Trossachs Hotel.
Maps: OS 1:50,000 Second Series. Sheet 56.
Summary: A short and easy hill walk. Some of the ground is wet and broken but the route is suitable for any walker of reasonable fitness.
Points of Interest: The area known as the Trossachs is rich in historical interest and has been romantically painted in the works of Sir Walter Scott in his book *Rob Roy*. Due to the amount of deciduous woodland this area is particularly fine during the autumn.

Drive north from Aberfoyle in Stirlingshire over the steep and winding road known as the Duke's Pass and stop for a moment at the top. In front of you lies a wonderfully rugged landscape, an area bristling with spruce, larch, oak and birch, for once intermingling in fine displays of acceptable forestry.

The hills are craggy, the summits throwing down bouldery bluffs and spurs, and great corries bite into the hillsides.

High on the south huge Ben Venue
Down on the lake in masses threw
Crags, knolls and mounds, confusedly hurled
The fragments of an earlier world.

31

So wrote Sir Walter Scott in describing this area which is generally known as the Trossachs. The word itself is derived from 'Trosaichen' which loosely translated means a transverse glen joining two others. This description roughly relates to the heartland of the Trossachs, the great jumble of rock and woodland which separates Loch Achray from Loch Katrine.

It's a wild looking area and its former inhabitants were equally wild. The Trossachs sits on the very edge of the old Highland Line, a geological and geographical fault which runs across Scotland from the south end of Loch Lomond to Stonehaven on the north-east coast near Aberdeen. The clans who lived north of this line were, even until a comparatively recent period, as Scott so succinctly puts it, 'much addicted to predatory excursions upon their Lowland neighbours'.

Although the Trossachs is situated on the edge of this line, a border country in effect, it was virtually sequestered from the world and, as it were, insulated with respect by society. *Graham's Sketches of Scenery in Perthshire,* published in 1806, explains:

Tis well known that in the highlands, it was in former times, accounted not only lawful, but honourable, among hostile tribes, to commit depredations on one another; and these habits of the age were perhaps strengthened in this district by the circumstances which have been mentioned. It bordered on a country, the inhabitants of which, while they were richer, were less warlike than they, and widely differed by language and manners.

Best known of these inhabitants was Rob Roy MacGregor Campbell, erstwhile chief of the Clan MacGregor. Rob Roy owed much of his notoriety to the pen of Sir Walter Scott, who painted a very colourful picture of the man. Nevertheless, he is undoubtedly one of Scotland's best-known heroes who became chief of his clan through sheer personality rather than by virtue of descent. The MacGregors were at one time outlawed for their misdeeds and they suffered great persecution. Most Highland clans were a rule unto themselves and resented any thought of law enforcement from the south. For political reasons the MacGregors suffered more than most and many of the men took to the hills, living in caves and howffs. Stealing was the only course open to them. Their nocturnal doings soon earned them the name, Children of the Mist.

And this Trossachs area is MacGregor country. Away in front of you a long line of hills approach from the east and at the western end of this range, sticking up like an af-

terthought, is the shapely crest of Ben A'an, our destination for this walk.

This isn't a high hill, a mere 1520ft (463m) above sea level, but it's a rocky top of immense character and offers more for its height than many hills twice its size. Ben A'an, in fact, isn't its original name. The old Gaelic name was Am Binnein (the rocky peak) but that was changed like many other local names to suit the poetic licence of Sir Walter Scott. Scott had considerable influence on this area and his novel, *Rob Roy,* and poem, 'The Lady of the Lake', greatly romanticised the whole area.

On the north shore of Loch Achray, close to the turreted grandeur of the Trossachs Hotel, the Forestry Commission have built a car park and erected signposts indicating the Ben A'an walk. The first section of the walk is steep and is often muddy but gains height quickly and directly.

Take your time and enjoy the song of the chaffinch as you climb uphill below the canopy of larch. After a while the steepness relents and a signpost indicates a viewpoint to the left. It's well worthwhile taking a look, for it's from here that you'll get your first glimpse of the summit rock of Ben A'an, framed by spruce and larch. From this viewpoint it looks steep and exposed, but the path climbs up the right hand side of it and contours round the back towards the summit itself.

Once out of the forest the views open up towards the craggy bluffs and corries of Ben Venue and the long stretch of Loch Katrine, the finest of all the Trossachs lochs. In late August and early September the heather blooms in purple magnificence, and contrasts with the vibrant greenery of the trees. Later on the grasses turn blond, and the leaves lighten into yellows and ochres, reds and russets, a time of the year when the Trossachs are at their most splendid.

Continue upwards and now the path begins to climb steeply again, up wet and broken ground, helped on your way by some sound path construction. Higher up much of the rock is loose and after heavy rain there is a lot of running water. Contour round the back of the hill, across some wet mossy areas, and then up the final few feet to the summit rocks.

The summit of Ben A'an is a superb rocky eyrie, with magnificent views towards the west and the north. On clear days all the Arrochar hills are clearly seen, from the unmistakable outline of the Cobbler to Ben Vorlich. Further north the Crianlarich hills come into view with the twin summits of Ben More and Stobinian particularly impressive. Loch Katrine stretches her way into the heartland of the MacGregor country and across the waters below you lies

Scrambling on the summit rocks with Loch Katrine in the background. (Photo: Cameron McNeish)

heather and boulder-scarred hollows. These urisks, explains Dr. Graham in *Scenery of the Southern Confines of Perthshire*, published in 1806, 'were a sort of lubbery supernatural, who could be gained over by kind attention to perform the drudgery of a farm. They were supposed to be spread throughout the Highlands each in his own wild recess, but the solemn meetings of the order were regularly held in this cave of Benvenew.'

South-east of you lie the waters of Loch Achray, one of the principal lochs of the Trossachs and it was close to these shores that the Clan MacGregor had their traditional assembly point. A fiery cross would be carried around the MacGregor lands by a team of runners, summoning the able-bodied men of the clan to action. When a chief deigned to summon his clan, upon any sudden or important emergency, he slew a goat, and making a cross of any light wood seared its ends in a fire and then extinguished the flames in the blood of the slain animal. This symbol, the Crean Tarigh (the cross of shame) (because disobedience to what the symbol implied inferred infamy), was then carried round the clan lands and areas which owed allegiance to the patriarch of the clan, by a relay of runners who passed the cross to each other with a single word, the place of rendezvous.

At the sight of the fiery-cross, every man, from age sixteen to sixty and capable of bearing arms, was obliged to present himself instantly at the given rendezvous. Anyone who failed to appear suffered the extreme punishments of fire and sword which were emblematically demonstrated to the disobedient by the bloody and burnt marks on the warlike cross.

Scott, in his 'Lady of the Lake', paints an exciting portrait of this ritual as Angus, heir of Duncan's line, was summoned to carry the first stage of the cross. According to Scott, Angus sped quickly along the shores of Loch Venachar to Coilantogle where he ascended the broad ridge of Ben Ledi, and then dropped steeply to the Pass of Leny to hand the cross over to Norman, heir of Arnandave. Poor Norman. He had just become married to a young lass called Mary and was just leaving St. Bridge's chapel when Angus thrust the cross in his hand and told him to get on with it. No matrimonial leave in those days.

It's well worth reading the works of Scott if you plan to visit the Trossachs, and it would certainly make the experience of climbing Ben A'an much more rewarding, taking you back into the history of what is an exciting and magnificent corner of Scotland.

the ancient pass of the Bealach nam Bo. This is the Pass of the Cattle, through which the MacGregors once drove stolen cattle to secret hide-outs.

Behind the Bealach, lies the rock-strewn Coire nan Uruisgean, the Corrie of the Urisks, or Goblins. This was reputedly the meeting place for all the goblins in Scotland, who gathered here to plan and plot amid the deep

BEN LEDI (Central Region) by Roger Smith

Distance: 7 miles (11km).
Ascent: 2500ft (750m).
Start/Finish: Forestry Commission car park, near Leny Water.
Map: OS 1:50,000 Sheet 57.
Summary: Ascent on track and hill path, descent on hill and forest path. Some steep ground but nothing too severe.
Points of Interest: Mature forestry; large glacial erratic boulders in Stank Glen; summit of Ben Ledi—fine views.

Above left: **The waterfall in Stank Glen. 'Stank' in Scots means a drain or watercourse.**

Above right: **Ben Ledi, the 'Hill of God' or 'Hill of light' where on May Day—the Celtic New Year—people from the surrounding settlements would climb the summit and light a fire to greet the spring.**
(Photos: Roger Smith)

Vast numbers of people are familiar with the outline of Ben Ledi without ever having set foot on it, or indeed even knowing what its name is. The hill and its prominent knobby top dominate the northward view from the M9 and M80 near Stirling and from the main railway line running into Stirling from both Glasgow and Edinburgh. Seen from here, Ledi rises above the Carse (plain) of Stirling, appearing as a southerly outlier of the mountainous Highland ground to the north.

That is indeed its geographical situation. As

you drive north through Callander (the magnificent railway line taking this route was regrettably closed in the 1960s) you encounter a very marked change in the scenery. From being a relatively flat and fast route, the A84 becomes a twisting switchback forcing its way through a narrow gorge (the Pass of Leny) to run alongside Loch Lubnaig, with high hills on either side.

Ben Ledi is the mountain dominating the western shore of Loch Lubnaig and its ascent is supremely rewarding, for the view from the summit in clear conditions is quite outstanding. The hill has a very long-standing Celtic significance too, as we shall see. North of Callander is another link with the Celtic past in the hamlet of Kilmahog—nothing to do with slaughtering pigs but a name deriving from 'the cell of St Chug', he being one of the lesser-known saints of that distant time. 'Kil' meaning cell is a very common element in place-names in Scotland.

There are several ways up Ben Ledi, but the route described here gives, to my mind, the most satisfying ascent and also the most rapid way down. It starts at the small car parking area provided by the Forestry Commission—

who own and work most of the mountain—reached by turning left half a mile or so past the Pass of Leny, over the Leny Water. From the car park two roads head north towards Loch Lubnaig (the name means loch of the bend). Take the left hand road, not the one leading to the Forestry Commission's holiday chalets.

The road leads past some cottages, including one called 'The Mancunian' clearly used by expatriate Lancashire folk and another ingeniously constructed by extending a parked caravan. In about a mile the road becomes a track leading to the farmhouse of Stank. This apparently unattractive name, like so many others in Scotland, should not be taken at face value. There are two possible derivations, both of them watery. 'Stank' in Scots means a drain or watercourse, and there is a Gaelic word *stang* meaning pools. Either would be appropriate for this beautifully set place, on a fine tumbling burn and surrounded by mature trees.

Do not walk as far as the house but take the forest road to the left. At a very sharp hairpin bend look for a green waymark on a rock opposite you showing the start of the path up

The large, glacial erratic boulders of Stank Glen. (Photo: Roger Smith)

Stank Glen. There has been much working of the forest here in recent years but the path is generally kept clear. It twists sharply upward through the trees to a point where it overlooks a fine waterfall.

The forest hereabouts—mainly conifers—will be subject to almost continual change in the years ahead as some blocks or 'coupes' are felled and then replanted. The aim is to provide a rotating crop on a sustained basis, and the Commission has restocking and landscaping plans for this forest all the way up to Strathyre for as far ahead as the year 2025.

Stank Glen is very beautiful at all times of the year. I have walked it in January snows and in summer heat when the air was drowsy with the hum of insects, and the pattern of light and shade through the trees was almost hypnotic in its effect. At other times when the clouds lour there is a feeling of being trapped in a dank, dark tunnel from which there is no escape.

At about 1500ft (450m) you come out of the main block of trees into the upper glen (there are still some smaller plantations ahead). From darkness and shade a step, it seems, takes you to light and space, and what a fine wild place this is too. The most common route is a slant half left up the hill slope, keeping left of Creag na h-Iolaire (crag of the eagles, though you will be lucky indeed to see them nowadays) to gain the ridge not far from Lochan nan Corp, of which more anon.

For a diversion I would certainly recommend following a narrow path up by the forest edge to reach a number of vast glacial erratics, boulders of extraordinary size left here by the retreating ice and now affording merry sport for scramblers. This is a great place for a break to eat your piece and maybe take a swig of burn water.

To the north the lumpy outline of Ardnandave Hill forms a fine rough skyline. Below the forest is spread, with glimpses of Loch Lubnaig and Callander clearly seen to the south-east. Sitting here at ease there is a great temptation to stop and go no further. But that would be a shame when such riches still lie ahead and above.

Pushing up north-westwards, the ridge is gained eventually, as ridges always are. Immediately the horizons broaden dramatically, with Stobinian and Ben More seen to the north, the Trossachs hills and forests further west and the ridge itself stretching out to Ben Vane, a Corbett well worth the walk across. Just a little way to the north (if you have reached the ridge at the usual place, and I can't guarantee that) is Lochan nan Corp.

A small and unremarkable body of water it seems, perhaps. Apart from the dimension that such things always add to the high hills, this one has its place in local history, as the name shows. 'Corp' means body—you might have suspected that—and the lochan is said to lie on a coffin route, used to transport bodies from the glens to the west over the hill and down to St Bride's Chapel near the Pass of Leny for burial. Once, so the story goes, a party using the route failed to see the lochan, it being covered in ice. They started across but their combined weight was too much and the ice broke, drowning some of them in the freezing water. If you have been here in winter you can easily imagine it happening.

Once you are on the ridge, the way to the summit is easily found by turning south and following the line of the old fenceposts which once marked a boundary between estates. The summit is crowned by an OS trig pillar and commands, in the right conditions, a view as fine as anywhere in the southern Highlands. To the far south-west the unmistakable outline of the Arran hills can be made out. To west and north an incredible array of peak upon peak crowds the horizon. Further east the great Ben Lawers group stand up proud and away back the high Cairngorms draw the eye irresistibly. What a magic country this is and how very good to be able to stand on such a summit and be presented with such a view.

Others came here in other times for other reasons. Ledi's name has long been a subject of dispute among Gaelic scholars, but a likely derivation is *Beinn le Dia,* the Hill of God or of Light. The root is the same as that for Beltane, the ancient Celtic festival marking the coming of spring. On the first day of May—which was the Celtic New Year—people from the surrounding settlements of Callander, Balquhidder, Brig o'Turk and elsewhere would ascend Ben Ledi to light the Beltane fire and greet the spring, the season of warmth and growth.

At midnight all hearth fires would be put out, to be relit from flames brought down from hilltop fires such as that on Ben Ledi. Cattle were driven between the old and new fires to keep them free of disease, and food was shared. Standing on the summit of Ben Ledi it is easy to imagine the shadowy figures in the flickering light of the Beltane fire offering their thanks for the passing of another long winter and the coming of the season of supreme beauty and growth, the spring. We lose such feelings at our peril, I believe.

Such pilgrims as seek to attain the summit of Ben Ledi nowadays tend in the majority to do so from the south. Hence my belief that the Stank Glen approach is the better, as you are unlikely to meet many folk going up that way.

On the descent things are rather different. A well-marked and much-used path is laid before you and there is no difficulty with route-finding. It is also rather a nice feeling to be going *down* when everyone else is coming *up!*

From the subsidiary top a few hundred feet below the summit there is a fine panorama of the Highland Edge spread before you. Westward stretches the expanse of Loch Venachar (the pointed loch), which points indeed—to the Trossachs and Loch Achray (the loch of the field). This whole area was made famous by Victorian travellers and writers, notably Sir Walter Scott. The farm at the foot of Ledi's southern ridge. Coilantogle, is mentioned in *The Lady of the Lake* as being linked with Clan Alpin, and he goes on to say: 'Here Venachar in silver flows, There, ridge on ridge, Benledi rose'—as indeed it does.

The descent continues steeply down the ridge until the angle eases at some rather marshy ground, and then swings sharply left to reach a stile at the top of the forest. The path continues down beside a chuckling burn which is easily reached if you want a very pleasant spot for a break.

Before long you reach a stretch of path which has had an interesting piece of maintenance carried out on it. It crosses ground which, through the pressure of many hundreds of pairs of booted feet, had become churned up and very muddy. The technique used to restore the path is called fascining and is believed to date back to Roman times. It involves gathering bundles of brushwood or undergrowth—in plentiful supply in a forest, naturally!—strapping them together and laying them across the muddy area to the width required. Poles cut from branches are laid lengthwise and the whole lot is bound together, with a layer of soil or fine gravel on top to provide a walking surface.

It all blends in very well, provides an excellent path, and is quite simple to prepare. This technique has been used in a number of locations on paths through forest—you will find other examples on Ben Venue and Ben A'an in the Trossachs. This technique was, incidentally, used to 'float' the railway across Rannoch Moor. As you walk across this stretch of path there is a definite, and not unpleasant, bouncing feeling—probably an aid to tired legs after a hill day!

The rest of the descent is soon accomplished, landing you back at the car park where you started. This is right on the line of the former Stirling-Crianlarich railway, which must have been a grand run up through the forest and alongside Loch Lubnaig. It follows the line of an old road made in the eighteenth century as part of the network developed by Wade and Caulfeild after the 1745 uprising.

The history and legend surrounding Ben Ledi, from the ancient Celtic rites of Beltane to the writings of Scott and the works of the railway engineer, add greatly to the pleasure of its ascent. The remarkable views from the summit confirm the pleasure that this friendly hill has given to so many people.

THE FIFE COAST (Fife Region) by
Roger Smith

Distance: 9 miles (14km).
Ascent: 350ft (100m).
Start/Finish: Start at Pittenweem Harbour, and finish at Crail.
Map: OS 1:50,000 Sheet 59.
Transport: Hourly bus service (No.95) from Crail to Pittenweem.

Summary: Coastal walk on roads and good tracks. Negligible ascent overall.
Points of Interest: Crail, Anstruther and Pittenweem fishing villages; museum in Anstruther; Caiplie Caves; Fife Ness.

Crail Harbour, a fishing village full of lovely old pantiled houses, narrow streets and plenty of places of interest to visit at the end of your walk. (Photo: Roger Smith)

Coastal walking has a pleasure all its own. The constant presence of the ever-changing sea at one side and the beauty of the coast itself at the other make a very happy combination. The settlements along the coast are always worth visiting and tend to vary themselves as you move from one part of the country to another.

The walk described here is perhaps not one of our best-known stretches of coastline – at least as far as walkers are concerned. I am happy to try to put that right, for I found it exceptionally enjoyable and very fulfilling despite its relatively short length.

The walk starts in Pittenweem, one of a

number of fishing villages on the Fife shore of the Firth of Forth. Fishing and its associated trades was for long the principal business of the area: it has declined in the past century, but Pittenweem still has very much the feel of a working harbour. There is car parking space just by the harbour, and just looking at the boats will pass a pleasant half-hour before setting off east to start the walk. A diversion to Cave Wynd will enable you to view the remarkable St Fillan's Cave, believed to have been the home of the missionary St Fillan in the seventh century. Keys to gain admission to the large cave with its well and stone staircase can be obtained from the Gingerbread Horse craft shop at 9 High Street.

To leave Pittenweem from the harbour, walk east along the road for about a quarter of a mile then take the path on the right through a small children's swingpark and along the edge of a field. Halfway across the field, turn right down some steps to join the golf course. Already the 'sea smells' are very evident and there is a fine view out to the Isle of May, a view which is a delight throughout this walk.

The walk continues along the shoreline for a mile or so to pass the headland known as Billow Ness and approach Anstruther. The keen ornithologist will already have had cause to stop more than once: the birdlife in the Firth is outstandingly good, with many varieties of sea-bird regularly to be seen. I particularly enjoy the extraordinary sight of gannets diving at tremendous speed, wings folded, and emerging with fish that had a few seconds beforehand been quietly going about their business held firmly in their beaks.

The path leads past a small sandy beach and into Anstruther (locally pronounced as 'Anster'). You will see from the map that there are two burghs, Anstruther Wester and Anstruther Easter. Each of these, and the small settlement of Kilrenny a little way inland, was a separate royal burgh until 1929: when Anstruther Wester received its charter in 1587 it was the smallest royal burgh in Scotland. Anstruther Wester was originally more important than its eastern neighbour, having its own church as early as the twelfth century.

Enter Anstruther Wester on Shore Road and turn left into Crichton Street to join the Pittenweem Road. At Elizabeth Place do not cross the bridge over the Dreel Burn but turn right into Esplanade and go down a flight of

Caiplie Farm in its glorious setting. (Photo: Roger Smith)

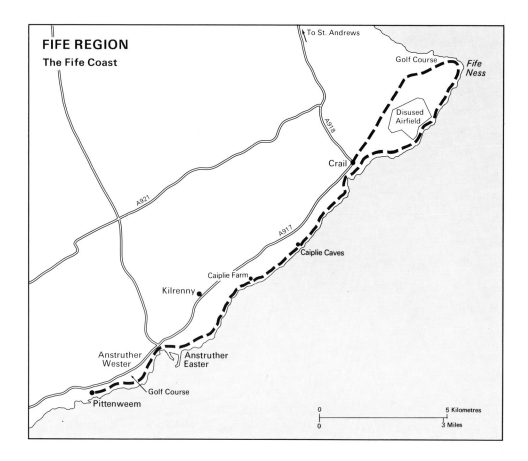

To St. Andrews

Golf Course

*Fife
Ness*

Disused
Airfield

A918

Crail

A921

A917

Caiplie Caves

Caiplie Farm

Kilrenny

Anstruther
Wester

Anstruther
Easter

Golf Course

Pittenweem

0   5 Kilometres

0   3 Miles

steps to cross the burn by the old stepping stones; this was originally the only way from the wester burgh to the easter. Anstruther's main harbour now lies just ahead, and a fascinating place it is too.

In the sixteenth century vessels traded from here to the Baltic, the Low Countries, France and Spain as well as to England. The royal charter for burgh status was granted in 1583, and as well as the usual basic subjects, navigation was taught to all pupils in the school here, as the great majority of them would pursue a career linked to the sea when they grew up.

On the east side of the harbour is the lifeboat house, which is well worth a visit. The station was established here in 1865. The present boat is the station's sixth; it was launched in the centenary year, 1965, and is named *The Doctors* after Drs Norah and William Allan, who with their brother Mr James Allan presented the boat to the town. This boat is now ending the term of its service and will be replaced within the next five years by a faster vessel equipped to maintain the Anstruther station's proud record of lifesaving.

A few yards away is the Scottish Fisheries Museum, which should certainly be visited.

The museum, which opened in 1969, is housed in an attractive group of buildings around three sides of a cobbled courtyard; the tourist information office is here also. The museum covers every aspect of the fishing industry, including whaling. As well as actual vessels on view there is a splendid collection of models, and the dark side of seagoing is seen in the memorial to Scottish fishermen lost at sea. A marine aquarium provides an opportunity to look at many sea creatures at close quarters. The museum is open daily all year round (afternoons only in the winter months) and has a tearoom should the walk here have already made you thirsty.

Back at the harbour, another attraction is the former North Carr lightship, now permanently moored here and open to visitors in the summer months. As you prepare to leave 'Anster', it is worth reflecting that exactly 400 years ago some 250 survivors of the ill-fated Spanish Armada fleet landed here. The men and their leader, General Juan Gomez de Medina, were well treated during their stay, after which they crossed the Firth to Leith to board a ship for Flanders.

Walk out of Anstruther along narrow streets named respectively James, John and George

Map to show the 9-mile walk along the Fife coast from Pittenweem harbour to Crail. Negligible ascent and good walking on roads and tracks make it an excellent family day out.

Where the houses end a sign says "Coastal walk to Crail. Please keep to the shoreline". This is exactly what we intend to do! A fine walk it is too, with the Isle of May drawing the eye all the time. (It is possible to visit the island, by the way, by boat from Anstruther. The island has a ruined chapel and monastery and, as might be expected, exceptionally fine birdlife.)

A mile along this lovely shoreline brings you to the farm at Caiplie, in a quite glorious setting. Sitting here having my lunch on a wonderful June day, I was joined by a farm dog which seemed just to want company. It did not beg for food, or bark: it just came and sat very quietly with me until I left. We were quite happy with each other's company and when I got up to walk on it walked back to the farm, perhaps to wait for the next traveller to pass.

It could be said that this walk lacks one element of coastal scenery—dramatic cliffs—but in another half-mile there is something every bit as good, and all the more surprising for its sudden appearance. A sandstone bluff is seen ahead. It doesn't look anything special, but when you get up to it you find it is fantastically eroded into stacks and arches which lean precariously against each other. This unique place can only be visited on foot and was for me the highlight of the walk.

These Caiplie Caves (also called Carlawchy) were originally, it is thought, used as a dwelling place in around 2000 BC. In one of the caves is a drawing of a large animal with spears sticking out of its back, and Greek and Latin crosses have also been found inscribed here, indicating use over a long period. One of those associated with the caves is St Adrian, the first bishop of St Andrews. He was murdered in AD 870 by Danish invaders under King Humber. More recently, in the mid-seventeenth century, the self-styled 'prophet' Alexander Penn lived in the caves. He was feared by the local people and was eventually exiled to Bass Rock, where he died. A truly fascinating place.

The best bit of coastal scenery is followed by probably the most attractive village—but not before another highly enjoyable mile of shore-side walking has been done. It leads you, by a splendid old flight of stone steps, into Crail, the last settlement on this stretch of coast. Crail has been described as 'probably the single most photographed spot on the coast of Scotland', and while that can never be proved, you will be an exception indeed if you do not reach for your camera when you get here.

The village itself is full of lovely old pantiled houses and narrow streets; it boasts a very handsome seventeenth century Customs House (in Shoregate, above the harbour) and

Top: **The Fisheries Museum at Anstruther which has actual vessels on view as well as a splendid collection of models and a marine aquarium.**

Above: **Caiplie Caves, one of which has a drawing of a large animal with spears in its back. It is believed to have been a dwelling place in 2000BC.**
(Photos: Roger Smith)

for a mile or so to the tiny harbour at Cellardykes. The name is believed to come from Sillerdyke, from the silvery appearance of garden walls (dykes) where nets hung. This was the harbour for the burgh of Kilrenny, and it is recorded that in 1837 as many as 140 boats regularly finished from here. Now there are just a few left, creel fishing for crab and lobster, and some craft used for leisure sailing. Just to the east of the harbour, on the seaward side, are the Cardinal Steps. These were formerly used by bishops and other eminent churchmen who sailed from Cellardykes—where they had a residence—to St Andrews.

the harbour itself is almost unbelievably photogenic, so that you might suspect it has been put up as a film set. But it's real right enough, and has been a place of work for fishermen for many centuries. Trading these days is much less vigorous than it used to be, with the boats working from here being mainly shell-fishers, but the harbour is very definitely still in use and not a museum piece.

It is a place to wander through and savour (and photograph!). The Collegiate Church, an eighteenth century building, has fine woodwork, and the small museum includes an intriguing relief model of old Crail. On Castle Walk, looking out to sea, is a most unusual painted panorama depicting the view in front of you. Some view too: May is of course prominent, the coastline we have been following stretches out to east and west, and across the Forth the East Lothian shore can be made out.

There are two or three miles still to do. Out of Crail, you pass Roome Rocks and the caravan park at Sauchope and step out towards Fife Ness, where the coastline turns north. Before then you walk alongside the site of Crail aerodrome, used as a fighter base during World War II. The control tower is still there, as are many of the buildings: what ghosts inhabit them nowadays, I wonder?

Just before Fife Ness is reached you cross the path of Dane's Dike, an old earthwork and fortification associated with the days when St Adrian was trying to bring Christianity to the area and the fierce invaders from across the North Sea came with other ideas on their minds. At Fife Ness itself is a coastguard station, and the place is visited by that special feeling that is always associated with the turning of a coastline round a tenable corner: I hesitate to described it as 'emotional' but in truth it is, in my mind at least.

The walk is now nearly over. Just round the corner from Fife Ness is the golf course at Balconie Links, which must surely have one of the most magnificent situations of any course in Britain. From the clubhouse you look out at a most wonderful seascape; I would think it is extremely distracting but it provides a great excuse if you hit a duff shot! Golf in such surroundings can only be a pleasure, whatever your actual sporting standards.

A minor road provides a very pleasant walk back to Crail, with generally very little traffic. It gives a view of the landward side of the aerodrome; you may well be joined by aircraft of the present day, as jet fighter trainers from the RAF base at Leuchars, near St Andrews, regularly pass overhead at low level, and helicopters shuttling to and fro on their always seemingly-urgent missions also frequent the airspace over the 'East Neuk'.

From Crail it is easy to return to Pitten-weem, using the No.95 bus, which leaves the main street at ten minutes to the hour. It is a very pleasant ride of about twenty minutes. Your walk here took rather longer, but if my experience is anything to go by it will be time you will not begrudge. I found the 'East Neuk' of Fife a most interesting part of the world and its coastline a very pleasing place to walk.

STRATHCLYDE REGION

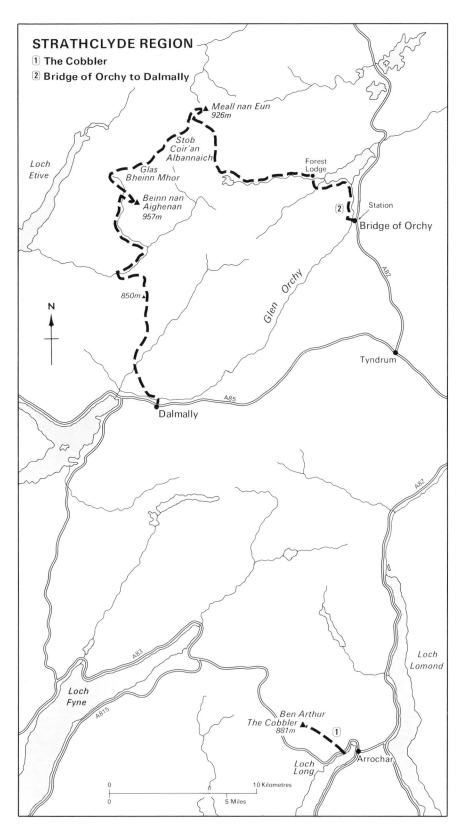

STRATHCLYDE REGION
1. The Cobbler
2. Bridge of Orchy to Dalmally

Meall nan Eun
926m

Stob
Coir'an
Albannaich

Glas
Bheinn Mhor

Loch
Etive

Beinn nan
Aighenan
957m

Forest
Lodge

2. Station

Bridge of Orchy

850m

Glen Orchy

Tyndrum

A85

Dalmally

N

Loch
Lomond

Loch
Fyne

A83

A815

Loch
Long

Ben Arthur
The Cobbler
881m

1.

Arrochar

0   10 Kilometres

0   5 Miles

Map showing 2 walks in the
Strathclyde region: The
Cobbler (p44) and Bridge of
Orchy to Dalmally (p47).

The 5-mile walk to the top of
Ben Arthur (The Cobbler), is a
circular one which begins and
ends at Buttermilk Burn.
Scrambling skills are needed to
reach the top but otherwise
it's a superb short hill walk
amid rocky mountain
surroundings.

For the 27-mile mountain
walk from Bridge of Orchy to
Dalmally you should allow 2$^{1}/_{2}$
days. The country is largely
uninhabited but route finding
is straightforward in good
weather and not unduly
difficult in bad. The mountains
themselves present no special
difficulties.

THE COBBLER (Strathclyde Region) by Cameron McNeish

Distance: 5 miles (8km).
Ascent: 2500ft (760m).
Start/finish: Beside Loch Long at the But-termilk Burn.
Maps: OS 1:50,000 Sheet 56.
Summary: A superb short hill walk amid rocky mountain surroundings. Scrambling skills are required to climb the main summit.
Points of Interest: Very good views of Ben Lomond and the rest of the surrounding peaks known as the Arrochar Alps. Extensive views down Loch Long towards the hills of Cowal.

Above: **Ben Arthur, popularly known as The Cobbler, is possibly the only hill of its height in Britain that requires the skills of a rock scrambler to reach its summit.** (Photo: Cameron McNeish)

The Ordnance Survey calls it Ben Arthur, but it's known to all and sundry as the Cobbler. It's a Glaswegians' hill. High up on the rocky flanks of this wee hill you're likely to be greeted with the broad vowels of Clydeside, for the Glasgow people claim this as theirs: close enough for a day trip in the twenties and

thirties, when hordes of working class Clyde-siders would come on the train to Arrochar and gaze up at the Cobbler's alpine shape. It was their wee hill, and it still is.

The Glaswegians are a bit possessive about their hills. When Munro-bagging became something of a cult activity they lost Ben

Lomond, their Beacon Hill to the new hordes or 'bashers'. The 'ither' Ben, to distinguish it from Ben Nevis, had become cosmopolitan.

It's unlikely that the Cobbler will solicit such popularity because two features of its topography go against the grain of mass popularity; its height and its ruggedness.

The Cobbler lacks the altitude above sea level to elevate it to Munro status. At 2891ft (881m) above the sea water of Loch Long it's as big a mountain, if not bigger than scores of the Munros which get a bigger start because of their landward height, but because it's not a Munro it will be ignored by many. Hurrah!

The Cobbler is also an incredibly rocky mountain, possibly the only hill of its height in the country that requires the skills of a rock scrambler to stand on its summmit. The final few feet have caused many a happy rambler to turn back and settle for the lowlier North Peak. Like the Inn Pin on the Cuillin Ridge on the Isle of Skye, the central summit of the

Cobbler has disappointed many a visitor, and why not for the Cobbler is on many accounts a climber's hill and not a walker's hill.

So why include it in a book of classic walks? Every walker that I've introduced to the Cobbler has managed to pluck up the courage to scramble the final feet to the top. It's actually not difficult at all and only requires a head for heights which most walkers have anyway, and even if you don't make it to the very summit there's too much that's good about the Cobbler to miss it completely.

But to the history. Despite a visit by the Abraham brothers, those brilliant rock climbers from the Lake District, earlier in the century, the Cobbler was virtually unexplored when the first explosion of working class climbers hit it in the 1930s. Members of the Clydeside-based Creag Dhu Mountaineering Club put up many of the initial rock climbing routes and during the post-war period this club totally dominated the route-finding on the hill,

Below left: **Walkers stop to enjoy the view from the north summit of The Cobbler, the only summit that can be climbed without having to scramble or rock climb.**

Below right: **The Middle Peak of The Cobbler, the actual summit, showing the narrow 'window' which offers scrambling access to the summit.** (Photos: Cameron McNeish)

sleeping at night below the Narnain Boulder and in and amongst the natural 'howffs' which are to be found in the rockfalls in the corries. Read Alastair Borthwick's amusing account of this first foray to the Cobbler in his book, *'Always a Little Further'*, one of the great classics of outdoor activity books.

I first saw the Cobbler when I struggled up nearby Ben Lomond for the very first time. Away across the gulf formed by Loch Lomond this almost surrealist-looking form dominated the small range of hills known as the Arrochar Alps. Despite the fact that its neighbour Beinn Narnain is much bigger in height, it's the odd shape of the Cobbler which captures the eye and the imagination.

It's this odd shape that gives the Cobbler its nickname. Some suggest that it resembles a cobbler working at his last. There are three distinct summits, the left one formed into a definite pyramid, while the Central Peak, the true summit, just looks like a rather dull flat-topped rock. The right hand, or North Peak is an immense overhanging prow which, with a coating of snow and ice, looks utterly alpine.

I soon discovered that the easiest route to the hill was via Arrochar, a sadly neglected-looking village which straggles around the head of Loch Long. Like many other villages in the area, Arrochar suffers from the presence of the Ministry of Defence (MOD), and the upper reaches of Loch Long are used for torpedo testing. In fact it is opposite the torpedo testing station that a prominent footpath runs up through some forestry to the open country just below the hill.

On a recent visit, on a rather hot day, I followed the course of the Buttermilk Burn (which the path follows) in the hope of getting a cool scramble. It was marvellous. The Buttermilk Burn is an interesting, winding burn, with many of the better features of a Lakeland gill. In fact there were one or two sections where I had to forsake the route itself for the ease of the grassy banks. Try it if you feel like a change from the usual plod up the footpath.

The most straightforward route to the top of the Cobbler is by an obvious bealach, or col, between the North and Central Peaks of the hill. Follow the obvious path from the Buttermilk Burn, past the overhanging bulk of the Narnain boulders, and on upwards through the rocky litter and debris of the corrie itself.

By this time I'm sure you'll be enthralled by the rocky aspect of the hill. Rock dominates, and much of it is vertical. Follow the path onto the bealach, turn immediately right, and follow the well-worn path that leads to the flat platform of the North Summit. Take care here for the drops are sheer on three sides. Up here too is the spew-out point of a well-used and popular rock climbing route known as Recess Route, a vertical right-angled gully which almost brought me to grief several years ago.

I had started the climb which is graded as a Very Difficult route, not realising that the route moved off to the right after the first pitch to follow an easy ledge, an awkward move over a bulge, then an easy enough finish. After the first easy pitch I had climbed straight on, mistakenly, to the direct finish which was graded Very Severe. I really believed I was in bad form that day as it took me almost four hours to negotiate that final pitch onto the North Summit. There's a moral there. Read the guidebooks properly.

From the North Peak there are grand views in all directions. Ben Lomond dominates the scene to the south and closer at hand rise the other Arrochar Alps. Particularly impressive are Beinn Narnain and Beinn Ime. Across the corrie rises the Central Peak, the highest on the hill, and below sparkle the waters of Loch Long, reaching far inland from the sea.

Make your way back down to the bealach and up towards the Central Peak. The way to the summit isn't terribly evident, but soon you'll see it, a narrow gash, or window, in the rock. You must crawl through this, like the eye of a needle. Once through the slit you will find yourself on a traversing ledge which should be followed to the left, around the back of the rock to where a couple of easy holds lift you to the summit platform. It's an exhilarating finish to the hill, a real reward to those who enjoy an easy scramble.

The South Peak involves a bit of scrambling too, but is really for those who rock climb. However, it's very rewarding sitting on the Central Peak watching other walkers shake their heads and say, 'No thank you . . .'

But perhaps that's a bit unfair and egotistical. Even without the scramble to the summit the Cobbler has the ingredients of a classic. On my very first ascent of the hill I was accompanied by a small black and white collie dog, a real little character of a dog who appeared out of the mist and showed me the way to the top. He shared my lunch that day, and on the way down, near the bottom, he vanished as suddenly as he appeared. I liked the notion that this wee dog was like the very spirit of the Cobbler, cheeky, a bit cocky, and good company. For this hill is a bit like that, a wee hill with all the attributes of bigger hills. I would put it among my top five favourite hills in Britain, and would happily swop it for two hundred Munros.

BRIDGE OF ORCHY TO DALMALLY
(Strathclyde Region) by Peter Evans

From the summit of Stob Coir' an Albannaich, a walker enjoys the view to Ben Starav (furthest away) and Glas Bheinn Mhor. (Photo: Cameron McNeish)

Distance: 27 miles (43km).
Start: Start at Bridge of Orchy Railway Station, Glasgow to Fort William line.
Finish: at Dalmally Railway Station, Glasgow to Oban line.
Map: OS 1:50,000 Sheet 50.
Summary: A mountain walk over two and a half days through largely uninhabited, inaccessibly country. Escape from the mountains to lower levels if the weather turns foul is easy and the mountains themselves present no special difficulties. Route-finding is straightforward in good weather and not unduly difficult in bad.

Points of Interest: Inveroran Hotel, between Victoria Bridge and Bridge of Orchy is an ancient hostelry with interesting connections. The poet Wordsworth and his sister Dorothy were visitors. At the northern end of Loch Awe is Kilchurn Castle, a ruin open to the public, and just outside Dalmally, on the old road to Cladich, is a memorial to the Gaelic poet Duncan Ban McIntyre, once keeper at Ben Dorain, near Bridge of Orchy.

Tom began to stagger as if he were drunk, lurching from side to side on the path, the weight of his pack exaggerated by his weakened physical condition. I had never seen anyone in such a state before, but I realised fairly quickly what was wrong: he was dehydrated. It was one of the hottest summers on record for Scotland and Tom had gone too long on a long day without drinking. We would have to stop soon.

Although a couple of miles from our intended wild campsite in Glen Kinglass, Tom's plight needed urgent action. A short distance further on and I spotted a likely pitch for the tent. We gratefully unburdened ourselves of our packs, got the tent up and thought about preparing food. Tom made a beeline for the nearby burn and started replacing lost fluid. The burn was surprisingly full, and its rushing water delightfully cool. We both drank long draughts before returning to the tent.

Visions of hot food and a welcome rest: and then they struck! Midges! There'd been no sign of them all day but they were making up for it now. They swarmed around us in great hordes—the air was black with them. Tom was not fit to shoulder his pack and move on so there was only one thing for it: dive into the tent, do up all the doors, cover as much exposed flesh as possible, crawl inside the sleeping bags and seek refuge from the biting beasties.

We were tired and sleep came quickly. Next day we poked our heads out cautiously. Within seconds the black cloud had descended on us again. We broke all records for taking down a tent and packing rucksacks. It was a case of the great escape.

We moved like backpackers possessed, for only movement gave us respite from the midge hordes; stopping brought only misery, and no amount of magic midge repellent made any difference.

Finally, above 2,000ft (400m), in the bed of a burn reduced to a mere trickle by weeks of drought, we lost them. Peace at last. Out came the stove and within minutes our first decent meal for hours was being cooked. We ate, laid ourselves down on a hot boulder in the sun and dozed.

It had all started well enough. My first cross-Scotland backpack west to east had given me an appetite for multi-day trips. This one was an unashamed Munro-bagging expedition over two days that would complete my tally of Glen Kinglass Munros.

Glen Kinglass is a long glen running between Loch Etive in the west and Victoria Bridge near Bridge of Orchy and the A82 main road to Fort William in the east. The only

means of access to the glen is on foot or by Land Rover, for at its centre lies an isolated shooting lodge.

This is excellent backpacking country, the through route of the glen itself offering a good trip. Railway lines provide useful points of access, with stations at Bridge of Orchy on the Fort William line and at Taynuilt and Dalmally on the Oban line out of Glasgow.

Mountains there are aplenty, and the northern side of the glen is bounded by a chain of seven Munros. It's possible to do six of them in a day, but it needs to be a long one, you need to be fit, travelling light and in fair weather.

There is little habitation for miles, and this is no place for the inexperienced. In August 1984, a couple of months after our trip, a Dutch walker had an accident in these hills and was lucky to escape alive. One of his rescuers called it a thousand to one fluke that he was found.

Ton Peters was making his way across country to Fort William when he fell into a ravine on the slopes of Beinn nan Aighenan—one of the Munros crossed by Tom and me. He survived four nights in the open nursing a broken leg before the head stalker at Glen Kinglass lodge heard his cries for help and he was finally rescued and transported to hospital.

In the interim Ton had been washed over two waterfalls in a flash flood and in a supreme effort had hauled himself out of the ravine. His remarkable tale of survival was due largely to a calm temperament and an ability to avoid panic.

Fortunately such horror stories are rare, and accidents can happen to the best of us. But Ton Peters' experience teaches backpackers that they must go prepared and know how to cope with the unexpected. My friend Tom's dehydration is another case in point.

Day One

Our own trek began at Victoria Bridge. Deposited there by car, our first objective was Loch Dochard, around four miles from the eastern end of Glen Kinglass, where we would camp for the night. Starting from Bridge of Orchy, if you arrive by train, adds a further three miles to the walk. Anyone seeking overnight accommodation or a meal before starting the walk can do no better than the Bridge of Orchy Hotel. There is a good bunkhouse and food is served all day.

We reached Loch Dochard in the late evening, found a pitch for the night and settled down to a brew and the peace and quiet of the glen. This far in there is a real sense of wildness. The nearest habitation is a farm at Clashgour, a mile away, and you are surroun-

ded by mountains.

Prominent to the north are Stob Ghabhar, though this is not its best profile, and our first hill of the following day, Meall nan Eun. Stob Ghabhar is a fine hill with a superb corrie, hidden from the Glen Kinglass side. To get a good view of the corrie, its cliffs and the lochan at its base, combine an ascent of Stob Ghabhar with a climb of its neighbouring Munro, Stob a'Choire Odhair. Start with the latter and head along the connecting ridge between the two, giving a sight of Stob Ghabhar's rocky corrie virtually all the way.

Day Two

Breakfast over, Tom and I made ready for what would be our hardest day, landing us five miles further on down the glen after covering four Munros—Meall nan Eun, Stob Coir' an Albannaich, Glas Bheinn Mhor and Beinn nan Aighenan.

I had decided on an ascent by the burn between Meall nan Eun and Stob Coir' an Albannaich. This would allow us to leave our packs for the final part of the climb onto the first Munro, and they could be picked up again *en route* to the next.

The area around Loch Dochard is usually boggy, with remnants of the old Caledonian Pine Forest sticking up through the morass. But the sun had hardened the peat to a crust now and we had little trouble crossing to the start of our burn. It was running beautifully clear, sparkling in the sunlight, the colours of the base rocks picked out under the water.

It was already hot, the packs were heavy and we made slow but steady progress on deer tracks well above the burn and flanking Meall nan Eun—(hill of the birds). Suddenly Tom shouted: he had seen a wildcat dodge in among some boulders, but though we watched for a while it didn't reappear and I was annoyed that I'd missed it. Round a bend we surprised some deer, who bolted off across the hillside, pausing now and then to look back at us inquisitively.

At last we reached the bealach between Meall nan Eun and a subsidiary top, Meall Tarsuinn, deposited the packs and headed, light-footed now, for the summit of our first Munro. We scanned the view north-east to the Blackmount hills and then turned our eyes west along our intended route. It looked inviting so we wasted no time getting back to the packs. Then it was over Meall Tarsuinn, an annoying intervening bump impossible to avoid, and down to the bealach under Stob Coir' an Albannaich, where we took a break.

Stob Coir' an Albannaich (peak of the corrie of the Scotsmen) has quite a sharp aspect from this angle, but its ascent poses no problems and we plodded purposefully to the top. A broad shoulder drops to a bealach where we lunched before tackling Glas Bheinn Mhor—a grassy hill which, like Meall nan Eun, has little to commend it individually. But I think it was inveterate Munroist and writer Hamish Brown who said that there are no dull hills, only dull people, and the walker with vision and a feel for his surroundings can always derive something from the most featureless hill.

In the case of Glas Bheinn Mhor there are fine views north into Glen Etive. Its convex slopes keep the summit cairn out of sight until the last. The climb was laborious and we were glad to reach the top.

Almost due west of here is one of the best hills in the area, Ben Starav. Like Stob Ghabhar at the other end of Glen Kinglass, it provides an excellent day's outing on its own, in which case it is approached from Glen Etive. Some time previously I had completed a traverse of Ben Starav and Glas Bheinn Mhor with Roger Smith. Starting in Glen Etive, we walked out through Glen Kinglass to Victoria Bridge, where we had another car waiting.

This time, though, Ben Starav was not on the list and our thoughts turned instead to Beinn nan Aighenan, the bulky hill detached from the linear line of the rest. Although tired, Tom and I comforted ourselves with the thought of being able to ditch the packs for the climb.

Even so, when it came it was a trial. Fitter than Tom from a two-week backpack across Scotland the month before, I made better progress and arrived on top about a quarter of an hour before him. I rested and surveyed the scene, checking every now and then on Tom's progress up the hill. Our last Munro of the day had been climbed and I felt elated as I scampered down to the packs again in my trainers—carried mainly for wearing around the tent in the evening, but proving of further use now.

We still had about three miles to go alongside the Allt Hallater, a burn descending into Glen Kinglass. I discovered an unexpected track, unmarked on the map, which followed the line of the burn. It was while we were making our way along this that Tom started to falter and stumble and our camp was devastated by the midges.

Day Three

Dropping some two miles short of our intended campsite added that much extra mileage onto our walk out to Dalmally on the final day of the trip. Driven to an early start by the midges, we made for a bridge crossing the River Kinglass under Bein Eunaich, one of two Munros on the south side of the glen.

From the bridge, which crosses spectacularly high above the river, a path (marked on the map but very indistinct on the ground in places) crosses the hillside to join the Allt Dhoireann. It climbs to a high bealach at 2050ft (625m) then drops alongside another burn into Glen Strae.

Fed and rested we both revived considerably. Tom was a different person, restored to normal and set for the last part of the walk. A final pull to the bealach, over steep ground, and it was all downhill after that. A lochan at the bealach, featured on the map, had evaporated completely, leaving just the dry bed.

I had planned this as a relatively short day following our heavy day over the tops, but with the extra two miles from the previous day and our rapid departure without breakfast, the ascent to the bealach had been a real grind in the heat. Noses for Dalmally now though, we set off down in good spirits. The path on this side is much more distinct and easier to follow.

We stopped often to take draughts from the burn and Tom, in particular, was making sure he kept his fluid level topped up to avoid a repetition of the previous day's experience. The midges had obviously been confined to Glen Kinglass, for we were plagued no more by them and were able to stop several times on the way down. Tom even took advantage of a deep pool to enjoy a skinny dip in the deliciously cool water.

Ahead lay Loch Awe and the ruins of Kilchurn Castle; to our right rose the great mass of Ben Cruachan, a truly magnificent hill with a complex series of spurs jutting from it. If more time is available, an extended backpack could take in Beinn Eunaich and Beinn a' Chochuill, the two Munros we had already bypassed, then end with a traverse of Ben Cruachan and finishing at Taynuilt, its station providing transport out.

We reached Glen Strae, where a few people had taken advantage of the sunny evening to stroll along our path from the B8074 road. A couple of miles brought us to the junction between it and the A85 main road to Oban, and it was then just a short step to Dalmally.

We were early for the train so left our packs at the station and went to find a tea shop. Duly found we were served with liberal quantities of reviving tea, accompanied by equally liberal quantities of fruit cake.

Relaxing on the train I reflected on the walk. Whatever hardship is endured at the time seems to diminish in significance by the minute, and I was already planning my next sortie into the hills.

HIGHLAND REGION

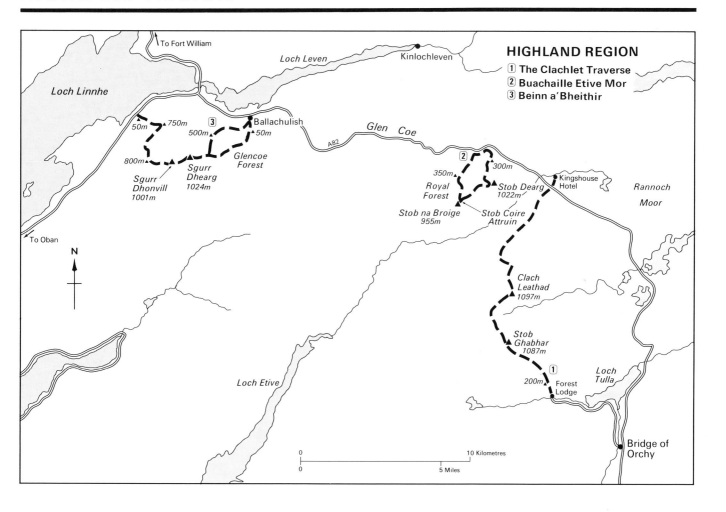

HIGHLAND REGION

1. The Clachlet Traverse
2. Buachaille Etive Mor
3. Beinn a'Bheithir

Map to show the following walks: The Clachlet Traverse (p52), Buachaille Etive Mor (p56) and Beinn a'Bheithir (p59).

    The 15-mile traverse of the Clachlet Ridge is a long and sustained mountain walk that requires good navigation skills.

    The 3,200-foot ascent of Buachaille Etive Mor offers a full mountain day for the fit walker who can tackle steep, rough scree.

    Two Munros are included in the 5½-mile mountain traverse of Beinn a'Bheithir. This is exhilarating mountain walking that requires both scrambling and good navigation skills.

THE CLACHLET TRAVERSE (Highland Region) by Cameron McNeish

Distance: 15 miles (24 km).
Ascent: 5500ft (1700m).
Start/Finish: Start at Victoria Bridge near Forest Lodge beyond Bridge of Orchy. Finish at Kingshouse Hotel. You can either hitch a lift back to Bridge of Orchy, or walk back by the old military road across the western fringe of Rannoch Moor.
Maps: OS 1:50,000 Sheet 50 and 41.
Summary: A long and sustained mountain traverse. Good navigation skills are necessary in misty weather. A superb ski tour in winter conditions.
Points of Interest: The area of the Blackmount Deer Forest has long associations with the ancient celtic story of Deirdre of the Sorrows, Meall a' Bhuiridh is nowadays a popular mountain for skiing.

Above: **Clachlet and Meall a Bhuiridh as seen from the A82.**

Above right: **On the slopes of Clachlet in January.**
(Photos: Cameron McNeish)

The crossing of the Clachlet Ridge starts at Inveroran Inn, on the old Glasgow to Fort William road which is now part of the West Highland Way. Park your car near the hotel, and try and arrange for another car to pick you up at the north end of the ridge, probably close to Blackrock Cottage on the White Corries ski road. If you can't get transport fixed up you can either leg it back to Inveroran along the West Highland Way, or stay overnight at the excellent Kingshouse Hotel, a hostelry that has improved ten-fold since climber Ian Nicholson took it over two or three years back. The Kingshouse also has a bunk house, at very reasonable rates.

From Inveroran you'll have to make your way by Victoria Bridge and then westwards along the track by the Linne nam Beathach to the Glasgow University Climbing Club hut at Clashgour. Then you start to work, climbing the long slopes of the first peak of the traverse, Stob Ghabhar. A rough footpath follows the waters of the Allt Toaig northwards, a path which ultimately carries you high onto the bealach between Stob Ghabhar's east ridge and its near neighbour, Stob a'Choire Odhair. Walkers who like a scramble will enjoy this eastern ridge of Stob Ghabhar as a means of ascent for much of it is shattered and broken into a fine tight ridge. Others will find a less exposed route by following the obvious line of the south-east ridge.

Just a few days before writing this I had tramped up the heathery slopes of Stob Ghabhar in mist and heavy rain. It had been a bit of a mental struggle to leave the car. But as so often happens the effort was worthwhile for as I sat behind the big cairn on the summit of

Ghabhar the mist just vanished, as though it was being sucked off the hillside by some great vacuum cleaner. At the same time the heavy overcast sky was torn apart by unseen forces to reveal great patches of blue. Where I had been immersed in a suffocating cloak of grey a few moments before I was now exposed and tiny in the great high-level world that had appeared around me. The suddenness of it made me feel a bit unsteady.

Golden plovers whistled mournfully and I put up a number of ptarmigan as I made my way northwards onto the long finger that stretches out towards the other hills of the Blackmount. I was glad of the clearance in the weather for this section can be a bit tricky to navigate. A narrow neck of land, the Bealach Fuar-chathaidh, connects the Aonach Mor ridge of Stob Ghabhar with the south-western slopes of Clachlet itself, and it can be easy to miss in bad weather, necessitating an unduly long and steep climb.

My day was really made when I had crossed this deep trench of the Bealach Fuar-chathaidh. I had stopped to have my lunch and across on the other side of the hill I saw a blue hare start to run uphill, zigging and zagging in a most unusual fashion. As I watched it I became aware that it was running from something and I soon saw what it was. About 100 feet above it a golden eagle drifted silently. How the hare knew it was there I'll never know, but boy, did it run. The eagle swooped lower and made a couple of half-hearted attempts at catching the hare but I suspect it maybe had one eye on me, and I had shaken its concentration. I watched it for a while lazily beating those great wings and drifting away until it was a mere speck in the sky.

One of the finest views I have ever seen from a car window was during a winter journey to Glencoe, crossing the Rannoch Moor from Bridge of Orchy to Kingshouse.

It was a day of intense brightness, with the snow-covered ground making us wear sunglasses so that we could discern the black band of the road. As the car negotiated the big long hill and bend from Achallader, and a blue Loch Tulla drifted behind, our breath was taken away by the magnificent array of peaks appearing in front of us.

We stopped, climbed out of the car into the cold air and drank in the view, Meall a' Bhuiridh and the Clachlet hills stood proud as though detached from the moor that they grew out of. The brilliance of the snow-plastered slopes contrasted with the dark blue of the sky behind, and the entire scene was framed to perfection by the shimmering waters of Loch na h-Achlaise in front. Ice floes on the loch

gave an Arctic feel, and I cursed the fact that I didn't have skis with me.

The skyline of that view, over the tops of Stob Ghabhar, Clachlet (Clach Leathad), Meall a'Bhuiridh and Sron na Creise gives a high-level walk that is one of the classics in Scotland. On one side of you the steep crags fall away to the vast emptiness of Coire Ba, the biggest corrie in Scotland, which in turn unfolds onto the great mattress of the Rannoch Moor. The flatness of that desolation gives a great feeling of height and space, a feeling that is emphasised by the deep glens and trenches of the Blackmount Forest on your other side. Here long and broad ridges link up the tops that make up this legendary deer forest. This is the fabled land of Deirdre of the Sorrows, these were the hills she and her lover Naoise roamed, hunting the deer and fishing the streams, before they were drawn back to Ulster and a terrible death.

The summit of Clachlet, 3602ft (1098m) above sea level, sits proud above the empty expanse of Coire Ba and the Rannoch Moor. A fine easterly ridge runs down steeply to the moor and the old military road at Ba Bridge and those who don't want a particularly long day, or who have to return to Inveroran for their car, would be advised to take this ridge off the traverse. But enjoy the situation first, with long unbroken views across the moor to the unmistakable outline of Schiehallion, as Neil Munro described it, 'like a skerry of the sea'. What a place this Rannoch Moor is, this huge blanket of peat and bog, broken by the long waters of Loch Ba and Loch Laidon. What a priceless wilderness asset to have, and yet much of it is unprotected by legislation. Quite simply there is nothing else like it in Britain. It is unique in its vastness and barrenness and to walk across its empty quarter is a worthwhile experience for anyone who enjoys remoteness. Out there the sounds of the deer, curlew, snipe and plover fill the air, and often the evening stillness is haunted by the melancholy cry of black throated divers.

The ridge walk from Clachlet towards Creise is a good one, along a broad and undulating ridge with views in front dominated by the Glencoe hills, the Buachaille Etive Mor with its great rocky ridges running steeply to the summit, and beyond it the sharp peaks of the Mamores. The crouched outline of Ben Nevis is obvious, with the graceful sweep of the Carn Mor Dearg Arete connecting it to its outliers.

A short distance after Clachlet, another ridge leads off eastwards to connect with Meall a'Bhuiridh, 3636ft (1108m). Again, you can descend to the military road by way of this top, but a word of warning, Meall a'Bhuiridh is

The Clachlet Ridge in spring from Stob Ghabhar towards the Glencoe hills. (Photo: Hamish Brown)

Glencoe's ski mountain, and the lower slopes bear the malignant scars of ski development. You can of course avoid the obvious infrastructure of the development, particularly by maintaining a south-easterly bearing. In many ways this descent is recommended for those who are unhappy with steeper slopes for the descent from the final top of the traverse, Sron na Creise, can be difficult in misty weather. The north ridge, which appears to be the obvious ascent and descent line, is particularly steep and indeed offers a superlative scramble for those who enjoy the middle ground between walking and climbing. The eastern face of the mountain is very steep and isn't recommended for descent. Walkers carrying on to complete the traverse on Creise should work their way slightly north-westwards to avoid the awkward sections of the north ridge.

Having given the warning, I'm sure there are many who enjoy scrambling as I most certainly do. The ridge itself requires care in places but it is comprised mainly of rocky steps, ramps and ledges and the rock is first class, sound with good friction.

I was sorry when I reached Creise, and had to descend. The weather had been steadily improving all day and the evening looked set to be fine. But I had a good night in the Kingshouse to look forward to, a meal and a dram in front of its great window that looks towards the pyramid of the Buachaille. A place to sit and contemplate, dream and think of great days yet to come.

BUACHAILLE ETIVE MOR (Highland Region) by Cameron McNeish

Distance: 9 miles (14km).
Ascent: 3200ft (975m).
Start/Finish: Altnafeidh, on the A82 Glasgow to Fort William road.
Maps: OS 1:50,000 Sheet 41.
Summary: A straightforward but full mountain day. The initial ascent up Coire na Tulaich is rough and steep and much scree has to be negotiated but under reasonable conditions there shouldn't be any difficulty.
Points of Interest: Superb views over the Rannoch Moor from the summit of Stob Dearg.

Also very good views across Glen Etive to the hills of the Blackmount Deer Forest, and towards the rest of the Glen Coe hills. A superb alternative ascent for competent parties is by way of Curved Ridge from the Jacksonville car park on the A82. This is a first class scramble and is without doubt the finest route up the mountain. This route becomes a real mountaineering expedition under winter conditions though.

Buachaille Etive Mor from Blackrock Cottage. (Photo: Cameron McNeish)

The Buachaille (the great shepherd of Etive) rises majestically from the western edge of the Rannoch Moor forming an impressive cornerstone between Glen Coe and Glen Etive. Its pyramid shape, thrown up from its solid, squat base, is the very epitome of a mountain in the classic sense.

Seen from the warm comfort of a car seat,

56

Top: **Looking down Coire na Tulaich, the easier ascent route of the Buachaille**.

Above: **The imposing north-east face of Stob na Doire.**
(Photos: Cameron McNeish)

the great walls, ridges, gullies and towers have an air of impregnability, offering few lines of accessibility to the casual walker. But this is the Buachaille's bold face, its climber's face, presenting what is possibly the finest climbing prospect in the country.

Rock, snow and ice routes of every grade of difficulty are there to be enjoyed on these great faces. The rock is rhyolite, generally coarse and sound, with superb square-cut holds of every size. For generations these cliffs have offered exciting sport to climbers from all over the country and the walker with some experience of scrambling and a head for heights can enjoy a real airy promenade amid the buttresses and bastions as well.

Curved Ridge is graded as a moderate rock climb but can be tackled with confidence by most walkers who have some experience of rock climbing. The route, as its name suggests, curves its way up from near the base of the mountain, following the crest of a solid broad

ridge with ample hand and footholds. Not only is Curved Ridge an exciting scramble in itself, but it forms an impressive gallery from which to watch the rock climbers in action on the steep and unrelenting Rannoch Wall. In many respects this is the classic climbing cliff of Scotland, scene of many early tussles as the pioneers of Scottish climbing got to grips with the new sport. Classic climbs such as Agag's Groove, January Jigsaw and the more difficult Whortleberry Wall trace their way up the steep rock, and on a good summer's day you'll see climbers queueing up to enjoy these superb routes.

Further on the steepness of Curved Ridge relents, and the route to the summit goes via the base of the impressive Crowberry Tower, and up some easily scrambled rocks to the 3345ft (1020m) Stob Dearg top of Buachaille Etive Mor.

Now you may be forgiven for thinking that the Buachaille is all about climbing and scrambling, and while in many ways it is the climber's mountain par excellence, the walker with no desire to use his or her hands can enjoy it too. In fact the apex of the familiar Buachaille pyramid is only one of four tops to the mountain. Buachaille Etive Mor is really a four mile long ridge which rises steeply above Glen Etive with its four tops nicely spaced out along its length.

The walker's breach in the Buachaille's defences is Coire na Tulaich on the north-west of the mountain, directly behind the whitewashed cottage at Lagangarbh. A good car park lies off the A82 Glasgow to Fort William road here, and a track crosses a footbridge over the River Coupall and continues to the whitewashed cottage, the Lagangarbh Hut, owned and jealously guarded by the Scottish Mountaineering Club.

This is a good spot to stop for a moment and plan your campaign. Ahead of you lies the open corrie of Coire na Tulaich, a wide corrie which steepens appreciably near its top. In winter the rim of the corrie can be considerably corniced, and great care should be taken. At other times though there are no real difficulties and a track runs up the corrie to the ridge of the Buachaille.

If you turn your eyes to the right, beyond the steep cliffs of Creag a' Bhancair, a broad V-shaped valley separates the Buachaille from its little brother, the Buachaille Etive Beag. This is the pass of the Lairig Gartain, the route of your return journey after traversing the four tops.

I always enjoy the wander up Coire na Tulaich. The lower stretches subtly climb rocky slabs and terraces before the path begins to zig-zag onto the steeper slopes. Beetling crags rise up around you, and behind the view is framed by a truncated V formed by the outer slopes of the corrie. Beyond lies the start of the Blackwater Reservoir, and the Loch Treig and Loch Ossian hills. The cottages at Altnafeadh and Lagangarbh already seem far distant.

The last few hundred feet of the corrie are over fairly steep scree. Some care is required and you would do well to avoid the obvious narrowing gully at the top of the slope. Scramble up the steep slope east of the gully to emerge on the fairly broad ridge. Ahead of you lie the jumbled tops of the Blackmount Deer Forest, to your left the broad ridge rises to Stob Dearg, the highest point on the Buachaille Etive Mor, and to your right the fine peak of Stob na Doire rises from the broad bealach.

The ridge leading to the summit of Stob Dearg is rock-strewn and rough, and a rough path wends its way through the rubble. As you approach the summit the ridge narrows nicely and after one or two false summits you reach the large cairn which appears to sit on the edge of nothing. The expanse in front of you is vast, the flatness of the Rannoch Moor giving this feeling of aerial space. On its outer edges the Bridge of Orchy hills, the Perthshire hills, the Ben Alder group and the Blackwater hills form the rough bounds, effectively containing this great mattress of peat and bog. Behind you, the Glen Coe hills lift their proud heads above the neighbouring ridge of Buachaille Etive Beag, culminating in the high peak of Bidean nam Bian, the highest hill in the old county of Argyll. Through the jaws of Glen Coe the newish Ballachulish Bridge is well framed, joining the two shores of Loch Leven, and beyond it rise the fabulous hills of Ardgour.

Make your way back down to the bealach and continue along the ridge towards Stob na Doire and the rest of the Buachaille tops. It's a superb high-level traverse, with no obstacles in the way at all. The views across Glen Etive are particularly grand, towards Ben Starav and Cruachan, high above the silvery waters of Loch Etive.

This is all the ancient land of Deirdre, and on a recent visit, in the autumn, I suspect it looked as Deirdre of the Sorrows would have loved it. The grass was a burnished bronze, as though we were looking at the world through a tobacco-tinted filter. Here and there dense patches of bracken flamed red on the hillside, and down below in the glen the larches had turned yellow.

On the opposite hillside, above An Grianan (the bower) Deirdre had her summer home. What a place to sit and soak in the autumnal

sunshine. But there are no Sons of Uisneach today. Only the rocks remain, and the red deer which roam these hills, the stags lustily full of the passion of October. This is the start of a hard time for the stags, already they look leaner. And no wonder. After two months of passion and fight, mating with every hind in the harem and fighting off every young staggie who fancies his chances at taking over the lordship of the herd, it's small wonder that they look haggard. And things won't get better. When the north winds blow bringing snow the deer are driven to the glen floor in search of food. It is the beginning of their terror time.

While the deer find it hard the birds must find it even harder, even the wily and resourceful raven. It's a rare day when you don't hear or see a raven on the Buachaille. On this day we watched a pair of them perform crazy but superbly controlled aerobatics. Up they would fly, into the air currents and then, wings folded back tight into their bodies, they would fall like a free-fall parachutist. Dropping like stones they appeared to twist out of the fall, flap their wings and regain their flight; and all this with a joyous croaking call. It was good to sit and watch them from our grandstand seat, and they seemed happy to perform for us.

How much better it is to watch the raven than suffer the 'sudden roaring noise of low-flying jets. These peace-shattering flights are an incredible intrusion into a landscape like this, an alien and frightening reminder that men are actually spending their lives being trained to kill. Even more frightening, in a slow-moving and purposeful way, was the huge RAF Shackleton aeroplane which flew at a very low level up the length of Glen Etive. As it flew over this land of Deirdre, burnished blond and beautiful with the autumn, it bought with it an aura of destruction, a stealthy oppression which was intensely ugly. Deirdre's sunny bower wasn't peaceful any more. The RAF destroy more than the enemy.

From the final top of the ridge, Stob na Broige, the easiest line of descent is to backtrack over Stob Coire Altruim to the bealach between that peak and Stob na Doire. From there you can descend the steep but straightforward slopes down into the Lairig Gartain and return to your car along the footpath which hugs the River Coupall.

Clambering up the Curved Ridge, an ascent route only for experienced scramblers. (Photo: Cameron McNeish)

BEINN A' BHEITHIR (Highland Region) by Peter Evans

Loch Leven from Beinn a'Bheithir with the Pap of Glencoe showing prominently.
(Photo: Cameron McNeish)

Distance: 5¹/₂ miles (9 km).
Ascent: 4300ft (1310m).
Start/Finish: Start at Ballachulish. Finish at Pier north of Kentallen.
Map: OS 1:50,000 Second Series Sheet 41.
Summary: An exhilarating mountain traverse involving some scrambling, covering two Munros. A linear walk requiring transport at both ends for the full route. The last two miles can involve awkward route-finding in mist.
Points of Interest: A walk offering excellent variety and superlative views of mountains and sea. Just a short step from Glen Coe, steeped in historical significance and giving many more opportunities for walking to suit all tastes.

At the portals of Glen Coe and standing sentinel over the narrows between Loch Leven and Loch Linnhe lies Beinn a'Bheithir (hill of the thunderbolt). Although referred to in the singular, Beinn a'Bheithir is really a long ridge stretching between the village of Ballachulish in the east and the hamlet of Kentallen, on the shores of Loch Linnhe, in the west. The ridge is composed of three main summits—two of them Munros—and offers the walker a superb day's outing with plenty of interest.

The hill can be tackled in a variety of ways, and those simply out to bag its two Munros can approach from South Ballachulish through monotonous pines, which defile the northern slopes lower down. But this is to do Beinn a'Bheithir an injustice, and by far the finest outing is a full traverse of some five and a half miles from east to west. The views are magnificent, there's some easy scrambling thrown in, and if you time your descent to catch the sunset, you'll be rewarded with a breathtaking panorama out to sea, as a warm glow fills the western sky.

My first acquaintance with Beinn a'Bheithir came at Hogmanay, when the hill presented itself as a good way of ending the year in fine style, as well as adding to my tally of Munros. With an early start I could savour the walk and still be back in time for the night's festivities, spiritually refreshed and ready to tackle a new year. And so it proved.

Ballachulish was not showing much sign of life when I arrived—a tingle of anticipation in my stomach, for I intended to reach the summit ridge by a sharp spur which shoots down towards Gleann an Fhiodh and has some rocky steps on it. At this time of year it would be holding snow and probably ice.

I left the car and walked along the track above the River Laroch. Dogs barked in the farm as I made for the open hill, the spur of my planned ascent rearing up into a cold, clear sky. It looked forbidding, icy, difficult. I reassessed and took out my binoculars for a closer inspection. That sealed it: I considered the approach too risky for a solo walker and opted instead for the broader expanse of Beinn Bhan, to the right. It, too, leads to the first summit of the day, Sgorr Bhan.

As you meander slowly up to Sgorr Bhan, the first views open up over your shoulder. Stop for a welcome breather and take in the prospect. The shapely Pap of Glencoe is obvious in the foreground; across Loch Leven are the Mamores, and if you're lucky and the day is clear, you'll spot the distinctive whaleback of The Ben himself, Ben Nevis.

The summit of Sgorr Bhan (not named on the 1:50,000 map) has a useful cairn for sheltering from the wind. I took full advantage of it, settling down for a hot draught of coffee from my flask and a few sandwiches before pressing on. These are often the moments that provide the best memories when you're alone. You can sit and ponder on the meaning of things, and be humbled by the mountains and the elements.

The elements made themselves felt in a hail shower and I huddled into the cairn for protection. It passed quickly but I could see another building up from the north-west which would probably hit me in about half an hour I guessed. It was time to move on. I gathered up

my rucksack and headed for Sgorr Dhearg, at 3361ft (1024m) the higher of Beinn a'Bheithir's two Munros. A graceful, sweeping curve of snow leads to the trig pillar in winter.

A drop of about 800ft (240m) leads to the grassy bealach between the two Munros—a pleasant spot for a break if you're so inclined, and a good opportunity to gird the loins for the pull up to Sgorr Dhonuill. At 3284ft (1001m), this peak is not much lower than its neighbour and gives a more entertaining ascent. Steep grass gives way to a jumble of boulders and a mild scramble to the summit cairn. Crags overhang the northern corrie of Sgorr Dhonuill. The path sticks to the edge of the crags, with a steep drop on the right, but the walker is always safe and your way through the boulders can be as close or as far from the edge as your nerve dictates.

Today the boulders were iced and I negotiated them with care, staying away from the edge. On top I met a group of four walkers who had come another way. We saw black clouds rolling towards us and zipped up waterproofs and pulled down bob caps ready for the onslaught. It was a vicious little shower, obliterating the views while it lasted but soon passing to leave the air clear again.

The others set off for Sgorr Dhearg and I sat for a while longer, finishing my food and feeling satisfied with the day's achievement: I was very definitely on a high.

Without the benefit of transport at the other end of the ridge I was unable to do a traverse, so descended to the bealach once more and picked my way south to the edge of the forestry plantation on this side of the hill. Then I headed east along the track into Gleann an Fhiodh and rounded Sgorr Dhearg to my starting point, completing a fine circuit. I wandered down to Ballachulish with a spring in my step in the company of a shepherd who was going down off the hill into the village. He showed interest in my day and we exchanged good wishes for the new year. I whooped it up with the rest at a Hogmanay party that night, but the memories of my walk still lingered; they'd be there long after the party was finished and forgotten.

Two years passed before I was able to enjoy a full traverse of Beinn a'Bheithir. Two cars made it possible, and I was accompanied by a couple of friends. This time we made for the spur that I had avoided when I first climbed Sgorr Bhan. A path leads up over steps of stratified slate, giving some sporting scrambling towards the top, though any difficulties can be avoided by less adventurous walkers.

A light covering of snow meant care in the ascent, adding another dimension to the

Top: **An unusual view of Beinn a'Bheithir from Sgor na h-Ulaidh, at the south-west end of Glencoe.** (Photo: Roger Smith)

Above: **Sgorr Dhonuill from Ballachulish.** (Photo: Hamish Brown)

Top right: **Sgorr Dhearg (left) and Sgorr Dhonuill, Beinn a'Bheithir's two Munro peaks, seen from Ballachulish.** (Photo: Donald MacCulloch)

Right: **Sgorr a'Choise, which faces Beinn a'Bheithir across Gleann an Fhiadh, and from which fine views of the higher hill can be obtained.** (Photo: Donald MacCulloch)

excitement. Finally the angle eased and we walked up the easier slope leading to the top and a well-earned rest. Sgorr Dhearg and Sgorr Dhonuill fell in turn and I was looking forward to seeing the seascapes from the last section of the ridge.

We had been in mist for most of the day, but as we lost height from Sgorr Dhonuill, and with it the snow covering the summits, the air cleared and become suddenly warm. Waterproofs were peeled off as we made ready for what was obviously going to be a pleasant, leisurely end to our walk.

This last section of the ridge forms a cirque around Gleann a'Chaolais. Navigation can be tricky in mist because the ground undulates, with no distinct reference points. It is dotted with a series of small lochans, which can help providing you can work out which is which! In clear weather, however, there is no difficulty. Walkers wishing to complete the horseshoe of

Beinn a'Bheithir should cross the bumps and hollows and make for Creag Ghorm, the last summit on the ridge.

It is the vista to the south-west that now draws the eye, with water as the dominant theme in the direction of Oban, some thirty miles away. It was truly magnificent on the evening of our walk, and the sea sparkled as the sky turned first golden and then deepened to a fiery orange.

There is no one obvious descent line from Creag Ghorm. The ground to the west is steep, but by no means impossible given sure, deliberate footing, and is certainly preferable to doing battle with the trees on the lower northern slopes. Make for the pier on Kentallen Bay, a mile or so north of Kentallen itself. Take your time and have your camera at the ready: I guarantee the shutter will be clicking like mad.

HIGHLAND REGION – 2

Map to show the following 2 walks: Comyns Road and the Gaick Pass (p63), and Loch an Eilein and Rothiemurchus (p68).

Allow 2 days for the 30-mile, low-level walk from Blair Castle to Ruthven Barracks. As most of the walking is through remote countryside, good navigational skills are necessary.

The 8-mile nearly circular walk to Loch an Eilein and Rothiemurchus is an easy and beautiful low-level walk on well-prepared forest tracks, that offers abundant birdlife.

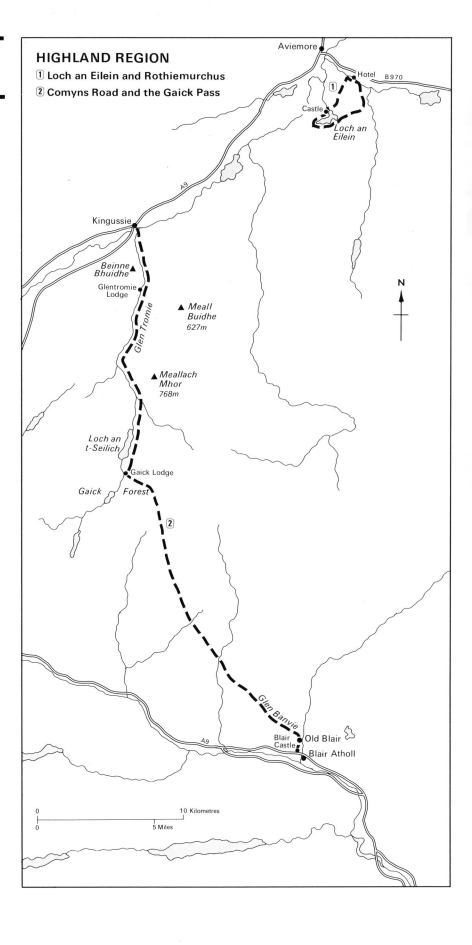

HIGHLAND REGION

① Loch an Eilein and Rothiemurchus

② Comyns Road and the Gaick Pass

COMYN'S ROAD AND THE GAICK PASS
(Highland Region) by Cameron McNeish

Leaving the Whim Plantation on Comyn's Road. (Photo: Cameron McNeish)

Distance: 30 miles (48km).
Start/Finish: Start at Blair Castle, Blair Atholl. Finish at Ruthven Barracks just south of Kingussie.
Maps: OS 1:50,000 Second Series Sheets 35, 42 and 43.
Summary: A predominantly low-level walk through very remote countryside. Climbs to its highest point at just over 2000ft (610m). Footpaths much of the way but other sections require good navigation, especially in bad weather.
Points of Interest: Ancient byeway but now walked only by the odd backpacker. Blair Castle is well worth a visit as is Ruthven barracks at the end of the walk. Also well worth visiting the Highland Folk Museum in Kingussie at the end of the walk. Finish of the walk can be linked easily to the start by rail, the Perth–Inverness line stops at both Kingussie and Blair Atholl.

Until General Wade built his new road over Drumochter Pass between Atholl and Badenoch the main route through the wild and remote Grampians was by way of a high-level bridleway called the Minigaig. This route ran more or less due north from Blair Atholl in Perthshire to the Castle at Ruthven, near Kingussie in Badenoch. Cattle drovers made their yearly journey southwards to the great trysts at Crieff and Falkirk, and those journeying from the MacPherson and Shaw lands of Speyside would use this ancient trail.

But another track, even more ancient than the Minigaig, crosses this empty quarter. A sixteenth-century manuscript, MacFarlane's Geographic Collection, refers to 'a way from the gate of Blair in Atholl to Ruthven in Badenoch made by David Comyn, for carts to pass with wine and the way is called Rath na Pheny, or Way of Wagon Wheels. It is laid with calsay in sundry parts.'

David Comyn was Lord of Badenoch in the thirteenth century, and as he was passing through Atholl making his homeward way north he stopped at the roadside inn at a place called Kilmaveonaig, just outside Blair Atholl. He was apparently so delighted with the quality of the ale that he asked the landlord where the ingredients came from. The malt, said the landlord, came from Perth, and the water, which gave the ale its particular flavour, came from the stream which ran through the village.

Obviously being of a compulsive nature, Comyn immediately decided that this ale was so good he must have it at his estate in Ruthven, and that he would transport it over the pathless tract of wilderness between Atholl and Badenoch. He had a road surveyed and built and it became known as Rathad nan Coimeinach, or the Road of the Comyns.

As a modern walking route it is a good one, crossing as it does the vast deer forests of Atholl and Gaick. These are wild areas, the rounded hills here and there reaching undulating plateaux of over 2000ft (600m). The glens are lonely and uninhabited, fragments and tracings of old buildings reminding us of the days when the sheiling system was in use. Once children laughed and played in these glens, the women would sing ás they looked after the cattle, but that is long gone. Today only the bleat of a sheep or the plaintive call of a whaup echo through the empty glens.

Day One

Blair Atholl and Kingussie, which is only a mile or so from Ruthven, are both on the main London to Inverness railway line, so are ideally placed to allow you to walk over Comyn's Road from Blair Atholl to Kingussie, returning by train to your starting point at the end of the walk. Some hardy walkers tramp the entire distance in one day, but it is a long and wild walk and you are advised to spend two days over it, camping out somewhere in the middle.

Blair Castle is the home of the Duke of

Blair Castle, the ancient home of the Duke of Atholl and starting point of the Comyn's Road walk. (Photo: Cameron McNeish)

Atholl, and it has something of a chequered history. The oldest part of the building, Cumming's Tower, was built in 1269 by John Comyn of Badenoch, and various alterations and additions have been made since. King Edward visited it in 1336, Mary Queen of Scots in 1564 and the Marquis of Montrose garrisoned his Royalist army here in 1644. A less sociable call was made by Oliver Cromwell in 1652, and Claverhouse spent the night there before the Battle of Killiecrankie in 1689.

The castle is a good place to start this walk, especially if you spend a couple of hours wandering around it, soaking up the history of it and learning something of what this countryside must have been like in the earlier centuries. Great oak woods surround the castle, and our route out of the castle grounds takes us through these woods, past Diana's Grove to where a track strikes off northwestwards beside the Banvie Burn. This track climbs fairly gently through dense natural woods of pine, larch and birch, and keeps in sight of the burn and its cascades, pools and deep-set ravines, all darkly shaded in bottle green.

After a short walk you'll reach the Rumbling Bridge, a stone humpbacked bridge which was built in 1762. Its name comes from the fact that in times of spate, you can actually hear the rocks on the bed of the Banvie Burn being 'rumbled' along. Our route doesn't cross the bridge, but passes it and continues through a gate into the Whim Plantation, which is actually marked on the OS 1:50,000 map.

A locked gate marks the end of the plantation and you'll have to scramble over it. Ahead of you the track splits in two, with

Above: **Ruthven Barracks, the site of an ancient stronghold of the Comyn family. The present structure was used for the garrisoning of troops during General Wade's road building exercises. The highlanders shown here are from the White Cockade Society.**

Right: **Much of the walk takes you over heather-covered moorland with low rolling hills, in the constant company of grouse and deer.**
(Photos: Cameron McNeish)

Comyn's Road stretching straight on. The other path, the beginning of the Minigaig route, drops down to the burnside where it crosses over the Quarry bridge, built eight years after the Rumbling Bridge.

Once clear of the trees, and the comparative softness of the Atholl Estates policies, the landscape changes dramatically. Here the calls of the lapwings and the curlew replace the sweeter tones of blackbird and thrush, and the bottle green of the forest gives way to the ochres and purple of the bare moorland. Ancient ruins, like bony skeletons of a bygone age, line the river banks, piles of rubble where people once lived out their entire lives. Zigzags on the hill opposite indicate another old path where peat cutters once laboured up and down with their loads, cutting the fuel from Tom nan Cruach (the hillock of peat stacks). The peat for the cottage fires would be cut here, and so would the peat for the great halls in the castle. It would be cut in the summer months, and stacked up in piles to dry in the sun and the wind, before being carried down for burning.

The track continues to rise gently, through a pine wood, before bending tightly southwards. Comyn's Road leaves the track here, on a newly bulldozed road, and heads north-west downhill into Glen Bruar, past the old shieling of Ruichlachrie. It's a short distance from here to the Bruar, and the river is easily forded at the old ruin called Cuilltemhuc. Stop for a while here and consider an old Atholl story of the laughing man of Cuilltemhuc. A hundred years ago, so the story goes, a man was found blind drunk in a water trough laughing his head off. No-one ever found the reason for his mirth and it seems he died convulsed in a hearty fit of glee. It's maybe as well he didn't share his joke before he died.

The next section of Comyn's Road has suffered the toll of the years and the luxuriance and wide-spreading growth of heather. The direction is north-westwards though, through the peat hags, boggy areas, and ubiquitous heather, over the hillside to the bothy at Clunes, where a bulldozed track has revitalised Comyn's Road again.

Clunes (pronounced Cloonis) bothy is not a well-known one but if offers comfortable shelter in bad weather. Unfortunately it's probably not far enough into the walk to justify spending the night.

The evidence of Comyn's Road has largely been obliterated hereabouts, like so many ancient paths have been, by the forced gouging of modern bulldozed tracks. Designed for Land Rovers these tracks have little aesthetic attraction for walkers, but sourly serve the purpose of carrying keepers and sportsmen deep into the deer forests.

This is grouse country, and grouse butts dot the hillsides; an area to avoid in late August, September and October.

Follow the bulldozed track from Clunes, over the crest of the low ridge and down to run parallel with the waters of the Allt a'Chireachain, where it's joined by the faster-flowing Allt a'Baidh. Leave the track at this point, and scramble down the slippery slopes to the confluence of the streams, where a rubble of rocks and boulders makes rudimentary stepping stones across to the northern bank.

You'll notice the remains of some old ruins here. These are old shielings which were once known as the Kirrichans. The 1792 Statistical Account describes a typical Atholl shieling; 'Lower down is heath, peat bog, valleys full of pretty good pasture, and here and there a green spot, with huts on it, to which the women, children and herds retire with the cattle for the summer season.'

The Kirrichans is indeed a green spot, and it's good to stop here for a few minutes. To the north, the long ridge of Sron a'Chleirich (the nose of the priest), rises gradually, and it's over this ridge, at 2600ft (792m) that Comyn's

Road runs. The ground is a bit boggy and rough as you make your way up to the foot of the ridge, and the path can't be traced at this point, although it does appear again just below the summit of the Sron. Be careful with your navigation here, as low cloud and mist can often turn this featureless plateau into difficult terrain. It's a good idea to take a compass bearing from the trig point on the summit of Sron a'Chleirich to where the track meets the county boundary on Bac na Creige, the Bank of the Rocky Hill. An old rusty fence indicates the county boundary so look out for it.

As you cross the boundary into Badenoch you are entering the deer forest of Gaick, a place old in legend and superstition. Follow a northerly bearing until you start dropping down slopes which lead to the Allt Gharbh Ghaig, which runs into Gaick. As you make you way down the slopes enjoy the steady transformation of the landscape that takes place. From barren plateaux you enter a world of steep-sided glens, with broken crags and foaming burns. The hillside opposite, Meall Odhar Aillig, spouts bright white waterfalls, some tumultuous and roaring, some mere dribbles, while below, the river roars its way down the narrow defile.

A good footbridge crosses the Allt Gharbh Ghaig, a metal affair overlaid with turf. Cross it and carry on down the glen until you reach the alluvial flats of Gaick itself. With red deer roaming the hills, the trumpeting of peewees and the noisy chuckling of wheatear, it's hard to imagine that this area of Gaick once held the reputation of being the most supernatural place in Scotland. Tales abound of the Leannan Sith, the Faery Sweetheart who captures the hearts of hunters in the deer forest, or the Sprites o' Gaick, the tiny eleven folk who dress in "green siren suits" and milk the red deer hinds in the lonely corries.

The Comyn's link with the supernatural reputation of Gaick could well have been forged in the late fourteenth century when Walter Comyn of Ruthven, in a mood of cruel sensuousness, decreed that all the women of Badenoch between the ages of twelve and thirty should work in the fields stark naked. He had to go to Atholl and the day of his return was marked for the infamous exhibition. But he didn't return. His horse did though, terrified and foaming at the mouth, and trailing in one of the stirrups the torn off leg of the Comyn! A search party set out and Comyn's body was eventually found high in Gaick, with two gorged eagles preying glutinously on it. Comyn's gory end was put down to witchcraft, the eagles being the evil familiars of two of the mothers of the harvest girls. An age-old

Gaick Lodge, remote and lonely at the head of Loch an t-Seilich. (Photo: Cameron McNeish)

Badenoch curse, 'Diol Bhaltair an Gaig ort'—
'Walter's fate in Gaick on you'—recalls the old
story.

Tall tales indeed, and it seems likely that the
old stories and legends were put about to
discourage strangers in these parts. Remember
Comyn was carrying wagon-loads of ale across
this empty quarter. Robbers weren't uncom-
mon, and it was general practice to put about
ghost stories to deter highwaymen.

Despite the stories and Gaick's reputation,
this is a good spot to camp for the night. Close
by stands Gaick Lodge, remote and lonely at
the head of Loch an t-Seilich. On all sides of
this flat strath the hills rise to over 2000ft
(600m), steep-sided and smooth, perfect examples of potential avalanche slopes. One of
Scotland's first recorded avalanches took place
here in 1800 when the Black Officer, Captain
John MacPherson of Ballachroan was avalanched with four companions. The bothy they
were staying in was devastated by a huge
avalanche, although at the time the disaster
was put down to supernatural forces.

Day Two
An estate track runs down the length of the
east bank of Loch an t-Seilich to Glen Tromie,
but according to historians, Comyn's Road
takes the more direct route along the west
bank, before rising over the shoulder to
Bogha-Cloiche, to descend into Glen Tromie
down the long heathery slopes.

I must admit that this looks a fearfully steep
route on the map, but in reality a pony track
runs across the slopes starting from the
footbridge over the river directly west of Gaick
Lodge. Loch an t-Seilich is dammed at its
northern end, as part of one of Scotland's very
first hydro-electric schemes, built in 1940.
From the loch, a five-mile tunnel burrows
below the mountains to Loch Cuaich in the
west, and then west to Dalwhinnie and by an
aqueduct to Loch Ericht.

Glen Tromie is a fine place, the river banks
drooping with the branches of birch, alder and
juniper. The hill slopes are gentle and there is a
tranquility missing from the rest of the Gaick
area. The track passes by some ancient
settlements before climbing up onto the Nose
of the Winds, Sron na Gaoithe, the last climb
before the steady descent to Ruthven and the
end of the walk.

As you climb out of the glen, you'll pass a
prominent cairn, marked on the OS map as
Carn Pheigith, Peggy's Cairn. Tradition has it
that this mound of stones marks the burial
place of one Peggy, a suicide of the fourteenth
century. It was once customary to build a
mound of stones over the graves of the dead, to
protect them from wolves. It was also the
tradition to toss another stone on top as you
passed by, hence the proverb, 'Were I dead,
you would not throw a stone on it', meaning,
you don't think very much of me.

It's a gentle climb over the Sron, and as you
pass the crest of the ridge the views at last open
out northwards towards the Monadhliath hills
and the Spey Valley. Make your way downhill
towards the gaunt outline of Ruthven
barracks. General Wade reconstructed the
building for his dragoons on the prehistoric
mound which Comyn had also used in the
thirteenth century, but it was only to stand for
another twenty-five or so years before being
burnt down in 1746 on the orders of Bonnie
Prince Charlie on the run from Culloden.

It's a short walk from Ruthven round to
Kingussie, where, if you have the time, a visit
to the Highland Folk Museum would be well
worth your while. As you pass under the
tunnel below the modern A9, it's worth
reflecting on the differences between
thirteenth-century highways the like of which
you have just walked, and the modern dual
carriageways. I know which I prefer.

LOCH AN EILEIN AND ROTHIEMURCHUS
(Highland Region) by Cameron McNeish

Distance: 8 miles (13km).
Ascent: Negligible.
Start/Finish: Lay-by at Coylumbridge on the A951 Aviemore to Glenmore road.
Maps: OS 1:50,000 Sheet 36.
Summary: An easy and beautiful low-level walk on well-prepared forest tracks.
Points of Interest: Rothiemurchus Estate pro-

vides a visitor service with its HQ at Inverdruie. The ancient pine woods are of interest in themselves and their associated birdlife is typical of the old Caledonian forest. Watch out for crested tits, crossbills, capercaillies and siskins. Ospreys are occasionally seen above Loch an Eilien, although they rarely fish there.

Above left: **Loch an Eilein from Ord Ban with the Cairngorms in the distance.**

Above right: **Youngsters enjoy the waters of Loch Ghamhna, near Loch an Eileain.**
(Photos: Cameron McNeish)

Loch an Eilein castle stands on an island about 50 yards from the shore. The building dates from the 14th century and local legend says it was once the home of Alexander Stewart, known as the Wolf of Badenoch. (Photo: Cameron McNeish)

and in some areas there are small remnants of stunted Caledonian pines. In Glen Affric in Ross-shire there is a sizeable forest left but by far the finest example we have today of the former glory of the great forest is at Rothiemurchus in Speyside.

From the foot of the northern corries of the Cairngorms a great plain runs in a north-westerly direction towards the River Spey and the Monadhliath hills. Much of this plain is densely forested, the upper reaches in Glenmore by the modern conifers of the Forestry Commission, a thick almost impenetrable mass of trees. In contrast, in the lower reaches of the glen, the natural pines of the Caledonian Forest are comparatively well spaced, with a thick and abundant undergrowth of juniper and birch scrub. Regeneration here is excellent but not so good in the higher reaches of the forest where red deer browse during the winter months.

Wildlife is superb. You won't see the beasts of the forest's glory years but if you are observant you could well spot roe deer, red squirrel, otter and possibly even pine marten. Many of the birds are rare species, so this forest of Rothiemurchus has become something of a Shangri-la for ornithologists. Here you'll see the birds of the titmouse family, the great tit, the blue tit, the coal tit, the long tailed tit and the comparatively rare crested tit. Crossbills feed on the pine cones and you are likely to get the chance of seeing siskin, lesser redpolls, capercaillies and perhaps even the symbol of Speyside, the osprey, flying over the forest towards one of its feeding lochs.

The Rothiemurchus Estate was once owned by the Shaws but was later taken over by the Grants, who still own and run the estate today. The upper reaches of the forest are looked after, under agreement, by the Nature Conservancy Council. The name itself, Rothiemurchus, is said to mean the Fort of Muircus, from the Gaelic Rata-Mhurchuis, but who Muircus was no one seems to know.

The most popular walk in this area is around Loch an Eilein, the Lake of the Island, but I propose that we extend this walk a bit to take in some of the other areas of Rothiemurchus. We begin at Coylumbridge which is situated about one and a half miles (2½km) south-east of Aviemore on the Glenmore road. Just before you reach the bridge at Coylumbridge, a signpost at the side of the road informs you of the direction of Braemar via the Lairig Ghru. This then is the start of the Lairig Ghru Pass, the 30-mile (48km) walk which takes you through the heartland of the Cairngorms to Deeside in the south.

There is a parking lay-by here, and with the

Thousands of years ago, much of the area that we now know as the Scottish Highlands was covered in thick forest. The Scots pine reigned supreme on hillside and glen and offered shelter to such exotic beasts as wolves, bears, elks, wild bears and lynx. Beavers swam in the lochs and the golden eagle lorded it over all.

And then the slow destruction began. Man realised that these vast forested areas not only gave shelter to wild animals but to vagabonds and outlaws too. Wood was also needed for building, and there appeared to be a plentiful supply. The pines were felled. The wolves, bears, boars and many other species became extinct in Scotland and the red deer, once a forest dweller, took to the hills in fear.

Very little is left of that ancient Caledonian Pine Forest. Here and there we come across the bleached remnants of the roots in peat bogs, end of our walk finishing only half a mile down the road this walk is almost circular.

Take the Lairig Ghru path and follow it past the campsite and past the tiny Lairig Ghru cottage. Soon after the cottage the path splits in two and we take the left hand branch, still signposted to the Lairig Ghru.

Away ahead of us, beyond the great pines, you can actually see the cleft in the hills that is the pass itself, between the high hills of Creag an Leth-Choin and Sron na Lairig. To the right of Sron na Lairig rises the great bulk of Braeriach, the second highest mountain in the Cairngorms, and the third highest mountain in Britain.

Continue on the path over the large area of meadow. To your right you'll see some fine examples of luxuriant juniper and it's often a good idea to scan them with your binoculars for this is a good area for spotting crested tits, the small sparrow-like bird with the obvious crest on its head. Cross the small stream and head into the forest, keeping your eyes and ears open for the sound of chattering squirrels.

After a while the path leaves the gnarled blood-red pines behind and continues through a plantation of fairly recently planted sitka spruce. See the difference between the natural forest and the man-made commercial planting. These fast-growing trees do offer protection to many forms of wildlife but in aesthetic terms are far inferior to the type of natural forest we have been enjoying.

As we leave the commercial forest behind we come to a divergence in the ways. A path runs off to the right, towards our destination of Loch an Eilein. It's probably worthwhile wandering on for a few hundred yards to the Cairngorm Club footbridge which carries the Lairig Ghru path over the Allt Druie. A sandy beach by the river makes a good spot for lunch and in times of spate the river is an inspiring sight as it powers its way down towards its confluence with the mighty River Spey at Aviemore.

Our way now runs westwards over an undulating moorland of heather and pine. Small lochans are scattered here and there, usually inhabited by mallard and quite often goldeneye duck. To our left the hills begin to rise from the heather moor, the start of the long Sgorans ridge which ultimately colmi-nates on Sgoran Dubh Mor and Sgur Gaoith above Glen Feshie.

The track that we are now walking on is an ancient one, the Rathad nam Mearlach, or the Caterans Road. In the sixteenth and seventeenth centuries, clansmen from the west would often take this road to the rich pasture lands of Morayshire, where they would steal the cattle and return westwards with their booty. This quiet trail was well sequestered from the more populous route through Spey-side. You can still walk much of the trail, starting in the Pass of Ryvoan near Glenmore, passing south-east of Loch Morlich, through Rothiemurchus and past Loch an Eilein, and westwards by way of Glen Feshie, Dalwhinnie, Loch Ericht and the Bealach Dubh of Ben Alder to Loch Ossian and the ancient clan lands of the west.

Very shortly you'll spot the waters of Loch an Eilein through the trees, and you have a choice of routes. If time is against you or if you feel weary, you can turn right and take the footpath to the car park at the foot of Loch an Eilein. Alternatively, turn left and take the path which encircles the loch. If you have the time I would encourage you to walk around the loch, for it is one of the most scenic in the highlands. You can't go wrong on this path for it follows the shore of the loch for most of its route, splitting only at the head of the loch where a footpath continues towards Glen Feshie by the shore of Loch Ghamna, a small loch which is joined to Loch an Eilein by a short stretch of stream.

As you almost complete your circumnavi-gation of Loch an Eilein you will come across the remains of the castle ruins standing on its island fifty yards or so from the shore. The building dates from the fourteenth century and some local legends have it that this was once a keep of one Alexander Stewart, known as the Wolf of Badenoch. Stewart was the bastard son of Robert II of Scotland, and was eventually excommunicated from the Catholic Church for burning down Elgin Cathedral. More recently the castle ruins were used by one of the last ospreys before the old Scottish stock became extinct early this century. It's encou-raging to know that ospreys are again breeding in Scotland in good numbers and can even be seen from time to time fishing in the waters of Loch an Eilein.

At the end of the loch there is a small information centre which is run by the estate, and a car park. Leave the car park by the bridge that runs over a stream, follow the road for a hundred yards or so, and then turn right. Follow this track past some houses to the public road at Blackpark. Continue down the road to Inverdruie and from there to Coylum-bridge if you have to collect your car.

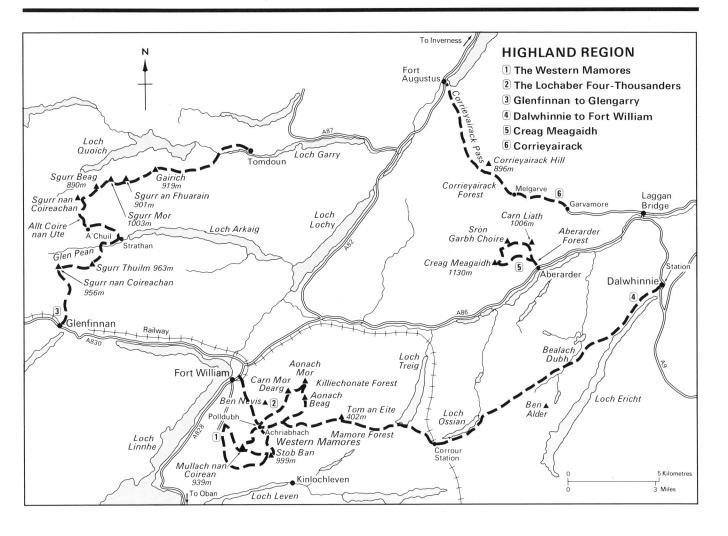

HIGHLAND REGION

1. The Western Mamores
2. The Lochaber Four-Thousanders
3. Glenfinnan to Glengarry
4. Dalwhinnie to Fort William
5. Creag Meagaidh
6. Corrieyairack

Map to show the following 6 walks: The Western Mamores (p73), The Lochaber Four Thousanders (p76), Glenfinnan to Glengarry (p79), Dalwhinnie to Fort William (p86), Creag Meagaidh (p91) and Corrieyairack (p94).

Two Munros are climbed on the Western Mamores walk, which although only 9 miles long is up steep rough ground and ascends 4,000ft.

The Lochaber Four Thousanders is a serious mountain walk of 8 miles that becomes a very serious mountaineering route in winter conditions.

The 37-mile route from Glenfinnan to Glengarry takes 3 days with overnight stops at bothies (or tent). A rough traverse of empty country with magnificent hills to climb and old routes through glens to be explored.

Three days are also needed for the Dalwhinnie to Fort William route, although because it is a predominantly low-level walk, 40 miles are covered.

The 16-mile walk over Creag Meagaidh is a moderate hill walk over broad ridges and plateaux.

The 17-mile walk from Garvamore to Fort Augustus over the Corrieyairack requires transport back to the start. Although it is an easy mountain pass in good weather, in winter conditions it can be exposed and difficult.

THE WESTERN MAMORES (Highland Region) by Roger Smith

Distance: 9 miles (14 km) *or* 12 miles (19km).
Ascent: 4000ft (1200m).
Start/Finish: A: Achriabhach, Glen Nevis.
B: Blarmachfoldach, on minor road S of Fort William.
Maps: OS 1:50,000 Sheet 41.
Summary: Hill paths and rough steep ground.

Mullach nan Coirean generally grassy but Stob Ban very rocky. Alternative route returns by old track and minor road.
Points of Interest: Ascent of two Munros, with spectacular views. Old military road now part of a long distance path on alternative route.

Facing page: **Sgurr a'Mhaim and the Devil's Ridge from Stob Ban.**

Facing page: **Snow on Mullach nan Coirean from Glen Nevis.**
(Photos: Hamish Brown)

The full traverse of the range known as the Mamores is one of the great hill days in Scotland. It is demanding and immensely rewarding and is undoubtedly a 'classic walk' in every sense, giving fine peaks, magnificent corries, stunning views, and some interesting scrambling in several places. At just over 20 miles (33km) with many thousands of feet of ascent however it is perhaps too extreme for this book. I have therefore chosen a gentler expedition at the western end of the range to give a sample of its pleasures.

There are eleven Munros in all in the Mamores, one of the biggest 'bags' available in a single day to the committed collector. This walk traverses a mere two but I doubt if you will go away from it feeling unsatisfied. And there is of course always the option of continuing further along the main ridge to bag a few more tops if you are so inclined.

The Munros climbed are Mullach nan Coirean (summit of the corries) and Stob Ban (light peak). The latter is named from the distinctive pale quartzite of its upper slopes, the same rock that forms the Grey Corries on the north side of Glen Nevis and many other Mamore peaks, including the shapely Sgurr a'Mhaim, so often mistaken by casual visitors for Ben Nevis in the belief that the quartzite rock is actually snow.

It is from Glen Nevis that the ascent starts—at Achriabhach, from where the hill is gained via a long and not altogether inspiring walk up through the forest. Enter the forest by the gate opposite the houses, and walk along the forest road for about 150 yards. Here, on the left, there is a path leading up through the trees that short-cuts a rather tedious section of the forest road to regain it higher up.

Turn left onto the road, go round a bend and carry on in a north-westerly direction to the end of the road, by a burn. The whole of this forest section is a pleasant enough walk through maturing conifers, giving time to reflect on the pleasures of the high tops ahead.

There is a path on the east bank of the burn which leads to the forest edge. The best way from here is to turn left along the fence marking the forest boundary until the north-east ridge of Mullach nan Coirean is reached, in about half a mile. It is a straightforward traverse.

Once on the ridge it is just a matter of putting one foot after another and tramping steadily up to the summit, a distance of about a mile and a half. As you rise you get fine views across the glen to mighty Ben Nevis and can appreciate the vast bulk of Britain's highest mountain and the distinctive shape of the summit plateau, with the cliffs of its northern side hacked out sheer by forces of unimaginable strength aeons ago.

There are also fine views of some of the other Mamore peaks, notably Stob Ban and Sgurr a'Mhaim. The ridge joins its more westerly counterpart just before the summit, which has a moderate-sized cairn. It is worth taking the stroll across to the westerly top, Meall a'Chaorainn, which is just 10ft under 3000, for the splendid views of Loch Linnhe and the hills of Morvern across the loch. This will add a mile or so to the walk.

To continue to Stob Ban, leave the summit of Mullach nan Coirean along the clear ridge running south-east and rounding the corries to the north that drop down into Glen Nevis. A minor top is crossed, after which the ridge becomes stonier in character and also a little narrower. At the col below Stob Ban a rather extraordinary thing happens. The rock beneath your feet changes, in a step, from the red granitic mass of the Mullach to the distinctive grey quartzite that so characterises the Mamores. It really is a strange sensation to go so suddenly from one rock type to another, so much so that I've stepped back and forth several times for the sheer fun of doing it! (Under snow, of course, the change would be less evident.)

Stob Ban looms ahead, a peak of vastly

Above: **Ben Nevis from the north ridge of Mullach nan Coirean.** (Photo: Donald Bennet)

different character from Mullach nan Coirean. It is rough, steep, and very rocky. The way up is well enough defined, going east and then more southerly up a rocky ridge below which, to the north, are extensive crags falling for almost 1000ft (300m). A certain amount of exploratory climbing has taken place on these crags but so far the mountain has remained generally quiet—possibly because the quartzite tends to be unsound in places and there is so much magnificent climbing elsewhere in the area, notably on Ben Nevis.

From being an unremarkable 3300ft or so in height, Stob Ban has achieved statistical interest with metrication in that it is given the figure of 999 metres for its summit. This is however of minor interest beside the vista of the rest of the Mamores ridge stretching ahead of you: a great temptation but unless you have prepared for it, best left to another day.

The initial part of the descent from Stob Ban, along its eastern ridge, needs some care as the rock is very broken and the way down has been worn by the passage of untold thousands of pairs of boots. This was my hundredth Munro, gained at the end of an exhausting day in August heat when I had started from

Kinlochleven and traversed most of the Mamores. There was a great feeling of satisfaction at attaining Stob Ban's summit, tempered somewhat by the knowledge that I had a long trudge back ahead of me! At that time I had not climbed Mullach nan Coirean but it looked impossibly distant to my weary eyes.

The easiest way back to Glen Nevis is to carry on to the col between Stob Ban and Sgor an Iubhair—a relatively recent addition to the list of Munros—and from here take a well-defined stalker's path winding down the east side of the burn in Coire a'Mhusgain, which deposits you in the glen only a few hundred yards from your starting point. From this path there are splendid views of the Devil's Ridge, which leads from Stob Choire a'Mhail out to Sgurr a'Mhaim and makes a fine scrambling traverse with little real difficulty.

There is another way of tackling the two peaks climbed on this walk, and it is worth mentioning as in some ways it gives a more satisfying, though longer, round walk. It starts from the minor road which leads south out of Fort William and is in fact part of the eighteenth-century military road from Kinlochleven. Parking places are not always easy

Ascending Stob Ban in winter.
(Photo: Hamish Brown)

This leads you onto the ridge going up to Meall a'Chaorainn, an easy ascent, and from there it is a simple walk round the corrie head to the summit of Mullach nan Coirean. This approach seems to me somehow more satisfying than the more direct stomp up from Glen Nevis.

The walk across to Stob Ban is of course the same as before, but to return it is necessary to retrace your route from the summit of Stob Ban back down to the col with the magical change of rock type. From here descend the grassy corrie to the south. A dyke helps with the initial part of the route, which is a little wearisome as the slope is somewhat unremitting. The burn in the corrie develops a number of fine small waterfalls as it descends.

Eventually you gain a clear, stony track near the former steading of Tigh-na-sleubhaich. You are now on the old military road, built under the direction of Major William Caulfeild, between 1749 and 1752, with a workforce of 300 soldiers. The notable traveller Thomas Pennant, passing this way in 1774, described the hills as having 'their sides covered with wood, and the bottoms of the glens filled with torrents that roar among the loose stones'. The wooded slopes are bare now but the torrents are still very much in evidence.

This track is now part of the West Highland Way footpath which stretches for nearly 100 miles (160km) from the outskirts of Glasgow to Fort William, and after two centuries there are again groups (though much smaller, and not soldiery pressed into service but eager volunteers!) working on the maintenance of the route. It leads back past Lairigmor (the military road is visible slightly higher up the hillside as a grassy track) and through a section of forestry to the start of the public road at Blar a'Chaorainn, from where it is a simple stroll of a couple of miles back to the start point of the walk.

It is fascinating to reflect on those who trod this way before and to try to envisage all the activity when the road was being constructed. As with a number of these routes, it did not stay in service for very long. The easier though longer route down Glen Coe came into use in 1785 and the old road was left to the more adventurous travellers on foot to discover and enjoy: as people are still doing today.

to find but you should be able to get off the road somewhere around Blarmachfoldach so that you can gain access to the hill by the south-east side of a forestry plantation.

THE LOCHABER FOUR THOUSANDERS
(Highland Region) by Cameron McNeish

Distance: 8 miles (13 km).
Ascent: 4500ft (1370m).
Start/Finish: Car park at Polldubh in Glen Nevis.
Maps: OS 1:50,000 Sheet 41.
Summary: A serious mountain walk over very rough ground. A very serious mountaineering route in winter conditions.
Points of Interest: Ben Nevis is, of course, Britain's highest mountain. The view from the summit is an extensive one and the ruins of the old weather observatory make an interesting historical point. The views of the Mamores and the Grey Corries from the Aonachs is extensive. Look out for eagles, and listen for the song of the snow bunting in spring time.

Ben Nevis from Aonach Mor.
(Photo: Cameron McNeish)

While the Cairngorms have always been able to boast of their 'four fourthousanders' in Ben Macdui, Cairn Gorm, Braeriach and Cairn Toul, the Lochaber equivalent hasn't always been quite justified. While Ben Nevis, Carn Mor Dearg and Aonach Beag most certainly top the magic 4000ft plimsoll line, until fairly recently Aonach Mor was a full twelve inches below it, at 3999ft (1219m) to be exact.

Am I being pedantic? Am I taking a Cairngorm allegiance too far? The Cairngorms/Lochaber rivalry is nothing new, ask modern climbers. The die was cast a long time ago when it was believed that 4300ft (1311m), Ben Macdui was the highest hill in Britain. Subsequent surveys upgraded Ben Nevis to 4406ft (1343m) and many Cairngormers' hearts were broken as a result.

Fairly recently the Ordnance Survey (OS) have resurveyed the Lochaber area for their new metric maps and Aonach Mor has been promoted to just over 4000ft, or its metric equivalent. So now we have two groups of four thousand quads, and another target for those who enjoy making long-distance treks out of such things.

Incidentally, the new metrications give Ben Nevis the equivalent of 4418ft (1347m) above sea level, but the vast majority of walkers appear happy to remember it as the traditional 4406ft (1343m). Perhaps I'm really being pedantic if I suggest that we remember Aonach Mor as 3999ft?

And there's another anomaly in this mountain story. Aonach Mor, the Big Ridge, is actually lower in height than its neighbour Aonach Beag, the Little Ridge. Many writers have suggested that this is because Aonach Mor has a larger acreage and more bulk but I refute this suggestion to a certain degree and point out that the Gaelic is quite correct in its description. Aonach Mor is simply a long broad ridge as its name suggests. Aonach Beag is a much shorter, smaller ridge. In fact all the ridges of Aonach Beag are narrower than the broad arm of Aonach Mor. These hills were all named long before the hills were surveyed for height, so in essence distance above sea level doesn't really come into it.

To the majority of visitors, Ben Nevis will be the *raison d'etre* of this round. But I don't propose to dwell too long on the Ben for it has been well documented elsewhere. Unfortunately too many people see Ben Nevis as a dull and repetitive slog up a tourist track. By linking it to Carn Mor Dearg and the Aonachs one can experience a much greater appreciation of it as it really is, a majestic and awesome mountain of the first order.

For this reason I would suggest to you that you forgo the dubious pleasures of the tourist track from Achintee, and take a steeper but more rewarding start to this round. Take the motor road up Glen Nevis to its end at Polldubh and leave your car here in the large car park. Not only does this offer a different starting point from the hundreds of tourists, but it also means that your car is handily available at the end of the walk without necessitating a long walk on the road back to it.

Now prepare yourself for some hard graft. You'll only walk a dozen paces or so from your car before you start climbing. No easy preamble here to warm up the muscles, it's heads down and get on with it.

This route is known as the Waterslide Route following the 1500ft (457m) slide of the Allt Coire Eoghainn which spews forth from its corrie of the same name high above you. A faint track climbs up the right hand side of the burn and it's a hard pull first thing in the morning. The views across the glen make it very worthwhile though, across to the impressive Sgurr a'Mhaim, Stob Ban and Mullach nan Coirean of the Mamores.

Coire Eoghainn is itself a majestic place, with boulder screes far above you leading onto the summit slopes of the Ben. From the lip of the corrie bear off north-east, and you'll soon find yourself in a jumble of scree and boulder which leads to the summit slopes. Take care hereabouts especially in winter conditions as an unchecked slide could have fatal consequences.

If you are correct in your navigation you should be coming across the marker posts which are there to guide climbers from the summit to the start of the Carn Mor Dearg Arete. The summit will be familiar to most, either from previous ascents or from published photographs. From the top, retrace your steps back down to the marker posts and follow them down steeply to the start of the airy crest that is the Carn Mor Dearg Arete.

For walkers whose only experience of Ben Nevis is from the tourist track then the Carn Mor Dearg Arete will be a revelation. This narrow ridge swings gracefully around the head of Coire Leis, a thin and airy crest which doesn't fall below 3478ft (1060m), and if you're lucky enough to get clear weather too, the great cliffs of the North-East Buttress will rise high and steeply above you. Beyond it lies the long line of Tower Ridge followed by the full and impressive array of crags, cliffs, gullies and snow-fields for which this great hill is so justly named Number One.

Wander around the arete to Carn Mor Dearg itself, sit for a while and enjoy this great

mountain scene. Nowhere in the country is there anything so dramatic. Here, throughout the generations, has been the scene of told and untold dramas. Here was the playground of the early Scottish Mountaineering Club stalwarts, and here too, in this same arena, is the playground of modern rock gymnasts. Away below lies the Charles Inglis Clark Memorial Hut, and the path that runs up the Allt a'Mhuillin, so often used as a means of climbing onto the Carn Mor Dearg Arete.

The eastern ridge from Carn Mor Dearg down to the bealach of Aonach Mor is steep and fairly tight and can be quite interesting, especially when snow has built up on the lee side. Dropping over 1200ft (366m) in under a mile I always thank the Lord I am descending and not ascending, although there is a sharp pull up to the bealach between the two Aonachs. I mention this for there are a number of climbers who prefer to climb the Aonachs first, leaving the arete fom Carn Mor Dearg to the Ben as the grand finale.

Aonach Mor is a long broad plateau of a ridge, and the summit cairn lies about halfway along it. The plateau is flanked by steep sides and good navigation is called for in dank weather. It's been suggested that the only safe way off the hill in winter conditions is back down to the Carn Mor Dearg bealach.

A fairly obvious path threads its way through rocky outcrops from the col to the summit plateau of Aonach Beag, and once again great care is required in misty weather. The bald pate of this summit can be atrociously icy and steep cliffs on most sides tend to give walkers a great feeling of insecurity. Add to that the fact that cornices often build up over the edges into great overhanging waves of snow, and the summit cairn lies very close to the cliff edge of the north-eastern corrie. The western edges of Aonach Beag are sheer, so great care really should be taken when navigating off the hill. Take the south-west ridge as a descent route to Steall and upper Glen Nevis.

Throughout the ascent of Aonach Beag you'll notice a new face of Ben Nevis rising above the wall of the Carn Mor Dearg Arete. Not the familiar crouching hulk that is the view from the south and west. Here the North-East Buttress of the mountain throws up a graceful spire into the sky. It is, in my opinion, the finest feature of the mountain, spiced by the fact that you can't see this angle from any road, making the effort of climbing here so worthwhile.

From the ruined cottage of Steall, follow the Glen Nevis path back to Polldubh, above the magnificent gorge that has been described as the 'finest half mile in all Scotland'. It's a worthy end to a worthy day, a day in which you may have seen Ben Nevis in a new light.

How does it compare with the Cairngorms' Big Four? Well that's another story entirely.

GLENFINNAN TO GLENGARRY (Highland Region) by Roger Smith

Strathan, the west end of Loch Arkaig. (Photo: Roger Smith)

Distance: 37 miles (60km).
Ascent: 12,500ft (3800m).
Start/Finish: Start at Glenfinnan Station. Finish at the Tomdoun Hotel, Glen Garry.
Maps: OS 1:50,000 Sheets 40, 33, and 34.
Summary: A tough traverse of rugged, empty country with magnificent hills to be climbed and old routes through glens to be explored. Overnight shelter only in bothies or by camping.

Start on good track: finish on forestry track and minor road.
Points of Interest: Glenfinnan, start of the 1745 Rebellion, has monument and visitor centre (NTS). Wild glens, superb hills, much recent forestry planting in glens. Two or three bothies. Fine old inn at finish.

There can hardly be a finer area of rough, wild country anywhere than that traversed by this walk. Much of it is on OS 1:50,000 Sheet 40 (Loch Shiel); the upper right-hand part of that sheet is an area of 150 square miles (400 square km) which contains only one road (the A830 along its southern edge) and a maximum of six occupied houses. It was all very different 200 years ago and to me the empty glens resound with a sadness that will never leave them.

For the purposes of the modern explorer on foot, the emptiness is a bonus and a challenge, and the excitement of the map is the way it is filled with splendid mountains and finely carved glens. The closeness of the area to the western seaboard means that the views in that direction are outstanding, and the sunsets are of a quality not found elsewhere in Britain. The wild, remote character of the area means that it is not a place for the inexperienced, but for those who feel at ease in the hills there is no finer landscape anywhere.

I cannot walk these hills and glens without being aware of their history, or at least the main strands of it, and that sense of the past looking over my shoulder, so to speak, is nowhere stronger than at the start of the walk, at Glenfinnan. The monument here—surely one of the most-photographed scenes in Scotland, if not in the world—marks the spot where Prince Charles Edward Stuart raised his standard on Monday 19th August 1745, at the start of his attempt to win back the throne of Britain, which he believed had been unlawfully taken from him.

The Prince had arrived secretly from France, landing in Loch nan Uamh, a dozen miles to the west. At first there was a reluctance to rally to his cause, but when key figures such as Cameron of Lochiel and Ranald MacDonald of Kinlochmoidart pledged their support, others joined then, and when the standard was raised there were over 1000 men behind the Prince. The campaign rapidly gathered strength, took Perth and Edinburgh and advanced south as far as Derby, where it petered out. On the retreat things began to decline and it all came to a terrible, sad end at Culloden in April 1746.

The story of the campaign, and especially of its beginnings, is very well told in the neat visitor centre at Glenfinnan run by the National Trust for Scotland, and I do urge you to go there if you can. It will help you to realise how this land came to be as empty as it is today.

After Culloden, Prince Charles ran and hid before his pursuers for many months, sheltered by loyal followers who risked their own lives. He traversed, on foot and with minimal equipment or supplies, all of this country and much else besides and by the end of that time he must have been a fit man of the hills (he was 25 at the time). Despite being hunted, surely he must have grown to know and love these wild west Highlands during those long summer days?

I cannot claim to know the area as well as

he, but my love and respect for it grows with every visit. The walk described here cuts across its heart and gives a very good impression of its essential character. It is not easy country. The hills are rugged and steep, and frequently rough, and there is very little shelter. Each peak ascended can be counted an achievement.

The start, at Glenfinnan, is impressive enough: but it has two further bonuses. One is that you can reach it by train, on the marvellous West Highland Line from Glasgow, with a change of train at Fort William. The train trundles along at a steady pace on the single-track line, stopping frequently at small stations. If you take the evening train, as my companion and I did when we made this through walk, you get to Glenfinnan in time for your second bonus—a pint at the excellent Stage House Inn before starting the walk.

We did the walk in midsummer, in a wonderfully settled spell of weather. It is a time of year in Scotland when there seems to be almost endless daylight. And even at 11pm, when we left the inn, there was quite enough light for our walk-in up Glen Finnan itself. There is a good track up the glen for much of the way, extended to serve the lodge, of which more later. The first notable landmark is the railway viaduct, a very fine piece of engineering dating from the 1860s and carrying the line in a vast sweep across the glen.

As with so many other glens, the character of Glen Finnan is being changed by forestry planting, which has been carried out on an extensive scale on both sides of the glen. Let us hope that as the forests grow they add to the attractiveness of the scene rather than the reverse. The planting extends for about three miles up the glen, though it has been kept some way clear of the glen bottom.

On the OS map, at the point where the Allt a Chaol-Ghlinne tumbles down to meet the river, you will see a building marked as Corryhully. This was our first night destination: it is a bothy, or unlocked shelter, a special feature of the Scottish hills (there are, to be fair, a small number in England and Wales also). Most of these buildings are maintained on a voluntary basis by the Mountain Bothies Association, and right well they do it too. Corryhully is an estate bothy, and a notice on its door welcomes walkers and asks them to leave the bothy in a clean and tidy condition.

By the time we got there it was midnight. The last light was still fading from the western sky and the warm air could almost be touched, so mild was it. We arranged our sleeping bags, brewed up and turned in ready for an early start.

Corryhully Bothy, Glenfinnan.
(Photo: Roger Smith)

Day One

Being out in the hills always encourages an early start: when the sun rises at 3.30am the encouragement is even greater! We were up and preparing by six and ready to go shortly after seven. An early start was desirable for a further reason: it was clearly going to be another scorcher, and we thought it wise to gain as much height as we could before the heat began to sap our strength.

There was no point in hurrying. With a long day before us, energy would need to be conserved and a steady pace, with a good number of stops, was essential. We made our way up the glen noticing with a start the new lodge up on the hill. With the greatest respect to the architect, it can hardly be said to blend in with the surroundings, being of a design more commonly seen in the suburbs of towns. But it was soon left behind and our thoughts were on higher things anyway!

Our first objective was Sgurr nan Coireachan (peak of the corries), to be gained by the fine ridge of Sgurr a'Choire Riabhach. We did not find the path marked on the map leading up to the ridge and made our own route. It is just as steep as the map shows and we gained height only very slowly. We had drunk as much as we could before setting out and were carrying water with us but I was already beginning to wonder if we would have enough for the ridge traverse to come. Rationing water in the west Highlands would be an odd game to play, for sure!

Eventually we crossed the subsidiary peak and made for the summit of Coireachan, a new Munro for both of us. We were more than ready for a rest when we got there, but a stop would certainly have been demanded anyway. The views, particularly out to the west, were stupefying. Loch Morar stretched away towards the sea (which it does not quite reach, a neck of land intervening) and drew the eye naturally to the wondrous glitter of the islands. The Cuillin of Rum stood out proud and clear, with the flatter shape of Canna to the north and the extraordinary prow of the Sgurr of Eigg to the south, a weird right angle in the sea.

To the north was a fantastic jumble of peak upon peak—Knoydart, Kintail, Affric, names to roll around the tongue and to conjure up magical memories in the mind. We stayed resting by the trig pillar for quite some time, trying to take it all in—and inevitably failing—and using our cameras as aids to bring at least some of this splendour back later.

At last we moved, reluctantly. Munro number two, Sgurr Thuilm (peak of the rounded hillock) waited three rough miles away to the east, with several 'tops' to be overcome *en route*. This is a grand ridge walk, never difficult but never dull either, with plenty of rock underfoot and enough twists and turns to keep the concentration up.

On the approach to Sgurr Thuilm we passed two other walkers coming down—the only people we were to see on the whole walk. Sgurr Thuilm overlooks Glen Pean and dominates the eastern approach to that glen, which has also been afforested in part. The fugitive Prince is known to have been in this area for some days and to have slept out on Sgurr Thuilm.

We were not intending to do that—our objective was another bothy in Glen Dessarry, but we were some way from it yet. The next aim was to get off the hill, find some running water and make the most of it. We staggered down Sgurr Thuilm's rough east ridge for a while then cut off north down to the Allt Choire Chaisil. In its middle reaches we found a quite delectable spot where we took an hour out enjoying one of the great pleasures of long through walks—the time spent doing absolutely nothing.

Refreshed and revived and with our thirst quenched (temporarily, at least) we wandered down the burn into Glen Pean. This is another glen, now empty of people, which was once full of life, particularly in the summer months when the higher shielings (grazing grounds) were occupied. Where the footbridge crosses the River Pean by the junction with Gleann a'Chaorainn, the narrow pass over to Glen Finnan, a stand of birch provided welcome shade and we rested again for a few minutes.

Ahead was Strathan, one of the most isolated places in Scotland, reached by a rough twelve-mile road along Loch Arkaig and standing strategically at the junction of the west end of that lovely loch with east ends of Glens Pean and Dessarry, both long used as through routes on foot to the west coast. Dessarry is a wider strath and here too were once many dwelling-places, the ruins of which can still be found.

West of Strathan is a tangle of forestry and new tracks, and a digger was working as we threaded our way across and into Glen Dessarry. The OS map has not yet caught up with the developments here, and care is needed if you are not to be ensnared in plantations and fences.

It was by now late afternoon and we were beginning to look forward to reaching our second bothy of the trip, A'Chuil. As it was such a marvellous fine weekend, we expected to have company—a thought that did not trouble us. There is a good track up the glen (which again has much forestry planting, going a long way up) as far as the last house, Upper Glendessarry, which had occupants, though it is not permanently used.

We passed quietly and cut down to the river to get across to the bothy. The Dessarry can be difficult to cross after heavy rain but we did not need to bother with the bridge—the river ran low and quiet over the stones and we hopped across dryshod with no difficulty. As we came up to the bothy, a lovely neat building, there was surprisingly little sign of life, and indeed we had it to ourselves. We could only surmise that everyone was at Sourlies, over the pass in Knoydart.

We were happy where we were, and made the most of it. Our gear sorted and evening meal prepared and eaten (and greatly welcomed after the exertions of the day) we made coffee and talked over our plans for the morrow. It had been a wonderful first day but the heat had taken quite a lot out of us. Standing at the bothy door in the soft evening light we looked at the great mountain wall across the glen. We had to climb that!

Over-ambitious plans to take in the twin tops of Sgurr na Ciche and Garbh Chioch Mor were soon shelved. We would start with Sgurr nan Coireachan and work along the ridge east from there, aiming to finish perhaps at a third bothy in Glen Kingie, with Gairich left as our target on the walk out. It looked as if a deep corrie—Coire nan Uth—might provide the break in the wall we needed. The morning would give us the answer.

I sense there might be some puzzlement among readers here. Why am I talking of Sgurr nan Coireachan when that hill has already been climbed? The answer is simply that there are two hills of that name in the area. This is by no means unusual nor illogical. Hills were named by people from below, and if 'peak of the corries' was the appropriate name for your hill, what matter if the folk two glens away to the south had a similar peak with a similar name?

The bothy book made much mention of a resident mouse so we made sure our food was well packed away. If he did visit us during the night we didn't hear him, and he certainly took nothing. Perhaps he wouldn't have liked packet meals and teabags anyway: times are hard for the modern bothy mouse.

Day Two

Another early start, another glorious day. Our preparations were a little slower than the day before and the walk up the glen seemed a bit of a struggle, especially as we crossed the river at the wrong point and had to fight up through heavily ditched young trees, cursing, until we

On the ridge between Sgurr nan Coireachan and Sgurr Thuilm. (Photo: Roger Smith)

reached the main path—said to have been made to carry herring from the coast through to market.

We cut across the shoulder of the hill east of Coire nan Uth and looked down. Yes, it would go. In fact it gave us a fine route up, with a drink, of course, readily available and higher up even a bit of scrambling on some rocks worn smooth by the water. At the high lochan which fed the burn we stopped to gather our strength ready for the big effort ahead.

82

Chioch Mor stood out boldly, both being very definite shapely peaks (Cioch or Ciche means 'pap', though these rough breasts never nurtured any child).

We could make out part of the amazing stone dyke that runs between the two peaks, dating from the days when landowners guarded their boundaries jealously. What a labour it must have been to build. It can be a useful route-finder in mist. To the north lay Loch Quoich, a large reservoir set in the most sublime surroundings imaginable. Our cameras were kept busy.

We returned to our packs, picked them up with some reluctance and turned east. We had four distinct, large hills to climb, and only one of them (Sgurr Mor) a Munro! There is a path marked along the crest of the hills for much of the way. If it was on the map I knew it must be a stalker's path and if it was, it would help us greatly. Such paths were made in the nineteenth century with great skill, always taking the easiest and best route up the hill. It had to be possible for ponies laden with dead stags to use them, or men with similar burdens. It seems a pity that so many are falling into disrepair now.

An Eag (the notches) was not too difficult, and on the descent we could see the path winding its zigzag way up Sgurr Beag. It was indeed a great help—for a 'little peak' this was a mighty big hill! About this time we saw one of the great sights of the Highlands—a soaring eagle. It never came really close to us but was nonetheless a marvellous sight as it displayed its utter mastery of the air. When it decided to move, in a few moments it was away over the far side of Glen Kingie. It is a privilege to watch these magnificent birds in their natural habitat.

We wished heartily that we had the eagle's wings to take us over to Sgurr Mor. We were both beginning to struggle a little, Peter perhaps rather more than me. Even with the path to help it was a long hard grind up to the top of what certainly is a 'big peak'—a great sprawl of a hill just topping the 1000-metre mark and by some way the highest point of the whole trip.

We reached the cairn and collapsed. It was only four o'clock in the afternoon but there was no point in trying to go much further. We looked at the map and discussed options. We very much wanted to 'bag' Gairich, an isolated Munro not easy of access. To go to Kinbreack bothy for the night was a substantial diversion, and a more direct line would be preferable. Peter hit on the answer. The weather was settled and unthreatening—why not bivouac out somewhere below Gairich? That way we

The other Sgurr nan Coireachan from Dessarry.
(Photo: Roger Smith)

There was one advantage in tackling the ridge this way—once on it, we could leave our packs for the scramble up to Sgurr nan Coireachan, thus substantially reducing the effort involved. That we did. The ridge was soon reached from the lochan and, packs dumped, we enjoyed the climb up to the summit. Again the views were quite superb. To the west was the wild expanse of Knoydart—the Rough Bounds as the area is called, and well named too. Sgurr na Ciche and Garbh

would hold our line and conserve some energy.

It was a simple solution and a good one. Bivouacing is great fun in the right conditions, and conditions could hardly have been more right at that moment. All that was left (and it was quite enough!) was to climb Sgurr an Fhuarain, the final top on the long ridge and find a spot between it and Gairich to park ourselves for the night.

It took us quite a long time to carry out that straightforward task. Even coming downhill off Sgurr an Fhuarain we were weaving about with tiredness. We cut down a promising-looking burn, avoiding some rotten old snow still hanging about high in the corrie, and found ourselves a good spot lower down, leaving a short descent in the morning before the climb of Gairich.

We were tired enough to grab a couple of hour's sleep before attending to the evening duties of cooking and eating. The evening was warm and still and we looked forward to the pleasure of sleeping out under the stars, and of our last hill and the walk out to Glengarry the next day.

Day Three

Sleep came easily, as did early waking. For a few moments I had no idea where I was. Even when I remembered things looked different. Then I realised why. A mist had come in during the night and for the first time on the walk there was a chill feeling in the air. This was disappointing, but not disastrous. I looked at my watch. Five o'clock: might as well be up and doing.

We had a hill to climb and a fair walk out after it to reach the Tomdoun Hotel in Glen Garry by lunchtime, where a friend had kindly agreed to come and give us a lift back to Fort William. An early start was therefore desirable, but in the dank gloom of the mist—such a contrast to the sparkling light of the two previous mornings—it was hard to energise ourselves, the more so as neither of our two small stoves seemed inclined to work at all well!

It took us an hour or so to get organised but by six we were moving down to the bealach of A'Mhaingir, where an old right of way cuts through the hills. Westward, it leads nowhere any more, as the enlargement of Loch Quoich to form a reservoir has truncated it: just one of the prices to be paid for the benefit of electricity produced through hydro power.

The bealach was a mass of peat hags and we were glad that we had chosen to bivouac higher up and not down here. The evening before, I had pinpointed the start of the stalking path up onto Gairich Beag and I was

pleased to find it without too much difficulty. As we climbed, we began to discern a lightening in the atmosphere and at about 2000ft (600m) I could not resist hurrying ahead. I was pretty sure of what I would find.

And I was right. In a step I broke through the mist into glorious sunshine. This is one of the truly magical hill experiences. Everything below us was swathed in woolly murk but above, where we were heading, was clean air and sunlight. I knew that the view from the top would be worth all the effort of the past three days put together and I raced ahead, heels suddenly winged, over Gairich Beag and across the broken ground to the sharp pull up to the summit of Gairich itself.

What I saw brought from me a spontaneous cry of elation, and I rushed back to urge Peter to get up as fast as he could (I'm sure he was anyway, poor chap). We stood at the cairn and marvelled. In a full circle of the compass, hills stood proudly up in the bright sunlight above a swirling mass of cloud. Already the sun's warmth was providing the benison to break the cloud and Loch Quoich appeared and then disappeared again as if by magic.

Directly to the east, a silvery shaft of sunlight lit up the full length of Glen Garry as it penetrated the veil of cloud. We swung south-east: and there was Ben Nevis itself, shoulders humped above the mist as if daring it to hide the proudness of our highest mountain. Could I capture this scene on film? I had only a couple of shots left in my camera, and I had to try. I lined Peter up by the cairn, pressed the shutter and prayed. As it turned out, it wasn't perfect, although not bad for a semi-automatic camera: but it doesn't approach the majesty of the scene as we viewed it.

Only the very early riser who is already deep in the hills is privileged to see such a scene, and we felt humbled to have been there and shared it. We had the best of it, without doubt: even as we got ready to start our descent the mist was dissipating more and more rapidly. By the time we reached Glen Kingie it would almost all be gone.

But that was some way off. The first part of the descent was an entertaining scramble down a narrow ridge which we both enjoyed. After that the ground levelled out and we became aware of the miles still to be covered. We took a slanting line south of the lochan on Bac nam Fod, aiming for somewhere near the start of the forestry track shown on the map. What the map didn't show, unfortunately, was that the planting had been extended further up the hill. By the time we realised this we were committed to our line of descent and there was nothing for it but to scale the fence and plunge into the

Peter Evans on the summit of the Glenfinnan Sgurr nan Coireachan. (Photo: Roger Smith)

with our joy of a couple of hours earlier! With a last glance back at Gairich, now completely free of mist, we set off towards Glen Garry. It took us another hour or so to reach the bridge over the Kingie, where we took what might be our last break. A path is shown here following the south bank of the river, but there was no sign of it on the ground and we decided to stick with the forestry road even though it was a longer route.

There's not a lot is to be said about it. Admitedly we were both tired, but it was still a monotonous trudge through endless conifers. The trees were quite mature but that did nothing to help—there was so little variety in them, not enough to bring any pleasure to the eye. We were both heartily glad to reach the gate at the forest edge and see the bridge across the River Garry. After that there would be just a couple of miles on the road to the hotel—and a welcome pint of beer.

Glen Garry is MacDonald country, with the MacDonnell branch of the clan being prominent here. They supported the Stuart cause and went all the way to Culloden with the Prince. Their war cry was *Creag an Fhithich,* which means the Raven's Rock. In times past there were hundreds of people living in the glen, and further west into Glen Quoich and Knoydart, which had a population of over 1000 in the late eighteenth century. Under 100 people live in all those vast acres today.

A MacDonald of those times would have been most surprised at the welcome we received at the Tomdoun, a great hostelry for walkers. Not that it lacked warmth, quite the reverse, but it was delivered in a Welsh accent! The inn changed hands a couple of years ago and the new landlord is indeed a Welshman. This pleased Peter, who is Welsh himself, and a couple of pints were very happily consumed while we waited for our lift (there is a postbus if you aren't so lucky).

It had been a great walk, and it is one I recommend to anyone. You will be very lucky if you get the conditions we got, but the country is so outstanding that the walk would still be worth doing. Obviously in very poor conditions the route might need to be modified but using the old passes through the hills instead of climbing them would still give a very satisfying walk. I hope it is not too long before I wander those empty hills again and reflect on the history of the people who once lived there.

furrows and ditches of the young plantings to get down to the road.

I cannot pretend there was any pleasure in it and we were both cursing roundly by the time we escaped from the treelets. What a contrast

DALWHINNIE TO FORT WILLIAM (Highland Region) by Cameron McNeish

Distance: 40 miles (96km).
Start/Finish: Start at Dalwhinnie Railway Station. Finish at Fort William
Maps: OS 1:50,000 Second Series Sheets 41, 42
Summary: A predominantly low-level walk through fine remote countryside. The going can be very wet underfoot after heavy rain and the area around Tom an Eite is often regarded as the wettest place in Scotland. The route doesn't pass through any habitation and all food must be carried. There are a couple of very fine bothies *en route.*
Points of Interest: Superb wild areas around the Bealach Dubh offering superb views westwards beyond Loch Ossian. Many hills to climb *en route* including Ben Alder, the Mamores, The Grey Corries, the Aonachs and Ben Nevis. Good areas for observing wild life including red deer, wildcat, red fox, ptarmigan, peregrine falcon and golden eagle.

Backpackers camped near Loch Ossian with the Bealach Dubh in the far distance. (Photo: Cameron McNeish)

Dalwhinnie is a bleak and desolate corner of the old district of Badenoch. It has little to offer other than a good transport café, a small store and a railway station. A couple of hotels give lie to the belief that no one would ever actually want to spend the night there.

In spite of this reputation, Dalwhinnie has something of the atmosphere of an old frontier town. The country that surrounds it is nothing short of superb. To the east, over the historic backbone of Druim Alba, ancient rievers' trails trace their way towards the rich pasturelands of the east, of Speyside and Moray. Over there lie the mighty Cairngorms, and northwards, across the dim outline of the Monadhliath hills, lies the empty corner that gives way to the Great Glen. Westwards, beyond the long sheath of Loch Ericht, lies another empty quarter, a land of rugged and remote hills and some of the most isolated mountains in Scotland.

Day One

A good Land Rover track borders the northern shore of Loch Ericht, an estate road which services Ben Alder Lodge, 6 miles (9¹/₂km) down the glen. In high summer bright yellow broom waymarks the road, and the sound of sandpipers is never very far away. The bleached stumps of ancient pines stand as ancient memorials of their former glory, stalwart reminders of the great forest that covered this part of Scotland hundreds of years ago, long before the green blight of over coniferisation.

I've often walked this stretch of track, enthusiastic to reach the delights of Pattack and Ben Alder. Conversely, I've often cursed its monotony in the other direction when trailing home after days out. How great is the motivation of anticipation.

Only the trees change in this part of the world. The conifers grow taller. The old grey lodge stands remote and aloof beside the loch, and the heart quickens at the sight of the track swinging west and onto the flats of Pattack, with the jaws of the Bealach Dubh between the Lancet Ridge and Ben Alder drawing you onwards.

Charles Edward Stuart passed through here after the tragedy of Culloden. Hard walking brought him from the Great Glen over the Laggan hills and through by Loch Pattack to Ben Alder. There he was welcomed by Cluny MacPherson, himself a Jacobite who had taken to the heather. A rocky bower high on the south-facing slopes of Ben Alder was his erstwhile home, and it was here in Cluny's Cage, that Charles found shelter from his continuous struggle against the elements. Soon, however, word was brought to him that a French frigate awaited him off the western

Steall, with the mighty waterfall roaring down the slopes of the Mamores. (Photo: Cameron McNeish)

seaboard to ferry him 'over the water' and back to France.

An obvious track carries you over the peat flats beside Loch Pattack and on towards the obvious target of the Bealach Dubh. I say obvious, but there are times when rain clouds wipe out any view whatsoever. When the sun shines though this is delightful country. Skylarks are rarely out of song in the summer months, and the place becomes alive with meadow pipits. Often there are swans on the river, and white garrons roam the moors. Further afield the great herds of red deer roam, and in the autumn months their roars echo from the hillsides.

As the path swings in to run alongside the slow-moving Allt a'Chaoilreidhe, you'll pass the old bothy at Culra. This may make a good opportunity to stop for the night, unless you have a tent and desire to find a higher-level camp up on the Bealach Dubh. The bothy is a dry one, and is fairly roomy and comfortable, with a couple of rooms to choose from.

Day Two

Leave the bothy and cross to the south bank of the river again. The track continues westwards over the bumps and moraines of the ancient glaciers that once scoured this great pass, and now herald the introduction of the pass proper. To your left the great bulk of Ben Alder rises high, one of the remotest of the Munros. Follow the track up and through the dark jaws, and then witness a view of great splendour unfold before you. Far down the long glen in front of you lie the waters of Loch Ossian, named after the bardic son of the great Fionn MacCumhail, better known in Scotland as Fingal. Beyond the loch rise some of the highest hills in Scotland, the hills of Lochaber; the great peaks of the Mamore Forest, the Grey Corries and the Aonachs, and Ben Nevis the highest of all. This must have made a welcome sight for the Lochaber raiders and cattle thieves as they hurried home from their pillaging, their home hills well within sight.

But all wouldn't necessarily be well. At the foot of this long glen, just east of Loch Ossian, a clan skirmish took place in the seventeenth century. Some MacDonnells of Keppoch had set out on the Rathad nam Meirleach, the Cateran's Road, towards Speyside, intent on a raid into Moray. They hadn't gone very far when word was brought to them that some Grants from Speyside were in fact behind them in Keppoch, stealing MacDonnell cattle. Infuriated, they returned without delay, caught the Grants red handed and killed them almost to a man. But not quite. The surviving Grants made good their escape and scurried off by

way of Loch Treig to Loch Ossian where they met some strangers. They confided to the strangers that they were being chased by 'cursed MacDonnell heathens'. Unknown to them, the strangers were also MacDonnells, who immediately saved their fellow clansmen a long chase by despatching the Grants to a quick and bloody grave. Violent times indeed.

Loch Ossian indents the north-east corner of Rannoch Moor, a vast undulating glacial plain which forms an inhospitable expanse of peat bog and open water, a supremely lonely place where the deer roam freely. The loch itself is remote with no easy access other than the train which crosses the line from Bridge of Orchy to Spean Bridge. Loch Ossian certainly isn't bleak though. High hills surround it, and the edges of the loch are softened by woods. This area is all deer forest, and of course you are not particularly welcome during the stalking season. I once bumped into a shepherd on the track that runs alongside Loch Ossian and as we chatted he told me to look out for a white deer which had been seen several times in the Creaguaineach area near to Loch Treig. 'It'll no live long A'hm thinking,' he told me. 'The older stags'll kill it off as it's no wan o' them.'

A youth hostel belonging to the Scottish Youth Hostels Association sits on a tiny peninsula at the western end of the loch, a hostel of the type which is becoming rare. A wooden shack of a building, it has an atmosphere which is peculiar to this type of accommodation; the reek of the red hot stove in the kitchen cum common room, the steamed up windows, the bubbling pots and pans, and the conversations of a dozen different languages as young people mix together. How different it is in modern hostels, where the hostellers spend their evening huddled around a television or a pool table. A hostelling official told me recently that modern youth demanded 'sophistication'.

Thankfully, the Scottish Youth Hostels Association are intent on keeping hold of their simple hostels, and are striving to meet the cost of the upkeeping of these little gems like Ossian, Glen Affric, Carn Dearg and one or two others.

A mile or so from the hostel lies the railway station at Corrour, on the Glasgow to Fort William line, probably the most scenic railway line in the country. A path follows the railway north-westwards to the southern shore of Loch Treig, a long six-mile trough hemmed in on both sides by 3000ft (900m) mountains. The scenery hereabouts tends to be more bleak than beautiful, and the shoreline of Loch Treig doesn't help. But Loch Treig is part of the great reservoir system that meets the demands

Above:**Loch Ossian at Corrour with the 3647-ft Aonach Beag in the background.** (Photo: Frank Martin)

the loch to Creaguaineach Lodge, and cross the waters of the Abhainn Rath by the footbridge. This fine river has its source high in the Grey Corries, just east of Ben Nevis. This is usually a colourful stretch after the bleakness of Treig, and a grand spot for wild flowers. Look around and you'll find bright patches of chickweed wintergreen, yellow primroses, dwarf birch and butterwort.

The final 17 miles (27km) or so to Fort William are delightful, and there is a strong contrast between the rich pastoral scenery below Staoineag and the bare wetlands of Tom an Eite, the watershed between Loch Treig and Glen Nevis.

Staoineag bothy is one of my favourites. There are two rooms on the lower level, one of which is habitable with a fair degree of comfort. Upstairs, a floored attic offers additional space. The bothy itself sits high above the river amid the trees, and it's a great bird spot. Hereabouts you are likely to hear stonechats, pipits, lapwings, and tits, and I've never passed along this way without enjoying the bobbing of dippers on the river.

Day Three

Follow the waters of the Abhainn Rath through green meadows bright with primroses and harebell, the Scottish bluebell. This doesn't seem like a highland landscape, it is far too gentle, with the river meandering regally around the vibrant meadows, shaded by birch and rowan, surrounded by gentle slopes. But the gentleness doesn't last long.

Above the meadows the river takes on its Highland aspect again, and comes rushing through the narrowing gorges with desperation.

Continue following the river, with the distant Mamores and Grey Corries attracting you onwards. An old building lies at the spot marked at Luibelt, the protective clutch of pines beside it failing to save it from the decaying ferocity of the winter winds. Sheep share the grazing with red deer in an open landscape where winds continually play. The pull of the hills is all around here, the great ridge of the Mamores ahead, and the Grey Corries on the right, with the bald pate of Ben Nevis at last lording it over all.

The rough path on the north bank of the Abhainn Rath at Luibelt has to be swopped for the one on the south bank, and as there is no bridge, that probably means wet feet. Essentially that doesn't matter too much for in a couple of miles you will be walking through what I always reckon to be the wettest land in Scotland. From Tom an Eite, down beside the Water of Nevis to Steall, the path runs

Right: **The wire bridge at Steall in Upper Glen Nevis**. (Photo: Cameron McNeish)

of the aluminium industry in Fort William, and the water line rises and lowers constantly leaving an untidy rim. It seems odd that the waters of Loch Treig can help power the aluminium factory in Fort William, since the town is all of fifteen miles away, but in 1929, a long tunnel was built from here, through part of Ben Nevis, and down to the works. When it was completed it was the first tunnel of its type in the world.

Follow the track, past the rueful shores of

downhill in a scenic glen which offers magnificent views of the high tops of the Mamores.

Steall itself is a fine spot, with the little white-washed cottage, nowadays a mountaineering club hut, well placed below the raging waterfall. The wire bridge which must be negotiated to reach the cottage can offer hilarious and challenging fun, especially if you have to carry a large rucksack.

The meadows below Steall offer a fairly tranquil scene, despite the crashing and thundering of the huge waterfall which drops down from Coire a Mhail above, but the shady scene isn't without tragedy. A number of years ago, when the cottage was a croft, the crofter was cutting hay on the meadow opposite the house when his wife sent their young daughter down to summon her father for a meal.

Sadly, the young girl somehow slipped as she crossed the stream, and she was carried away by the waters. Her body was found five miles downstream.

Below Steall the Water of Nevis takes on its role as a thundering cateract as it flows from the meadow flats and gouges a tortuous passage through the granite. Over the centuries these waters have buried themselves deeper and deeper into the bedrock, and today the gorge itself is one of the finest aquatic sights in Scotland. The power of the water as it surges and roars through the narrow chasm must be stupendous, and thirty years ago the Hydro Electric Board were very keen to harness this water power for electricity. Thankfully various individuals interceded and made it clear that this particular area was a natural and a national asset, and anything which was done to reduce the scenic grandeur would be a calamity. Good sense prevailed, and the gorge is there for all to enjoy. All, that is, who enjoy a walk on a narrow track above the roaring waters. This stretch from Steall to Polldubh has been described as the 'finest half mile in Scotland', and W. H. Murray, the Scottish mountaineer and author once described it as the closest scene to the Himalayas he has come across in Scotland.

You'll enjoy the walk which slopes down beside the gorge, hugging the wet rocky walls, in places eroded by the tread of a thousand boot soles, and exposed to the crashing waters below. It won't be long till you leave the roar behind you, and reach the start of a 5-mile (8km) stretch of tarmac road to Fort William. This isn't an anticlimax though, tarmac road

or not. The thundering river makes a good companion, and the gnarled pines which fringe the road here and there are old and proud and full of character. The glen floor is covered in birch and pine, and the road twists and undulates its way northwards, past the Glen Nevis Youth Hostel, a camp site, a restaurant, and the finish point of the Glasgow to Fort William West Highland Way.

Fort William itself has all the luxuries of a tourist town, and of course a rail service back south. If you have the time, enjoy a night's rest in the town, then tackle the 4406ft (1343m) Ben Nevis the next day, the highest mountain in Britain.

The water-worn rocks of Steall Gorge above Polldubh in Glen Nevis.

Facing page: **Looking towards the cliffs of Creag Mhor, one of Creag Meagaidh's outliers from the summit plateau.**
(Photos: Cameron McNeish)

CREAG MEAGAIDH (Highland Region) by Cameron McNeish

Distance: 16 miles (26km).
Ascent: 4500ft (1370m).
Start/Finish: Aberarder Farm, Loch Lagganside.
Maps: OS 1:50,000 Sheet 34.
Summary: A moderate hill walk over broad ridges and plateaux.

Points of Interest: Superb views of the broad expanse of cliffs which make the focal point of Coire Ardair. Look out for red deer, golden eagles, buzzards, peregrine falcon, ptarmigan, and snow buntings. Creag Meagaidh is part of the National Nature Reserve operated by the Nature Conservancy Council.

Lying just north of the A86 Spean Bridge to Newtonmore road, Creag Meagaidh and her outliers make for a fine day's walk when the weather on the west coast is bad. Likewise when blizzards rage across the Cairngorm plateau, Meagaidh is often seen bathed in the warm glow of a bright winter afternoon.

She's a contrary mountain, straddling the historic Druim Alba, the backbone and watershed of Scotland, she can offer delights when other areas are bad, and conversely she can hold a miserable huddle of cloud when elsewhere is clear. And she can be a fearful bitch when she wants to be. This is the very hill which confused a star-studded cast of climbers including such names as Bonington, Patey, Clough, Beard and others when a New Year's Day stroll turned into an epic. This is also the hill where a top mountain centre group were avalanched two winters in succession, and this is the hill which keeps mountain rescue teams busy year in and year out.

Aye, she can be cussed when she wants to, but when she smiles she grins a great toothless grin which shows off her vast cavernous corrie to the best possible advantage.

What makes Creag Meagaidh so special to climbers and walkers is the great array of sheer cliffs she holds tightly in her vice-like corrie. One and a half miles in length and in places plunging 1500ft (450m) to the corrie floor, Coire Ardair is breached only by the long winding glen which approaches the cliffs, and a high 'window', a high-level pass caused by the action of glaciation, and more recently used by that worthy Highland wanderer Charles Edward Stuart on his post-Culloden epic from Cameron country to the hospitality offered by his Jacobite compatriot Cluny MacPherson in Badenoch.

Creag Meagaidh's interest to climbers is strictly a winter one. Then the cliffs of Coire Ardair boast some of the finest snow and ice climbs in the country. This was the playground of the late and great Tom Patey, and the Scottish Mountaineering Club District Guide to the area describes Coire Ardair as 'one of the most impressive corries in Scotland, its cliffs second only to those of Ben Nevis for scale and grandeur'.

In contrast to Ben Nevis though, the cliffs of

Coire Ardair are serviceable only in winter, when they become plastered with snow and ice. In summer they reassume their rotten vegetated state, and the rock climbing is limited. The rock, a horizontally stratified mica-schist, is badly frost-shattered and quite unreliable.

For the hill walker though, the round of Carn Liath, Poite Coire Ardair, Creag Meagaidh and Beinn a Chaorainn makes a marvellous round walk of some 16 miles (26km) offering four Munros and a day of very fine high-level walking.

Aberarder Farm on Loch Lagganside is the best starting point for the round. The Creag Meagaidh Estate and Aberarder Farm were bought by the Nature Conservancy Council (NCC) in 1986. Prior to this, a private forestry company had announced plans that would have meant a mass afforestation of the lower slopes of the mountain, and would possibly have endangered an extensive birch wood which carpets much of lower Coire Ardair. The NCC were keen to protect the birch wood and its associated plant life, as well as giving a measure of protection to the birds of the higher hills, birds like the ptarmigan, dotterel and golden eagle.

The NCC ownership also means that access is available all the year for walkers and climbers, for the policy on deer management on the estate is an interesting one. Instead of stalking and shooting the deer during the months of August, September and October as in most estates, the NCC actually entice the deer from the higher slopes and capture them. The beasts are then sent to deer farms throughout the country. This policy creates some local employment, brings a revenue to the NCC and of course allows you and me to wander these hills when other estates are no-go areas during the stalking season.

Behind the old farm buildings, a good track crosses the lower moorland and for a while runs close to the waters of the Allt Coire Ardair. This track climbs slowly and eventually winds round westwards into the heart of Coire Ardair. Our route leaves the track after a mile or so though, to tackle the long heather-clad slopes of Carn Liath, the Grey Hill. Unfortunately, Carn Liath isn't the most dramatic of hills but it does offer a marvellous

The magnificent north-eastern corrie of Coire Ardair walled with 1,000-ft cliffs in the Creag Meagaidh Nature Reserve.
(Photo: Cameron McNeish)

view down the length of Coire Ardair towards the great cliffs in the distance.

The summit of Carn Liath is boulder-strewn and gives a good start to the high-level traverse which takes you along the northern flank of Coire Ardair to Poite Coire Ardair. I recently enjoyed this high-level wander in sweltering conditions and noticed that what I thought were 'moving' rocks down below me were in fact red deer congregating on the remains of the winter snow patches in an attempt to keep cool. All along the ridge the eye is held by the great sweep of buttresses down below, rising as though sheer from the dark waters of Lochan a'Choire Ardair.

The cliffs of Poite Coire Ardair fall away steeply too, and this rise in the ridge is a good vantage point for the main cliffs of Creag Meagaidh. From the cairn, the slopes fall away to the 'Window', from where the summit slopes of Meagaidh are reached after a short sharp climb of about 500ft (150m).

Many souls have been lost on the extensive summit plateau of Creag Meagaidh. For lack of features in misty or cloudy weather Creag Meagaidh compares with the summit plateaux of Cairngorm or Ben Alder and navigation has to be needle sharp. Don't be confused by thinking that 'Mad Meg's Cairn' is the summit. This great mound of stones lies about 100 yards north-east of the true summit of the hill and according to one writer, 'resembles an Inca sacrificial mound or some such monument'. Many walkers have made navigational errors by thinking that 'Mad Meg's Cairn' is the summit cairn.

The 3700ft (1128m) summit of Creag Meagaidh is, as its central position suggests, a truly marvellous vantage point. With views ranging from the nearby Cairngorms to Ben Nevis and from Knoydart to Torridon it's well worthwhile choosing a clear day for this walk. Closer at hand, across Loch Laggan, lies the Ardverikie Forest, with Beinn a'Chlachar, Creag Pitridh and the long ridge of Beinn Eibhinn, Aonach Beag and Geal Charn beyond.

Continue walking west for one and a half miles, until you reach the Bealach a'Bharnish, a gentle descent of some 1000ft (300m) which connects to the north-east ridge of Beinn a'Chaorainn, the hill of the Rowan. If you do not want to continue for this extra Munro, a long ridge winds south west, then south from Creag Meagaidh, leading down to the Crag of the Old Woman, Creag na Cailliche, from where the Moy Burn can be followed back to the A86 at Moy.

Beinn a'Chaorainn has an undulating summit ridge with three tops; the centre one, according to fairly recent revisions, is the Munro at 3437ft (1048m). There are no real problems from the summit ridge back down to the roadside, but try not to be tempted to take a short cut over the moorland by Lochan na Cailliche; the ground is boggy and very difficult to walk over. Unless you can arrange a lift, you have seven and a half miles to walk on the road back to Aberarder Farm, so it's well worthwhile planning to use two cars in advance.

Nearest accommodation is at Roybridge and at Laggan. There are youth hostels at Kingussie and Fort William and a private hostel, Nancy's Hostel, is highly recommended. This is at Fersit near to Tulloch.

Public transport is limited to a weekly bus which runs from Aviemore to Fort William. The NCC allow the use of a field near to Aberarder farm for camping.

THE CORRIEYAIRACK (Highland Region) by Cameron McNeish

Distance: 17 miles (27km).
Ascent: 1500ft (450m).
Start/Finish: Start at the old Wade bridge at Garvamore. Finish in Fort Augustus. Two cars are necessary to provide transport back to the start.
Maps: OS 1:50,000 Sheets 34 and 35.

Summary: An easy mountain pass climbing to a height of 2507ft (764m). Can be exposed and difficult in winter conditions.
Points of Interest: Ancient Highland road with some very good examples of Wade bridges and construction work. The Corrieyairack area is good eagle country.

The old Wade bridge at Garvamore, the start of the Corrieyairack Traverse. (Photo: Cameron McNeish)

Imagine the Highlands of Scotland when the vast mountainous area north of Perth had few roads. With rebellious clans threatening the sovereignty of the King, and the impending call to the Jacobite cause, it's little wonder that the Government in the early eighteenth century thought it imperative to build a network of roads linking key garrisons.

The 1715 Jacobite uprising really forced the issue. Until that time the governments of the day had largely preferred to ignore the Scottish Highlands, believing it to be a land frequented by surly savages, but it soon became clear to them that the northern coasts were vulnerable

94

to French, Dutch or Spanish invasion, no doubt assisted by the age-old alliance between Scotland and Jacobite France, the Auld Alliance.

Something had to be done to police these northern parts and one man in particular was given the job of surveying and building a road network. General George Wade was an Irishman, and in 1724 he was given the considerable task of Commander-in-Chief of His Majesty's Forces in Scotland. Wade was a soldier, but he has gone down in history as a road builder, a reputation that is not completely justified. However, in the thirteen years he spent in Scotland, he was responsible for the surveying and completion of a number of roads, including a major link between Dalwhinnie at Drumochter, and Fort Augustus at the head of Loch Ness on the important route between Inverness and what we now know as Fort William, the Great Glen Road.

Wade appears to have been responsible for the original road from Dunkeld, north of Perth, to Inverness, now the busy A9 trunk road, and in 1731 he started work on the link road from Dalwhinnie to Fort Augustus, taking full advantage of the traditional 'drove road' that made its way past the Corrie

Yairack and up over a prominent shoulder of the Corrieyairack Hill.

Four working parties began construction in April, and by October the same year a celebration was held on the banks of the Allt Lagan a'Bhainne, above Glen Tarff on the north side of the pass, on completion of the major part of the road. Total cost was just under £3,300.

It is perhaps ironic that one of the first to take advantage of the new road over the Corrieyairack was Charles Edward Stuart and his Jacobite army, but that's another story. When Thomas Telford began the first real civil road system in Scotland in the early nineteenth century he chose to ignore the Corrieyairack, preferring the link road to the west from Laggan to Spean Bridge. He did us a great favour, for the Corrieyairack has been left to the deer and the golden plover, and of course the walker who enjoys solitude and the history of those wild and remote days.

The Corrieyairack proper begins at Dalwhinnie, and runs over moorland to Drumgask and Laggan, before penetrating the Monadliath hills beyond Garva Bridge. The first 10 miles (16km) however, are comparatively dull and are on tarmac roads to boot. If instead you take a car past the village of Laggan, past the

At the top of the zig zags near the summit of the pass. (Photo: Cameron McNeish)

Spey Dam and over the old Wade bridge at Garvamore and onto Melgarve where the tarred road ends, you will quickly come to the real meat of the Corrieyairack Pass.

From Melgarve you can easily walk to the summit of the pass in two or three hours, returning to your car the same day. This can then be repeated from the northern side, leaving your car in Fort Augustus and taking the track up through Culachy Forest. Alternatively, if you can arrange the transport, walk right across the pass in one outing, a worthwhile outing to get the real feel of the walk, and to witness the achievement of the eighteenth-century road builders.

There is parking space at Melgarve where the tarmac road ends, and just beyond lies one of Wade's bridges, now resplendent with its new wooden surface. The track here is rough and incredibly straight, which says a lot for the engineer's alignments. Below the loose rock on the road it is easy to see the cobbles of the old road, and even when the surface was in its prime it must have given the carts and wagons a rough ride. One notable gentlewoman who has left a record of her travels in the Highlands in the year 1798, The Hon. Mrs. Sarah Murray, has suggested that the road was indeed rough.

The whole road rough, dangerous and dreadful, even for a horse. The steep and black mountains, and the roaring torrents rendered every step his horse took, frightful; and when he attained the summit of the zigzags up Corrieyaireag he thought the horse himself, man and all, would be carried away, he knew not whither; so strong was the blast, so hard the rain, and so very thick the mist. And as for the cold, it stupified him . . .

Mrs Murray also tells frightful tales of travellers on the road perishing from the cold and of soldiers who often died because they over refreshed themselves with whisky before the climb.

After a while the track runs military fashion to the right and proceeds across the lower slopes of Geal Charn. Ahead, lying face on, is the Corrie Yairack itself, with the plateau of the Corrieyairack hill above it. Just as you think you must climb up over the corrie rim, the track turns left again and takes a series of zigzags, an amazing feat of engineering in such remote surroundings. It's claimed there are thirteen zigzags in all, but I have only ever been able to count eleven. What is certain is that you can quickly climb out of the valley floor and reach the high point of the pass at 2507ft (764m). Turn around and gaze back and catch something of the atmosphere of this place. Away through the glen you'll see the hills of the Grampians above Glen Feshie, then the

valley of the infant River Spey reaching almost into the Corrieyairack itself. An interesting deviation at the start of this walk, if you have the time, is to head westwards from Melgarve for some two miles to Loch Spey, the source of the mighty Spey itself.

It's a pity that the isolation of this Corrieyairack Pass has been spoiled by the goose-stepping line of electricity pylons that follow the route, and the Hydro Board hut that sits on the summit of the pass seems a little out of place. An austere sign is painted on its door: 'Men's lives depend on the equipment in this hut. Please don't interfere with it.' Dramatic stuff.

Dramatic too is the way the view to the north and west begins to unfold as you cross over the summit. A small cairn celebrates the top, and then it's downhill all the way to Fort Augustus. To the north-west you'll see Loch Garry and the high hills beyond and somewhere on those purple flanks another old military road runs to Bernera Barracks at Glenelg on the west coast.

From the summit the walking becomes much more gentle, no knee-jarring descent here. The surroundings are milder too. Only the sad crooning of the golden plover will remind you of the loneliness, and the croaking of ptarmigan indicate your height above sea level. Around you is deer forest, and come late September and October these parts echo to the sound of the rutting stags.

The bridge over the Allt Coire Uchdachan is Wade built, and strengthened somewhat more recently by that splendid body, the Scottish Rights of Way Society. Less romantically, a Bailey bridge was erected in 1961 by the Royal Engineers a little way north over the Allt Lagan a' Bhainne. This is the spot where the road builders held their triple celebration in 1731, to commemorate the end of the road building season and the end of the building of the Corrieyairack road, and to celebrate the King's birthday.

This was seemingly a popular spot with the road builders who nicknamed it Snugborough. The Gaelic in fact translates as Dell of the Milk.

The descent to Culachy begins shortly after here, and runs down beside the River Tarff across the shoulder of Liath Dhoire. The track runs fairly steeply hereabouts, passing some splendid waterfalls. This is a pleasant end to the walk, amid an air of green cultivation and civilisation after the empty miles of earlier. The contrast can be overwhelming. Once you are past Culachy House, take the metalled road and follow it to the public road into Fort Augustus.

Facing page: **Map showing the following 3 walks: Trotternish Ridge (p98), Beinn Alligin (p102) and Sandwood Bay (p105).**

The Trotternish Ridge is an easy one-camp 30-mile, high-level walk over the backbone ridge of the Trotternish Peninsula in northern Skye. It is one of the finest walks in the country with superb seascapes and fascinating rock formations.

The 7-mile traverse of Beinn Alligin offers some worthwhile scrambling on the crest of the ridge but a path bypasses most of it. A serious expedition in winter conditions.

Sandwood Bay offers a magnificent short, 6-mile walk on fairly easy terrain.

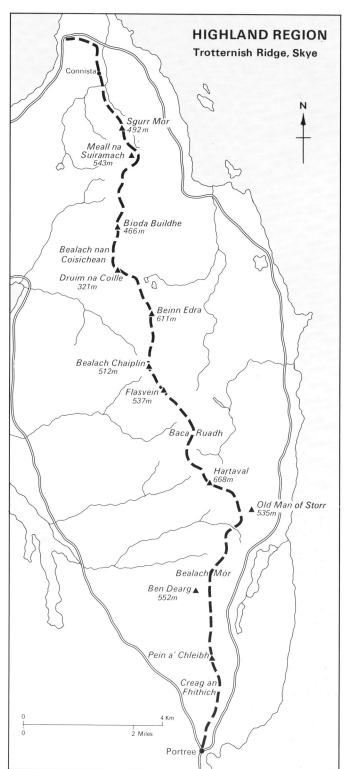

HIGHLAND REGION
Trotternish Ridge, Skye

N

Connista

Sgurr Mòr
492m

Meall na
Suiramach
543m

Bioda Buildhe
466m

Bealach nan
Coisichean

Druim na Coille
321m

Beinn Edra
611m

Bealach Chaiplin
512m

Flasvein
537m

Baca Ruadh

Hartaval
668m

Old Man of Storr
535m

Bealach Mòr

Ben Dearg
552m

Pein a' Chleibh

Creag an
Fhithich

0   4 Km
0   2 Miles

Portree

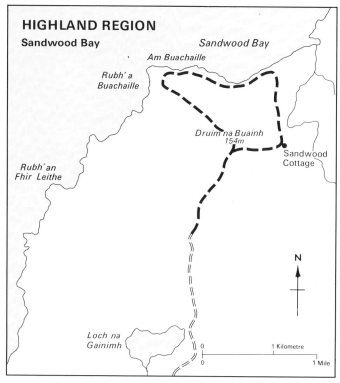

HIGHLAND REGION
Sandwood Bay

Sandwood Bay

Am Buachaille

Rubh' a
Buachaille

Druim na Buainh
154m

Sandwood
Cottage

Rubh' an
Fhir Leithe

N

Loch na
Gainimh

0   1 Kilometre
0   1 Mile

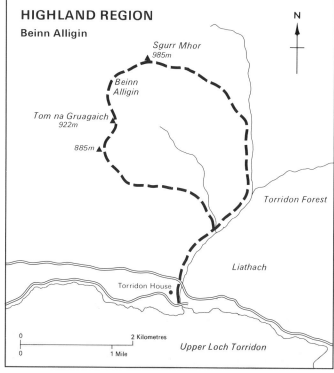

HIGHLAND REGION
Beinn Alligin

N

Sgurr Mhor
985m

Beinn
Alligin

Tom na Gruagaich
922m

885m

Torridon Forest

Torridon House

Liathach

0   2 Kilometres
0   1 Mile

Upper Loch Torridon

97

THE TROTTERNISH RIDGE OF SKYE
(Highland Region) by Cameron McNeish

Distance: 30 miles (48km).
Start/Finish: Start at Duntulm Castle, on A855 road near Kilmaluag. Finish at Portree.
Maps: OS 1:50,000 Second Series, Sheet 235.
Summary: An easy one-camp high-level walk over the backbone ridge of the Trotternish Peninsula in northern Skye.

Points of Interest: One of the finest walks in the country. Superb seascapes across to the Scottish mainland on one side and towards the Hebrides on the other. Fascinating geological formations of the Quiraing and the Storr rocks.

The start of the Ridge, on the basalt cliffs of Sron Bhiornal.
(Photo: Cameron McNeish)

Many walkers have described this walk as being without equal in the whole of Scotland. You'll bag no Munros on this great ridge, come across very little mountain majesty, yet there is something rather splendid and unique about it.

A glance at the OS map of northern Skye will show you the great feature of Trotternish; a long winding escarpment of basalt cliffs running in a southerly direction from the steep peaks of Sgurr Mhor and Sron Vourlinn near Duntulm, to the bare moorland above Portree. The steep east-facing cliffs of this great ridge are sheets of lava, immensely thick, intruded

Looking out through the ramparts of the Quiraing.
(Photo: Cameron McNeish)

Cuillin, to the great mountain masses of Torridon, Gairloch and Applecross on the mainland.

But the delights of Trotternish aren't just gentle. At the north end of the peninsula, opposite Staffin Bay, the wild towers and crazy pinnacles which form the battlements of the Quiraing, a collapsed lava slip, present an eerie prospect, while further south below the frowning cliffs of the Storr, another slip has culminated in the weird formations of the Old Man of Storr and his neighbours, eroded basaltic columns which throw their great spires skywards in a jumble of ghostly pinnacles.

Day One

The Trotternish ridge walk begins at the most northerly point on the peninsula, Duntulm Castle, a magnificent place of crashing surf and raucous gull calls. The gaunt ruins of the castle show a brave face to the north-westerly gales, clinging as they do to the rocky headland which rises sheer from the waters of the Minch. This was once a stronghold of the ancient Macdonalds of the Isles, a seagoing clan who were very much in control of the western seaboard of Scotland. From castles like this, the Macdonalds could taunt their enemies with little fear of real attack, and summoning their forces, sally forth on their war galleys to battle by sea in defence of their sovereignty.

We had driven up here from Portree, leaving one of our cars there for our return. From the ruins of the castle, we followed the scenic road eastwards for a couple of miles, through the scattered croftship of Kilmaluag to where a farm road turned off due south to a croft marked on the map as Connista. Beyond some thatched crofts lay the bulk of our first objective, the prominent basalt nose of Sron Vourlinn, the beginning of the long ridge which would eventually drop us off above Portree.

Sron Vourlinn is named after a Norse princess by the name of Bhiornal. Before she died she asked that she be buried in such a position that she could gaze across the mainland of Scotland towards her native Norway. Tradition has it that she was buried on the summit of Sron Vourlinn. There is nothing there to indicate it, but the view is as good as she requested. Away behind us in the green waters of the Minch lay the island of Trodday and beyond it the outline of the Shiants. On the distant horizon, the sun was just catching the cliffs of Lewis. A heavy haze hung over the hills of the mainland, but in front of us, flowing on like the crests of giant waves, lay the undulating noses of the escarpment of Trotternish.

between the upper and lower layers of the basalt plateaux after they were laid down. The upper basalt sheets have been cut back to the ridge and have left these long intrusive sills in a long line from Portree, up the length of the peninsula, and out to sea as far north as the Shiant Isles. While the east-facing cliffs are sheer, the western side of this great ridge is in complete contrast. Long grassy slopes run all the way to the rim of the cliffs. The summits aren't high, reaching 2358ft (718m) at the highest point, but on a clear day these comparatively lowly hills offer views as grand as the biggest of our hills, panoramas from as far west as St. Kilda, over the magnificent

From Vourlinn we followed the crumbling cliff edge south and then south-west until the slopes began to rise towards the craggy outline of Fir Bhreugach. By following the cliff edge uphill, we knew we would reach the summit of Meall na Suiramach, the hill which is often erroneously referred to as the Quiraing. The Quiraing (a fold, or pen) is in fact only the name for the collection of spires, pinnacles, rocks, and volcanic debris which has been broken away from the cliff edge.

The best way to enter the Quiraing is from below. From the cliff edge a slanting grassy slope ramps down through the cliffs, and you'll quickly reach the floor of the strange hidden valley which runs along the foot of the escarpment.

We wandered through this strange wood of spires and bluffs, these volcanic remnants. Only in Iceland have I ever seen landscape quite like this, the formations contorted and bent, strangely malevolent, like crooked fingers of rock beckoning you towards some nether world.

The normal route into the Quiraing follows a footpath from the Staffin to Uig road, the only east–west road to cross the escarpment. This was a mile or so south of where we were, and being impatient to get to grips with it we thought we would enter by the back door. A good sheep track follows the base of the cliffs southwards and we followed this for a short while until the cliff by our side had become broken and riven by great gullies and enormous rifts. We took the easiest-looking gully and entered the stronghold. Above us immense crags, blocks and spires loomed high, scree slopes leading us upwards into the giant amphitheatre. Great slices of rock, fissured, weathered and cracked stood apart from the main cliffs behind, and through these great fissures we could stare out to a scene of complete contrast, the pastoral green of the crofts of Staffin, with the blue waters of the bay beyond.

What a place this Quiraing is, a place of Titan verticalities, surrealist in its black and grey upthrusts. It seemed unreal to come across a high table of flat cropped grass, as smooth as a bowling green. This is the Table, the jewel of the Quiraing, and beyond it hung a veritable Hanging Garden of Babylon. Yellow globe flowers, red and white campions, blue butterwort and sprays of golden roseroot all contrasting with the glistening black of the wet cliff from which they hung.

We left the Table in silence, like mild Hobbits visiting Rivendell, the home of the elfin folk. Down dark corridors of scree we went, past the highest of all the pinnacles, the towering spire of the Needle, 120ft (35m) in height, tapering at both the top and the bottom. More slopes of scree slid us down to the track in front of the Prison, the southerly outpost of the Quiraing, a massive lump of rock like some ancient fortress.

A terraced track runs along the top of the slope, just below the foot of the cliffs and carries you down gently to the side of the Staffin to Uig road. On the other side of the road, the escarpment nose undulates southwards, as impressive as ever. Below us, some crofters were busy at the peat, digging and cutting the turf into manageable sizes, the long thin strips of their endeavour like little scars on the surface of the moor.

We didn't dally by the roadside, but pushed on beyond it to the slopes of Bioda Buidhe. Below us, in the lee of the cliffs, a profusion of rowan trees grew on ledges on the cliffs, remarkable in that trees are conspicuous by their absence in Trotternish. Apart from this long ridge it is a very open landscape, exposed to the vagaries of the Atlantic storms, storms which do everything in their power to discourage growth. These lonely rowans are the more attractive for it.

Several old hill passes cross this backbone of land from east to west, passes which were fairly well-trodden in days gone by. The Bealach nan Coisichean and the Bealach Uige are two of these old routes. Both are low points on the escarpment, at places where the cliff can be negotiated with little difficulty. To the south of Bealach Uige, a fence runs alongside the rim of the cliffs to the summit of Beinn Edra, the second highest point on the ridge at just over 2000ft (600m).

If you are taking this ridge walk over two days, then this is as good a spot to stop and camp for the night as any. Perhaps, if the weather is kind, you'll want to camp high on the escarpment, enjoying the views across to the mainland, or if it is windy, you can easily drop down from here to the lower ground below where the terrain tends to be boggy, but offers several dry islets of good springy turf.

Day Two

Climb back onto the ridge again and make your way south over the Bealach Chaiplin. I hope you enjoy better weather than we did, for we struggled along here on our second day pushing hard into strong winds and rain.

Be careful to keep well back from the crumbly cliff edge if the weather is bad; the mist and darkness make the thousand-foot drop look like a bottomless void. The ridge undulates gently from here, rising then descending in a series of gentle humps and

Top: **Duntulm Castle at the start of the Trotternish Ridge walk.**

Above: **The hills of Trotternish looking south from near the Quiraing.** (Photo: Eric Meadow)

bumps. We climbed on to the nose of Sgurr a Mhadaidh Ruaidh (the hill of the red fox) a name which sounds much more attractive and evocative in its Gaelic pronunciation. Try 'Sgoor a Vaddy Rooa'. . . This was the scene of an exciting children's book written by Allan Campbell MacLean, a story of skulduggery and adventure which was also successfully televised. A descent to the Bealach Hartaval brought us below the cloud level, and allowed us to catch a glimpse of the Storr rocks across a vast and deepset corrie, before steep slopes had us climbing into the murk again on to the summit of Hartaval itself. Many of the place names in Skye, indeed in all the Hebrides, are like Hartaval, of Norse origin, and it's claimed that there is still much Norse blood flowing through the veins of the Sgiannaichs. Indeed it wasn't till the battle of Largs in 1263 that Norse occupation of these islands was brought to an end, and until then, the Norsemen were settlers in Skye, with much intermarriage taking place between them and the Celts.

The Bealach a'Chuirn lies between Hartaval and the long slopes that lead to the summit of the Storr, at 2358ft (719m), the highest hill on the traverse. It's good to stop for a few minutes before tackling the slopes and enjoying the views, if the weather is clear. Westwards, long grassy slopes lead the eye by Loch Snizort and away across Vaternish to the distant outline of MacLeod's Tables.

The summit of the Storr has a trig point and away below, you can make out the spires of the Old Man of Storr deep in his impressive stronghold. You can find a way down from the escarpment to visit the old fellow in his lair, but we were wet through by this time and were anxious to continue onwards. We were content to shout our greeting from above, before turning west, and then south, around the corrie rim, to descend the grassy slopes to the Bealach Beag.

Below the cloud again, the remainder of our walk stretched out in front of us. The contrast between the dark bastions and weird summits of Storr and the countryside to the south is as acute as that between the Quiraing and Staffin. The Storr lochs, Leathan and Fada, lay like quicksilver, two lochs well stocked with brown trout.

The valley lies below, green and inviting; at its farthest end lies Portree and the twinkling waters of the bay. To the east is the sea, breaking softly on the skerries of northern Raasay, and beyond, the dim and shadowy outline of the hills of Gairloch, Rona, with her broken rocks, and Raasay of the purple hills lie between here and the mainland, and now and then, as the watery sun tried to ooze out from between the scudding clouds, a stray drift of light would shine on the distant coast of Applecross and the mountains beyond. A narrow sound squeezes its way below Portree beneath the sharp peak of Ben Tianavaig, and then turns southwards towards Broadford, where it becomes lost under the shadow of Scalpay. In that direction the Red Cuillin and the Black Cuillin should hold the eye, but on this particular day it was too cloudy. I hope you fare better.

Immediately in front, the ridge winds its way slightly south-westwards over a series of small bumps, before the way becomes barred by the steep outline of Ben Dearg, whose long ridge runs perpendicular to the main one. You don't have to climb it though, unless you really want to. An excellent alternative exists. Drop down below the ridge from the Bealach Mor where a terraced sheep track bypasses Ben Dearg and Beinn Mheadhonach behind it, to pick its way through the drumlins to the moorland above Portree. Any guilt that you experience about taking an easy option should be swallowed in the sheer delight of this track, the finest sheep-engineered track I have ever walked on. Running along below the cliffs it passes its way through a real garden of wild flowers; chickweed, wintergreen, alpine lady's mantle, mossy cyphel, least cudweed, wild thyme and pearlwort. Even the long ribbons of red scree which hang on the steep slopes are dotted with campion and starry saxifrage in season, and through this brilliant finery the track traces its way. Even as the flowers turn to the more familiar white bog cotton on the peaty moorland, so the track keeps on straight, before finally fading away as you begin to descend from the slopes of A'Chorra-bheinn.

Soon the houses of Portree, Port an Righ, the port of the king, come into sight, the town so named after a royal visit from James V in 1540; and a short walk on the tarmaced road past some modern bungalows takes you to the A855 Portree to Staffin road, a mile or so from the town.

Sheriff Nicolson, a well known Skye poet, once proclaimed that 'to ascend Storr and follow the mountain ridge the whole way until you come to the Quiraing is no doubt one of the grandest promenades in Skye, commanding wide views in all directions. 'There are those who say that Nicolson never actually walked the ridge himself, but his statement is correct. The walking is superb, the views second to none, and the astonishing labyrinth of towers and hollows which make up the Quiraing is well worth visiting again and again, one of the natural wonders of Scotland.

BEINN ALLIGIN OF TORRIDON (Highland Region) by Cameron McNeish

Distance: 7 miles (11 km).
Ascent: 4000ft (1200m).
Start/Finish: Car park at the Coire Mhic No-buil bridge.
Maps: OS 1:50,000 Sheet 24.
Summary: A superb traverse of a fine mountain ridge. If you stick to the crest of the ridge there is some worthwhile scrambling, but a path bypasses the most difficult of it. A serious expedition in winter conditions.
Points of Interest: Beinn Alligin offers magnificent views towards the other Torridon giants of Liathach and Beinn Eighe. Also good seaward views towards the Trotternish ridge of Skye. A magnificent area to explore in the autumn when the red deer rut is on. Area owned by the National Trust for Scotland.

The Horns, Beinn Dearg and Beinn Eighe in the distance. (Photo: Cameron McNeish)

The day before had been a hard one. We'd decided to try and make the best we could of the fine October weather as we had no idea how long it would last. Weather forecasting skills take a back seat to the vagaries of a Torridon climate and while it looked fine for a couple of days we reckoned it best not to risk it. After all it had snowed several days previously!

Despite pushing it hard we had enjoyed our

day. Beinn Eighe and Liathach in a day is tough enough by anyone's standards and we suspected we might be more than just a little bit sore the next day. An easy day was what we needed, and the traverse of Beinn Alligin, known admiringly as the Jewel of Torridon, fitted that bill beautifully.

The Torridon trio of Beinn Eighe, Liathach and Beinn Alligin must be one of the most magnificent groupings of mountains anywhere. It's also one of the oldest. Quartz-capped Torridonian sandstone offers an unusual mountain formation, a landscape of ribs, buttresses and spiky spires, intermingling with smoothly rounded battlements of enormous bulk.

These are big hills, in the fullest sense of the word. Leviathan big, prehistoric giants, and Beinn Alligin is the shapeliest of them. Her Gaelic name is Jewelled Hill and this was the first time I had seen her sparkle. How many hill walkers have climbed the Torridon hills without actually seeing them? So often it's hill walking by braille; you can feel the hills underfoot but you can't see them. This time it was different.

Today looked like bringing the jackpot in. As we parked our car just off the Diabaig to Torridon road the sun burst over the great whaleback of Liathach. Blue tits belled and chaffinchs landed at our feet, eager for crumbs. We wandered up through the green shadows of the pine woods from the roadside, following the path that soon shakes free from the trees to open onto the empty quarter of Coire Mhic Nobuil. What a wilderness this is. Mhic Nobuil goes under the title of a coire, but in reality it is no such thing. Instead it presents a broad and high pass through some of the most awe-inspiring scenery in the country.

After half a mile or so we crossed the Abhainn Coire Mhic Nobuil by a footbridge and began the stiff toil up heathery slopes towards Alligin's Coir' nan Laogh. Despite the sun the air was still vibrant and cool and the distant sounds of roaring stags had us scanning the hills all around in search of the herds.

Late August to October is normally the deer-stalking time in the Scottish Highlands, the time when we are requested by keepers and estate owners to keep away from the hills. But the National Trust for Scotland properties and

From the Beinn Alligin ridge looking down into Coire Mhic Nobuil. (Photo: Cameron McNeish)

some of the Nature Conservancy Council reserves impose no restrictions at all, so it's often good to keep these areas for the stalking months Beinn Alligin, Liathach and the western slopes of Beinn Eighe are all National Trust for Scotland properties, so there is normally free access for walkers. This access can be checked at the Information Centre beside the road junction at the foot of Glen Torridon.

I'm not sure whether it was the effects of our exertions the day before, or whether it was because the scenery was so good that we continually stopped to enjoy it, but it took us an abnormally long time to reach the first of Alligin's tops, Tom na Gruagaich (the maiden's hillock) at 3024ft (922m). It's good to remind yourself from time to time that these Torridon giants make you climb every foot from sea level . . .

The effort of reaching this first top was well worthwhile though. As we topped the quartzite summit, having just come up out of the confines of the shaded corrie, the abruptness of the unexpected view hit us like a slap on the face. It was so magnificently vast, so unobstructed and so crystal clear.

In front of us lay a great chunk of the western seaboard of Scotland. Across the sea lay the long arm of the Trotternish peninsula of Skye and beyond it, dancing on a mirror-like surface were the purple hills of Harris, a place of magic memories and dreams of big hill days yet to come. To the north the coastline meandered on in purple continuity, and if it is possible to see Cape Wrath from here then we saw it. Closer at hand, the Horns of Alligin, the Rathains, gave way to a thin-looking wedge of rock that is Beinn Dearg. Beyond lay Beinn Eighe. In the distance was the familiar jumble of hills that dominate the wilderness area behind Slioch, those impressive hills of the Great Wilderness between Little Loch Broom and Loch Maree, An Teallach, A'Mhaighdean, Ruadh Stac Mor and Beinn Tarsuinn. Remote hills, and impressive.

It was good to sit there and take it in, one of the grandest views in the Highlands. It really was a bonus to have this crystal clear weather. We stood there breathless from the grandeur of it, and eventually had to force ourselves onwards to complete the horseshoe that lay in front of us.

A careful descent from Tom na Gruagaich

was necessary, a steep bit of rough scrambling that caused us to shift our attention from the view to the more immediate terrain. A steepish climb pulls easily up onto the summit of the mountain, Sgurr Mhor, at 3232ft (985m) above sea level. Just below the summit the hillside is split by an immense rockfall of what must have been cataclysmic proportions. The rubble of it lies in the corrie floor below, great acres of boulders, rocks, and scree creating a mini-landscape of utter devastation, a testament to the powers of nature. What a sight that must have been. It's difficult to imagine what must have caused it. A lightning strike perhaps? It could have been simply the erosion caused by running water undermining the basic stability of the rock, or perhaps as has been suggested, the erroneous flick of Auld Nick's tail as he pursued a devilish quarry over the wild hills of Torridon? Whatever the cause, it never fails to impress, and you wander on your way in wonder, and in some considerable relief that you weren't camping below when it happened . . .

After Sgurr Mhor, the challenge of the Horns is taken up, a trio of enormous sandstone pinnacles built up like Cyclopean pancakes. Either enjoy the scramble over their crests, or bypass the most exposed of them by a track which scours round their southern flanks. My companion Bess isn't too keen about scrambling which I suppose is understandable since she has four legs to contend with, and she lets go with an almighty din of barking and whining whenever she becomes cragfast. So, for her sake, we usually compromise. Some easy scrambling, and some easy walking, over and around the Horns, ease us gently off the ridge, and back onto the lochan splattered moorland and the track to Coire Mhic Nobuil.

This track which runs down from the Bealach a Chomhlais is often muddy, passing as it does a fair acreage of bog, but by way of consolation it does offer superb views behind into the clenched corrie of Beinn Alligin.

We were particularly fortunate with the weather, for as we reached this track great black clouds came billowing out of the west, blotting the sun-speckled hills with that anonymous shroud of grey. But we didn't care for we had had the best of it. At last we had seen Alligin sparkle, a magnificent jewel in the crown that is Torridon.

SANDWOOD BAY (Highland Region)
by Cameron McNeish

Looking south from the cliffs above Sandwood Bay, a rugged coastline above the green swell of the Atlantic. (Photo: Cameron McNeish)

Distance: 6 miles (10 km).
Ascent: Negligible.
Start/Finish: Turning area at the end of the track from Blairmore near Oldshoremore.
Maps: OS 1:50,000 Sheet 9.
Summary: A magnificent short walk on fairly easy terrain.

Points of Interest: Sandwood Bay is one of the most magnificent bays in Scotland. The feeling of remoteness is powerful. Am Buachaille, the sea stack at the south end of the bay has interesting rock climbing associations and is worth a visit. Sandwood Cottage is allegedly haunted.

There is an element of the very north-west of Scotland that I find almost impossible to describe. I can tell you about the impressive cliff scenery and the relentless pounding of Atlantic surf on great lonely beaches; I can tell you about the bare moorland and the bird sounds that keep you company; I can tell you about raucous gulls and cheeky seals and otters which emerge from translucent green waters to play on rocky strands; and I can tell you tales of mermaids and ghosts of long-dead sea captains. I can tell you all these things and never actually touch on the real character of this lonely corner of Scotland. I can only urge you to go there and experience it for yourself.

Sandwood Bay lies several miles south of Cape Wrath, the most north-westerly point on the Scottish mainland. The bay itself is an extremely wide one and boasts a mile of beach, backed by a range of marram grass-covered sand dunes. North and south of the bay high sea cliffs face the vagaries of the Minch and the Atlantic gales and behind them, vast areas of rolling Sutherland moorland.

At the south-western end of the bar a 300ft (90m) high sea stack rises from the sea. This is Am Buachaille, a great spire of red sandstone first climbed in the sixties by the late Dr. Tom Patey, the late Ian Clough, and John Cleare.

Behind the beach and the sand dunes lies a freshwater loch, Sandwood Loch, a great favourite of fishermen, and sitting above it, Sandwood Cottage, more of which later.

So there it is, in many ways little different from countless bays all around the storm-lashed coast of Scotland. But there is something else about Sandwood Bay that has attracted me back on numerous occasions. Sandwood Bay is one of those very special atmospheric places: so much so that there are those who claim it is the principal hauling up place in Scotland for mermaids. You may smile, but a local shepherd, Sandy Gunn, was walking his dogs on the marram sand dunes when he saw the figure of a woman on a rocky strand which runs into the sea from the middle of the beach. He claims the figure was a mermaid.

There are also tales of hauntings, in particular that of a black-bearded sailor who reputedly walks up and down the beach wearing a cap and a blue reefer jacket. Sailors at sea and fishermen claim to have seen him on a number of occasions and believe that perhaps he was shipwrecked here at one time. Indeed the Scottish writer Seton Gordon tells of walking to Sandwood Bay in the twenties and of how astonished he was at the number of wrecks which littered the beach. They were old vessels he believed, lost on this coast before the building of the Cape Wrath lighthouse a hundred years before. Indeed he posed the question whether or not there could be Viking longboats buried in the sand. It was the Vikings who gave the name to the place, from Sand-Vatn or Sand-Water.

It isn't a long walk into Sandwood Bay. Take the Oldshoremore road beyond Kinlochbervie and drive to the tiny hamlet of Blairmore. A hand-painted sign by the roadside points out the direction of Sandwood Bay, four miles distant. However, if you are

prepared to risk your car suspension, a very rough track will take you two miles along that route, before the track dwindles into a very rough footpath.

It would be very easy to dismiss this rough walk into Sandwood Bay as being dull and possibly boring, especially on a grey overcast day. At first glance there is little more than monotonous moorland dotted here and there with the ubiquitous lochans, but when you stop, look and listen, there are delights galore.

On a recent visit we arrived at the start of the footpath in a deluge, and we were rather discouraged by the grey mists and general dourness of the day. However, once away from the comfortable temptations of the car things brightened up considerably. Chacking wheatears appeared to be everywhere, and we were excited to see black-throated divers on one of the lochans. Skylarks provided a background symphony and a pair of croaking ravens followed us at a distance.

In many ways the apparent dullness of this 2-mile (3km) walk into Sandwood Bay acts as a complete contrast to the bay itself. From the uniform greens of the moorland the eye is taken by the pale yellow sand and the white fringe of the surf as it breaks on the beach. On a good day the vast sea will reflect the blue of the sky, and on an overcast day the waters become brilliant green which matches the verdant green of the marram grass of the dunes.

As you begin to drop down towards the bay, you'll pass the remains of an old cottage, claimed at one time to have been the most isolated house in all Scotland. It's nowadays used largely by anglers and walkers as a bothy, and it's claimed to be haunted. Yes, you've guessed it, the place is haunted by a black-bearded sailor.

A few years ago a young man from Edinburgh had been enjoying a walking holiday in the North-West, and he spent the last night of his holiday alone in Sandwood Cottage. As a memento of the most isolated house in Scotland, he took a piece of wood from the staircase home with him and presented it to his mother. Shortly after, strange things began to happen in their home. At odd times during the day and night the mother claimed to smell the odour of strong drink and tobacco, and she had the distinct feeling that someone was in the room with her. On one occasion she woke in the middle of the night and could quite clearly see the outline of a figure standing in her bedroom; the figure was that of a bearded man wearing a cap. Apparently it was some time before she heard the tales of Sandwood Bay and could associate

pale grey monolith rising from a flat sea. The cliffs to the north appeared to evaporate in various shades of grey towards Cape Wrath and there was a stillness over the place that I'd never experienced before. I sat on the rocky strand and soaked it in, feeling the loneliness penetrate my very being, not an unpleasant loneliness, but rather a great peace. The steady, impetuous surge and suck of the outgoing tide mesmerised me and overhead common gulls hung in the slight breeze. A small company of ringed plovers paraded on the flat rocks, and in the near distance great clouds of fulmer petrels crowded the sea cliffs.

Rather than return to the car by the way I had come, I took to the sea cliffs to the south-west of the bay, and followed the crumbling edge and the purple thrift. As I came closer to the sea stack I began to realise what a superb climb it must have been. Nylon slings and old ropes still adorn the summit rocks of it, the remnants of many abseils as climbers have completed their adventure. Fulmars nest on the red sandstone ledges like the residents of high-rise flats, and their noise can be deafening when the wind is right.

A well-worn sheep track runs south along the cliff edge, and gives fabulous views down into the next bay, not a sandy one like Sandwood, but rocky and rough, the green waters glinting and contrasting with the black cliffs.

Follow these cliff edges south to the foot of this bay, until you come across an obvious stream. This flows from Loch a'Mhuilinn, close to where you have parked your car and while it offers a fairly rough return to our starting place, it does make a round walk of the route.

I hope, like me, as you leave this place you will be aware of leaving a small part of yourself behind. I don't know anyone who has visited Sandwood Bay without swearing to return. Return you must, because this place simply takes a grip on your very soul.

Am Buachaille, the Shepherd. This imposing sea stack was first climbed in the sixties by Tom Patey, John Cleare and Ian Clough and today still offers a fine challenge to rock climbers. (Photo: Cameron McNeish)

the strange goings-on in her home with that lonely cottage at the edge of Sandwood Loch.

You don't really appreciate the size and spaciousness of Sandwood Bay until you have dropped down from the hill, crossed the sand dunes, and set foot on the beach itself. It is immense, and feels incredibly lonely.

On that recent visit I mentioned, a thin mist hung over the broad expanse of the bay, and at its southern end the slim sea stack of the Herdsman, Am Buachaille, just appeared as a

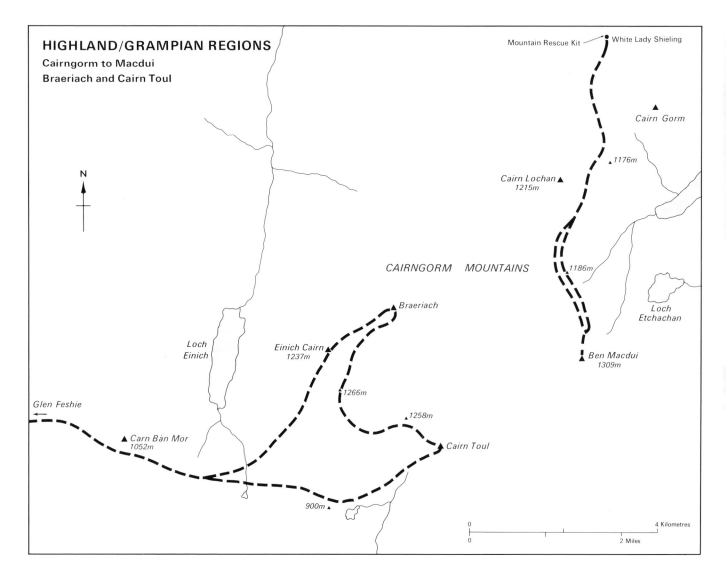

HIGHLAND/GRAMPIAN REGIONS
Cairngorm to Macdui
Braeriach and Cairn Toul

N

Mountain Rescue Kit — • White Lady Shieling

▲ Cairn Gorm

▲ 1176m

Cairn Lochan ▲
1215m

CAIRNGORM MOUNTAINS

1186m

Loch
Etchachan

▲ Braeriach

Einich Cairn ▲
1237m

1266m

▲ Ben Macdui
1309m

Loch
Einich

1258m ▲

Glen Feshie
←

Cairn Toul

▲ Carn Bàn Mor
1052m

900m ▲

0 — 4 Kilometres
0 — 2 Miles

Map to show the following 2 walks: Cairngorm to Macdui (p109) and Braeriach and Cairn Toul (p115).

The 6-mile walk from Cairngorm to Macdui is a straightforward walk to Britain's second highest mountain, over the Cairngorm Plateau. Good navigational skills are necessary and it is a serious walk in winter.

Braeriach is the third highest mountain in Britain and Cairn Toul, the fourth highest. This 18-mile walk is a long, hard mountain walk in remote country that becomes a very serious proposition in winter.

CAIRNGORM TO MACDUI (Highland/ Grampian Regions) by Cameron McNeish

Loch Avon from the edge of the Cairngorm Plateau. (Photo: Cameron McNeish)

Distance: 6 miles (9¹/₂km).
Ascent: 2500ft (760m).
Start/Finish: Cairngorm chairlift car park.
Maps: OS 1:50,000 Sheet 36.
Summary: A straightforward walk to Britain's second highest mountain over the Cairngorm plateau. Good navigational skills are desirable, particularly when the weather is misty. A serious walk in winter.

Points of Interest: The Cairngorm plateau is an Arctic environment with associated wildlife. Look out for reindeer, dotterel, snow bunting, ptarmigan and the occasional golden eagle.

The Cairngorms have suffered much in the past couple of decades, and as a result have been the victim of a bad press. Scene of a tragic accident in 1971 involving a large school party from Edinburgh; scene of high-level bulldozed roads which have gouged their way far into the fastness of the eastern massifs; scene of an expanding and aggressive ski development which erupted in the mid-fifties and goes on sprouting pylons, car parks, snow fencing and other unsightly paraphernalia; scene of general over-use, helicopters and tourism on a grand scale . . .

And yet, despite it all, despite the unmiti-

gated assaults by those who see cash before beauty, these big, wonderfully Arctic hills remain aloof. Despite a quarter of a century of attack, man has only succeeded in spoiling a corner of this wonderland. There is still much that is grand.

Ben Macdui is not only the highest of these Cairngorm hills, it is also one of the most central points in the range, and as such, offers a good introduction to all things Cairngorm. Standing at a height of 4300ft (1310m) above sea level, Macdui is second only in height to Ben Nevis (4406ft, 1343m). For a number of years it was believed that Macdui was in fact the highest, until a survey early in this century discovered a few more feet on Ben Nevis. Macdui supporters were displeased, and threatened to build a huge tower on the summit of Macdui to lift it above its western usurper. Thankfully they didn't.

The Cairngorms are high hills of course, having more upland areas over 2000ft, 3000ft, and 4000ft than anywhere else in the country. These are indeed big and Arctic hills with a spaciousness unknown anywhere else in Britain. Snow lies up here longer than anywhere else, and indeed there is a snow patch in the An Garbh Coire of Braeriach which has only melted two or three times this century.

Because of its central situation, Ben Macdui can be reached from the north or the south, from Aviemore or from Braemar. I have chosen to describe it from the north, for that is also the starting point for our next walk, Braeriach and Cairn Toul. I am also hypocritical enough to suggest that you start from the car park at the ski grounds high on Cairngorm. Robbed of its white cloak and colourfully clad skiers, Coire Cas of Cairngorm is a dull and depressing place, but thankfully you can escape from it quickly enough. Take the path from the bottom of the car park, and follow it around the foot of the Fiacaill Choire Chais and to where the Allt Coire an t-Sneachda rushes down from its broad corrie.

Already you will feel something of the Cairngorm character. Even at this stage you may well have heard the croaky call of the ptarmigan, the Arctic grouse which inhabits these high corries. Speckled grey in summer and autumn, these plump birds change to pure white in winter and are a regular companion on any Cairngorm jaunt.

A rough path now follows the Allt Coire an t-Sneachda up into the corrie, first through rock and heather, then through broad heath areas before leading you into a jumble of huge granite rocks in the corrie basin. No doubt you will wonder where to go from here, for it looks as though you are hemmed in on three sides by high rocky cliffs, but a track, appropriately known locally as the Goat Track, finds a weakness through the cliffs and lifts you up onto the Cairngorm–Macdui plateau.

It's a good pull up out of Coire an t-Sneachda, finishing on a series of zigzags where the rock is loose and there is always the danger of knocking boulders onto those behind you. A fair amount of care is required, but the situation of the path is a very fine one indeed.

Once on the plateau, a well-worn track runs around the broad slopes of Cairn Lochan towards the high level tarn called Lochan Buidhe, the highest named lochan in the country. This is a fine stretch. The walking is easy and flat and is all above 3500ft. This is the land of the dotterel and the snow bunting, the Arctic tundra where you can even see the occasional reindeer. Away to the south-east Lochnagar lifts its royal peak above the lower hills of Balmoral, and closer at hand the tor-studded whaleback of Beinn Mheadhoin (try Ben Vane) rises from the Loch Avon trench with its odd pimples of granite, celebrated in the old Scots song, Kate Dalrymple:

Snivel in her talk had Kate Dalrymple
Wiggle in her walk had Kate Dalrymple
Many a Cornellian and Cairngorm pimple
Was a hangin' frae the craggy face o' Kate
Dalrymple

Lochan Buidhe is a good place to sit for a few moments. Here the skies are wide and vast and it's hard to quite grasp that you are so high, but it's this very feature of the Cairngorms that makes it so special. The vastness of it can almost frighten. Imagine it in winter when the ground is covered in thick snow, when the mist is down and a wind tugs and pulls at you. It's a very different story then and sometimes even the greatest navigational skills and all the survival knowledge in the world won't protect you from possible tragedy. A Cairngorm storm is a frightening thing and these hills demand respect.

The contrast between the good and the bad is vast. On a good day there is almost a benevolence in the air. You can feel it, enjoy the holiday mood of it. On those days there is nowhere else to be but high in the Cairngorms.

As you start on the rocky slopes to Macdui from the lochan, the other big hills of the western massif come into view: Cairn Toul, Sgor an Lochain Uaine (Angel's Peak) and Braeriach, the subject of our next walk. These high hills form the walls of the An Garbh Coire (the big rough corrie), one of the finest corries in Scotland.

Facing page: **The cliffs of Coire an Lochan; beware of cornices.** (Photo: Cameron McNeish)

Above left: **Crossing the waters of the Feith Bhuidhe.**

Above right: **The Cairngorm Plateau in Summer is still an arctic environment.**

Right: **The white arctic wastes of the Cairngorm/Ben Macdui plateau in winter.**

Facing page, top: **On the granite boulders of the Cairngorm plateau.**

Facing page, bottom: **The cliffs of Coire an t-Sneachda.**
(Photos: Cameron McNeish)

A distant temperature inversion beyond the tor-studded whaleback of Beinn Mheadhoin. (Photo: Cameron McNeish)

After a spell of boulder-hopping, a short sharp pull takes you onto the western slopes of Macdui's north top. Traverse the slopes across the red granite scree, and if you take this walk in early summer you'll come across clumps of purple moss campion. This remarkable Arctic plant flowers amid the desolation of the scree adding a splash of colour to the grey and red granite. The name 'Cairngorms' is a comparatively new one, for these hills were until fairly recently known as the Monadh Ruadh, the red hills, so named after the redness of the granite. Away to the north, across the Spey Valley, lie the Monadhliath, the grey hills, because the granite of those mountains is tinged grey.

Soon you are on the final slope to the summit, a broad wide place with a huge cairn and a direction indicator pointing out hills as far away as the Lammermuirs beyond Edinburgh, and Morven in Caithness. The Lairig Ghru runs below you, linking up with Glen Tilt to form a long and superb pass through these hills from Aviemore to Blair Atholl.

From your vantage point you can trace the route away to the south below the big Perthshire hills of Beinn a Ghlo.

The broad summit of Ben Macdui is said to be haunted by a tall spectre by the name of Fearlas Mor (the great grey man). Several mountaineers and walkers have claimed passing aquaintance with the old fellow, but it's interesting that Prof. Norman Collie, who claimed to have seen Fearlas Mor at the end of the last century thereby opening up the floodgates to other spectre-spotters, was in fact a well known practical joker . . .

The return to the Coire Cas car park can be made different by retracing your steps to Lochan Buidhe, but instead of heading off north-east towards Coire an t-Sneachda, continue slightly north-west, around the broad shoulder of Cairn Lochan and down the broad ridge that forms the western wall of Coire an Lochain. From the foot of the ridge a rough path takes you back across the slopes to Coire Cas.

BRAERIACH AND CAIRN TOUL (Highland and Grampian Regions) by Cameron McNeish

A high-level camp on the Braeriach plateau. (Photo: Cameron McNeish)

Distance: 18 miles (29km).
Ascent: 4500ft (1370m).
Start/Finish: Achlean in Glen Feshie.
Maps: OS 1:50,000 Sheet 36.
Summary: A long and hard mountain walk in remote country. A very serious proposition in winter.

Points of Interest: Braeriach is the third highest mountain in Britain, and Cairn Toul the fourth. The Braeriach plateau, like the Cairngorm/Macdui plateau is Arctic in its environment, with associated wildlife.

Across the deep trench of the Lairig Ghru, the walker heading for Ben Macdui from Cairngorm will be enthralled by the great glacial cirque of An Garbh Coire (the big rough corrie).

Forming the walls and rim of the corrie are the big tops of Braeriach, the third highest mountain in Britain at 4248ft (1295m) and Cairn Toul, the fourth highest at 4241ft (1293m). In between the two lies an outlier of

115

Cairn Toul, Sgor an Lochan Uaine, or as it has become popularly known, Angel's Peak.

The walk from the summit of Braeriach around the rim of this high corrie to Cairn Toul is one of the classic high-level walks in all of Scotland. The blood red screes, the wide open skies, and the views down into the depths of the An Garbh Coire all combine to give it a very special atmosphere. It is also a long day, a walk which takes you into the very heartland of these western Cairngorms, far away from habitation in high-level country which is virtually unique in Britain.

It is possible to climb Braeriach and Cairn Toul from the car park on Cairngorm. That route is a long and arduous one though; through the Chalamain Gap, down to the Sinclair Hut in the Lairig Ghru, up the Sron na Lairige ridge to Braeriach, around the corrie top to Cairn Toul, and then back down into the bowels of the Lairig Ghru for the long walk back to the Chalamain Gap. It's a superb day's outing, but I've chosen a slightly easier day which will also show you a different facet of these high Cairngorms. The approach from the west, from Glen Feshie, shows you the sheer size and scale of these vast hills, especially the

section which traverses the lonely wastes of the Moine Mhor, the Great Moss.

Our route starts from the farmhouse of Achlean, midway up Glen Feshie. You can reach it by car from the Speyside village of Kincraig, by taking the Glen Feshie road from Feshiebridge on the B970.

'I see the ridge of hinds, the steep of the sloping glen: the wood of cuckoos at its foot: the blue height of a thousand pines.'

The words of this ancient Gaelic poem could well be describing any one of a thousand Highland glens but for some inexplicable reason I always seem to associate the verse with Glen Feshie. Perhaps it's the magical quality of the place which stirs the poetic appreciation, or perhaps it's the wildlife which always seems so abundant here, particularly in the upper glen.

Climb to the Great Moss from Achlean in Glen Feshie, en route to the big tops of Braeriach and Cairn Toul, and you'll probably witness for yourself a herd of red deer silhouetted against the skyline. In summer you'll undoubtedly hear cuckoos from the old pine woods of Badan Mosach. In addition the

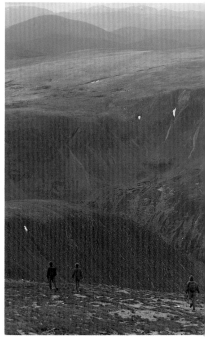

Descending towards the Great Moss, an Moine Mhor.

Left: **The cliffs of Braeriach with Cairn Toul in the distance.**

Right: **Sgurr Gaoith from Einich Cairn across the chasm of Gleann Einich.**

Right: **Looking down Loch Einich from the edge of the Great Moss.**
(Photos: Cameron McNeish)

air will be alive with the oystercatcher call, and the lower hill will be melodious with that marvellous call of the curlew. Not far from the rough track cock grouse will perch on heathery knolls, dutifully guarding their mates which will be brooding only a few yards away in the heather. Their rheumaticky coughs and grumps, not unlike the bickering of old men in a pub, will vibrate in the still morning air. Meadow pipits will slip furtively off their nests and flutter low over the ground in that hesitant flight of theirs, and high above, no doubt, skylarks will fill the air with their appreciative twittering, the most marvellous and stimulating of bird song.

The climb onto the Great Moss is long, but easy enough, up the old Foxhunter's Path and onto the broad shoulder of Carn Ban Mor. Stop and look back from time to time at the views which stretch up the length of Glen Feshie and beyond towards Ben Alder and Creag Meagaidh and even as far as Ben Nevis. Closer at hand the sun will dapple the broad whaleback ridges of the Monadhliath hills across Strathspey and below you the lower slopes of Glen Feshie will be speckled with tiny lochans and pools of water, as though someone has thrown down handfuls of white confetti.

As you breast the broad summit ridge of Carn Ban Mor, you'll be surprised at the vastness of the scene in front of you. The Great Moss rolls on as a high level plain, a great desert of tundra which is home to countless red deer, dotterel and blue hares, a place where the golden eagle hunts at leisure. In front of you Lochnagar will appear between the solid bulks of Cairn Toul and Monadh Mor and the great corries of Braeriach appear steep, rugged and ominously large.

Our route takes an uncompromising line straight across this Great Moss, following the burn of the Allt Sgairnich towards Loch nan Cnapan. It's well worth deviating slightly north-east to enjoy the views down the length of Gleann Einich. The loch lies deep in the trench, guarded by the steep ribs and buttresses of the Sgorans ridge on one side and the craggy corries of Braeriach on the other.

From Loch nan Cnapan walk virtually due east, through the bealach between Sgor an Lochan Uaine and Monadh Mor towards Loch nan Stuirteag, the loch of the gulls. This is a fine desolate place, a marvellous place for a lonely high-level camp.

From here a long pull takes us up the rocky slopes of Cairn Toul on what is in reality the back side of this fine hill. It has been claimed that Cairn Toul is the shapeliest of all the Cairngorms, but it's hard to believe from this angle. In actual fact the name means the Hill of the Barn, which suggests anything but shapely, but seen from Braemar and from the Cairngorms further east I suppose Cairn Toul with its double peak does seem to have more form than most of the other Cairngorms, which tend to be rounded. The name of the hill does in fact tell us that the people who named these hills probably lived in the west, and that makes sense for there were high-level shielings on the Great Moss at one time. Few folk in those days would have inhabited the barren Arctic wastes of the eastern massif, otherwise Cairn Toul may well have boasted a somewhat more evocative name than Hill of the Barn.

But Hill of the Barn she is and she is a cracker. She boasts three corries, Coire an t-Saighdeir (the soldier's corrie), Coire an t-Sabhail (the corrie of the barn) and Coire an Lochan Uaine (the corrie of the green lochan).

The summit is a good tight one, unusual in the Cairngorms, and the views eastwards to the great broad flanks of Ben Macdui are superb.

But the ridge calls and there is still a long way to go. A bouldery slope takes you off Cairn Toul and onto the slopes of Sgor an Lochan Uaine, the hill that shares the corrie of the green lochan. This hill has become known over the years as Angel's Peak, I think to spiritually combat the Devil's Point further south. As you descend its slopes gaze at the great snow patch high in the corrie below you. I say with some confidence that it will be there, for it has only melted completely twice this century. A local legend claims that when the snow melts completely in An Garbh Coire, then one of the Grants of Rothiemurchus will die.

The high-level walk around the rim of this corrie is a good one. Look out for patches of moss campion amid the scree and listen for the song of the snow buntings. Soon you'll find yourself amid the green flushes which indicate the source of the River Dee. High up here on the roof of Scotland this tiny spring produces a stream which crashes over the edge of An Garbh Coire and which eventually flows through Aberdeen into the North Sea, an important river which is famous the world over for its Deeside scenery and the royal connections with Balmoral.

Braeriach is the Bridled Upland, and it's an airy place. Stand by the summit cairn and gaze down the long empty miles of Glen Dee, past the bulk of Macdui and the long ridge of Carn a' Mhaim. Great cliffs of red granite thrust up out of the rough corrie in pinnacles and buttresses and the snow wreaths circle the upper corrie until late into the summer. The summit of Braeriach is actually made up from the apexes of no less than five corries and in the depth of winter it becomes a complex system of snow cornices.

The route back to Glen Feshie is simple enough, but will require some care in misty weather. Head for the point marked on the OS map as Einich Cairn, and then follow the rims of the corries back towards the Great Moss. It's a long downhill tramp, but much of it is on good springy turf and is among some superb scenery. From the Great Moss make your way back towards Carn Ban Mor and the track down into Glen Feshie.

GRAMPIAN REGION

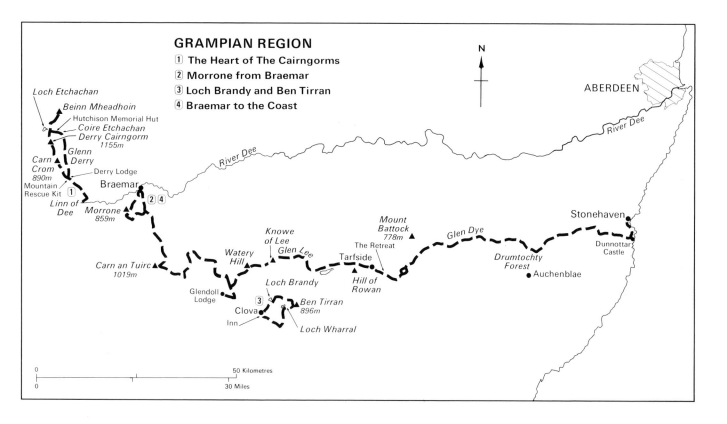

GRAMPIAN REGION
① The Heart of The Cairngorms
② Morrone from Braemar
③ Loch Brandy and Ben Tirran
④ Braemar to the Coast

Map to show the following 4 walks: The Heart of The Cairngorms (p120), Morrone from Braemar (p124), Loch Brandy and Ben Tirran (p127) and Braemar to the Coast (p130).

The Heart of the Cairngorms is a 20-mile walk on good tracks with some steep slopes, but nowhere is the going unduly difficult.

The ascent of Morrone from Braemar is on a minor road and good track with no severe gradients.

The 10-mile circular walk to Loch Brandy and Ben Tirran is on hill paths and rough ground. Green Hill and Ben Tirran are both excellent viewpoints.

The 3-day, 68-mile walk from Braemar to the coast includes a number of 3000-ft hills on the first day. The second day is spent in the hills and glens and the third descends to lower country ending with a magnificent castle and a short walk to the coast. Includes every type of terrain.

THE HEART OF THE CAIRNGORMS
(Grampian Region) by Roger Smith

A rock tor on the summit plateau of Beinn Mheadhoin.
(Photo: Roger Smith)

Distance: 20 miles (32km).
Ascent: 4000ft (1200m).
Start/Finish: Car park at Linn o'Dee.
Maps: OS 1:50,000 Sheets 43 and 36.
Summary: Walk in and out on good tracks. Central part of walk on hill paths and rough ground. Steep slopes on Beinn Mheadhoin but going is nowhere unduly difficult.

Points of Interest: Pine forest in Glen Derry; Choire Etchachan; ascent of Beinn Mheadhoin with 26ft/8m rock tor on summit; fine views from here and from Derry Cairngorm ridge on walk out; birdlife includes ptarmigan; likely to see large herds of deer in Glen Derry.

It is difficult for me to summarise my feelings about the Cairngorms. This great mountain range, which includes the largest area of land over 4000ft (1290m) in Britain, draws me back time after time, and never lets me down. If there is chemistry between people who are attracted to each other, than I believe there can certainly be chemistry between people and places.

So it is with me and the Cairngorms. Every aspect of the area delights and deeply satisfies me: the supremely beautiful glens with their pinewoods, the lochs at the glenheads or in remote mountain corries, the magnificent cliffs often encircling those lochs, and the hill summits: all are of the highest quality of mountain scenery. In all this grandeur, no area better summarises the appeal of the Cairngorms than Loch Avon and the hills around it. That is the prospect awaiting anyone who tackles the walk described here.

For choice, I would always approach the Cairngorms from the Braemar side rather than from Aviemore. The northern approach is spoiled for me by man's intrusions: roads, buildings and skitows, and the large numbers of people they bring, dull the magic. On the Braemar side it is different. There are still people, though not so many, but the main difference is the lack of intrusive structures. I feel it is essential that the area retains its wild character: present protective legislation is insufficient to ensure that it does, and I believe radical measures will be needed very soon. What these measures should be has exercised my mind for long hours while walking the Cairngorm glens and hills. I don't pretend to have all the answers, but I'll suggest one idea later in this chapter.

But now we should return to the walk. What a walk it is too. It penetrates deep into the heart of the Cairngorms, to a summit which cannot be claimed without substantial effort, approached by one of the area's finest passes and taking in on the return a splendid long mountain ridge.

The walk starts from the car park a little east of the Linn o'Dee, 6 miles (9½km) by road from Braemar. The Linn itself is worth looking at: a boiling race of water foaming under the old bridge, it is impressive at any time but when the snowmelt spates are running its power is awesome. In season you can see salmon and trout fighting the current as they make their way upstream to spawn, and if you are very lucky you may even see an otter in the area.

From the car park, walk east along the road for a quarter of a mile to the start of the track heading north to Derry Lodge. Turning on to this track is for me a moment of pure magic: here the hill day really begins. The four-mile stretch to Derry Lodge is a wonderful walk, despite much felling having taken place. There has been planting too, but it is sad to see so many of the old pines gone. The flats of Glen Derry are a favourite place for deer to assemble, and you will often see groups of two or three hundred gathered here to feed and rest.

After a walk of an hour or so, you enter a wood of magnificent mature pines surrounding Derry Lodge. The lodge, a fine Victorian building once much used by shooting parties, has fallen into disrepair in recent times and now presents a rather sad picture. It was rented by the Cairngorm Club for a while and I would like nothing more than to see it put back into working use. This seems to be an unlikely prospect, however.

Just past the lodge is a hut with a public telephone on the wall: placed here of course for mountain rescue purposes but still looking a little incongruous in this setting! A few yards further on a footbridge crosses the Derry Burn. This a real crossing of ways too. Ahead lies Glen Derry, the Lairig an Laoigh pass and the hills we are aiming to conquer. Westward is the approach to the other great pass through the Cairngorms, the Lairig Ghru. Not surprisingly, an informal campsite has sprung up here, and on a visit in late June 1987 I counted no fewer than fifteen tents pitched on the short turf. It is certainly a splendid site.

Our way lies ahead, over the footbridge and through the glory of the pines in lower Glen Derry. All this area is within the Cairngorms National Nature Reserve, one of the first established, in 1954, and now the largest in Britain. To walk through the pines here is to experience in microcosm what the old Caledonian Forest must have been like. Fenced areas indicate regeneration experiments, and it is to be hoped that the trees will eventually spread back higher up the glen. There is of course much wildlife, especially birds, and an interesting if rather mundane feature is a colony of black rabbits!

In about a mile and a half the trees thin out and the burn is recrossed by another footbridge, provided by the Nature Conservance Council (NCC) in 1959. The scene ahead is one of extraordinary contrast between the flat land of the glen bottom and the wild, rough hills above. Beinn Mheadhoin, our main target, is now clear in view, its unmistakable summit tors prominent. On the visit referred to earlier, I was overtaken in the glen by a trio of cyclists, who left their machines when they could take them no further and continued on foot. A sturdy bike can be a distinct advantage in the Cairngorms, with so many of the long approaches having reasonably surfaced tracks and paths.

A further 2 miles (3km) on up the glen is another parting of the ways. Many walkers will go straight on, using the Lairig an Laoigh (pass of the cattle) to go through to Glenmore. The path rises to over 2500ft (750m) on the slopes of Bynack Mor but despite this was certainly used as a drove route to get cattle through to Deeside on their way to the south.

Our walk leaves the Lairig to go left into the austere grandeur of Coire Etchachan, which climbs 1000ft (300m) to its loch, the highest in the Cairngorms and in a wonderfully remote situation. Partway up the corrie is the Hutchison Memorial Hut, a simple mountain shelter erected in 1954. Many people have been grateful for it in the past thirty years. The ferocity and unreliability of Cairngorm weather is notorious: a friend of mine once used the Hutchison Hut on the first day of October after his tent had been ripped to shreds by a 100mph-plus gale up by the loch. A week before the hills had basked in summer heat . . .

On reaching the loch, hop across the burn at its outflow (usually quite straightforward) and turn north to start the climb on to Beinn Mheadhoin. The name is one of those Gaelic puzzlers which actually turns out be quite simple—it's pronounced 'Vane' and means 'the middle hill'. Diligent study of the maps will reveal quite a number of similarly-named hills in Scotland, though none is as outstanding as this one either in setting or appearance.

The first part of the climb is a stiff pull but there's every excuse for stopping to admire the scenery. Across Loch Etchachan the cliffs of Carn Etchachan rise sheer for several hundred feet; to their left are the slopes of Ben Macdui, Britain's second highest mountain, and across the trench of Loch Avon (not yet visible) is Cairn Gorm itself. Underfoot the ground is pure Cairngorm. Anyone at all familiar with this area could be dropped here blindfolded and, once the bandage was removed, know immediately where he was. The pink, rough granite is unmistakable.

So too is the weird sound, between a cough and a belch, that is likely to accompany you on these hills at any time of the year. It is the sound of the ptarmigan, the mountain bird *par excellence*. On my June visit I encountered a hen ptarmigan with a brood of chicks. The young birds fluttered off peeping indignantly while their mother did her astoundingly brave 'broken wing' act, keeping just a few paces ahead of me until I was out of range of her family. If only I could have communicated to her that I meant no harm.

The plateau of Beinn Mheadhoin is a superb place. It has a genuine feel of wilderness with its bare rock and strange outcroppings of tors. It is not quite barren: in corners here and there if you look carefully you will (in summer) see alpine plants such as the saxifrage, defying the exposure and the thin soil to flower for a few brief weeks each year. From the southwest top of the mountain you get your first real view down into Loch Avon. This is one of the places

said to be inhabited by the *each uisge* or water-horse of legend, which carries unsuspecting folk away into the loch to their doom. The setting does nothing to make such stories seem improbable.

It is worth reflecting as you stroll across the stony plateau towards the summit tor, maybe exchanging greetings with other walkers, that just a century ago, on 22 June 1887, an ascent of Ben Macdui undertaken by a party of six people, initially to celebrate the Jubilee of Queen Victoria, led to a decision to form the Cairngorm Club—the first true mountaineering club to be formed in Scotland. Today there are around eighty clubs north of the Border with many thousands of enthusiasts among their members.

You pass several tors before arriving at the summit tor, which is about twenty-six feet high and appears from this approach to be insurmountable. In fact, a cleft on the northern side gives a reasonably straightforward, if still sporty, route to the top. You can't claim to have bagged Beinn Mheadhoin unless you've climbed it! These tors consist of granite bedrock more solid and more resistant to weathering than the surrounding ground. It is believed that they were formed when the climate was both warmer and wetter than it is today, after the time when the whole of this massif was submerged under the ice which carved out the deep glens.

Take as much time as you wish at the summit. It's a fine spot to linger and enjoy the extensive views available in clear weather: the whole Cairngorm scene lies around you. The return starts by going back to Loch Etchachan by the outward route. My June visit provided me with a very good example of how quickly conditions can change. All the way up Glen Derry and on to the plateau I had been sweating in shirtsleeves: on the way back down, although it was still only early afternoon, a chill wind sprang up and I had to don cagoule, hat and gloves to remain comfortable. It is essential to keep such equipment in your pack at all times in the Scottish hills.

At the loch, recross the outflow and take the clear, cairned path ahead. After about a quarter of a mile, when it bends right to go over to Ben Macdui, leave it and head up to the left to bag the 'top' of Creagan a'Choire Etchachan. The summit of Derry Cairngorm is now clear ahead and slightly to the left and is gained without undue effort, though it has to be said that the final climb, over a wild jumble of granite boulders, makes it impossible to get any sort of rhythm. Even in summer there is quite likely to be a snow patch on the col below this climb—an indication of how Arctic a

Top: **Loch Etchachan and Ben Macdui from Beinn Mheadhoin**. (Photo: Cameron McNeish)

descent. It is not a walk to hurry; the views change all the time, east into Glen Derry, ahead to the lower part of the glen, west across Macdui and Carn a'Mhaim to the wonderful group of Braeriach, Cairn Toul and the Devil's Point beyond the Lairig Ghru. Even in bad weather up here—and I've had my share, snowstorms in May among them—I am entirely happy and at peace in these hills, relishing every moment and drawing tremendous strength and refreshment from this superlatively wild land.

I hate to think of anything adverse happening to this part of the Cairngorms. The threat is certainly there, with the management under the present private estates being mostly one of benign neglect. The National Nature Reserve designation is based on a system of agreements which are at the least fragile and at best promissory. I fervently believe the area is much too important for that. I think we have a chance here, given the will, to create a *true* National Nature Reserve, with the whole area owned by the nation. The initial outlay to buy the land might run into millions but what is that beside a priceless part of our natural heritage? Alas, such bold schemes do not seem to be part of our thinking at present. Would that they were.

Such reflections accompany me on my visits to the Cairngorms, and will do as long as there is the slightest threat to the integrity of the area. At present there is little beside the raw elements to disturb the walk down Derry Cairngorm's south ridge to the final 'top', Carn Crom. It need not be scaled: there is a quite delightful wee path on its east flank which leads you safely off the hill to the edge of the pine woodlands and through a fenced area (ladder stiles provided), and thus back to the bridge by Derry Lodge.

Less exotic birds than ptarmigans are likely to be your companions if you take a break here, as I traditionally do. The resident chaffinches are well aware that people mean scraps of food, and are as tame as any town park birds—and no less delightful for that!

All that is left is the walk back out to the Linn o'Dee car park: no less beautiful than the walk in, and if you are like me, you will be taking frequent looks back at the wonderful hills you have traversed and will be vowing to return to them at the earliest opportunity. One wee tip—if you haven't the advantage of a bike to get into and away from the hills, and provided of course it isn't wintry, it is well worth slipping a pair of trainers into your pack. The effect on the feet for the walk out from Derry Lodge is quite magical!

Above: **Derry Lodge.** (Photo: Roger Smith)

climate the Cairngorms has. It is said that a drop of temperature over the year of only 1°C would be very likely to lead to the formation of a small glacier somewhere in the area. A sobering thought.

The summit of Derry Cairngorm commands another fine vista, especially to the south, the way ahead, with the fine southern ridge stretching away into the distance and hazy Glen Derry a superlative backdrop. To the right, Macdui's outlier, Carn a'Mhaim, appears small beside its massive neighbour, yet at 3328ft (1014m) it is in the highest third of the Scottish 3000-foot summits.

Derry Cairngorm's southern ridge stretches for some two miles from the summit, with several intervening bumps to add spice to the

MORRONE FROM BRAEMAR (Grampian Region) by Roger Smith

The summit of Morrone.
(Photo: Roger Smith)

Distance: 7 miles (11 km).
Ascent: 2000ft (600m).
Start/Finish: Centre of Braemar.
Maps: OS 1:50,000 Sheet 43.

Summary: Ascent on minor road and good track, descent on hill path. No severe gradients.
Points of Interest: Summit of Morrone—weather station, outstanding views.

This walk could be summarised very briefly: walk up the prominent hill south-west of Braemar, enjoy the view from the top, and walk back down again. However, it deserves a little more than that in the way of description, and while it is by no means among the most arduous walks in this book, it will occupy half a day very nicely and give a lot of pleasure in so doing.

'Morrone' or 'Morven' occurs frequently as a hill name on the maps of Scotland. Such hills are often conical in shape—or appear so from at least one angle—and easily visible from towns or villages. The name simply means 'the big hill'—another variation of Ben More—and such prominences are just that, the big hill which you see looking out from the settlement.

Their shape and position very often make such hills outstandingly good viewpoints, and Braemar's Morrone is no exception. At 2815ft (859m) it is accorded Corbett status, and it stands well clear of its neighbours. Its ascent is well worthwhile, but before climbing it you can find out what the weather is like on the top without leaving the village. Morrone has a weather recording station on its summit sending regular readings out and these are displayed on a wall panel in the main square just by the post office.

Leave Braemar by Cluniebank Road to follow the Clunie Water along its west bank. The manse, which you soon pass on the right, has a notice saying 'Keep deer out. Please close the gates' which can't appear on too many church buildings in Britain! Before long you reach Braemar Golf Club. Most of the course is on the flatter ground to the east of the road, and a very picturesque setting it has too, with the stubby hill of Creag Choinnich (mossy crag) prominent to the north-east. A little care is needed as you pass the first tee—the drive towards the green goes over your head!

Before you have gone a mile the houses thin out and soon after that the golf course is left behind. There is little traffic on this small back road and with such fine scenery all round it is no hardship to wander along it before tackling the climb ahead. At Balintuim a sizeable spruce plantation has recently been put in but the planting appears to have been done by hand rather than with mechanical ploughing, thus avoiding the hideous scars inflicted on the landscape by the latter method.

Across the burn at this point is Auchallater,

start of the 'Jock's Road' path through to Glen Clova described elsewhere in the book. As for us, the road should be left by the track on the right just after the end of the deer fence, to start the ascent of Morrone. I am rather against vehicle tracks in the hills but this one—put in when the weather station was erected—is not at all a bad example of its kind, and over the years the regrowth of heather and other vegetation has lessened its impact considerably.

In summer you will find an excellent variety of birdlife in this area. Oystercatchers wheel over the burn, their bright orange bills and sharp call unmistakable. Lapwings abound on the lower slopes of the hills, and the white rump of the wheatear will accompany you higher up as you climb. Just after turning on to the track up to Morrone, I once put up six grouse chicks almost from under my feet. I don't know which of us was the more startled!

The track swings right and then back left to take the ridge north of Coire na Meanneasg, climbing steadily all the time. Before long the radio mast on the summit of Morrone comes into view. It is disconcerting to find the track then turning directly away from its eventual objective, but don't worry, the change of direction is merely to ease the gradient a little and is only temporary!

Reaching the top of the ridge brings the first real expansion of the view, westward up the Dee Valley and south to the hills around Glen Ey. Carn Bhac and the two Beinn Iutharns, Mor and Beag, can be picked out by aligning the map.

A flat, stony col leads to the final hump before the summit. At this altitude the soil is very thin and regrowth is poor, so the erosion caused by the track is more noticeable. Five minutes' steady effort brings its reward at the summit of Morrone. The radio mast and associated buildings are not especially attractive, to be sure, but mountain weather is an under-researched science in Scotland and we should not begrudge sharing a few summits with the equipment needed to increase our knowledge. Better forecasting could save lives in the future.

But back to the view. Directly ahead to the north are the tors of Ben Avon and the vast flat summit plateau of Beinn a'Bhuird. From looking in that direction I would advise swinging right about, to keep the best to last.

Thus you look east, down the Dee, and south of that to the fine group of hills around Lochnager, then Cairnwell, then south-west to the dramatic cleft of Glen Tilt, an ancient and still much-used through route for travellers on foot.

West is the upper Dee and the wild empty country around the head-waters of the Feshie and the Tarf. I've wandered through there a few times, and I have to admit that much as I love being in the hills, at least part of the pleasure in that particular area comes in retrospect, when the toil of struggling through deep heather and across seemingly endless peat hags has been forgotten!

But to the north-west of us as we stand on Morrone's top is majesty indeed. The supreme grandeur of the main Cairngorm massif does not merely impress: it almost overwhelms the eye with its magnificence. Beinn Mheadhoin, Derry Cairngorm, Macdui, the deep interruption of the Lairig Ghru, Devil's Point, Cairn Toul and Braeriach: what can one write about such beauty that can ever do it justice? It is a privilege beyond price to be able to drink it in: majestic music in mountainous form that I find very humbling and refreshing at the same time.

The summit of Morrone is a place to linger, especially if the elements have been kind to you. In winter, despite its closeness to Braemar, it can be viciously esposed, and then you can be grateful for the windbreak provided by the buildings up there. It's worth a winter climb if conditions are reasonable, for the views are incredibly fine with snow on the hills.

Before starting the descent, read the notice-board indicating the boundary of the Morrone Birchwood National Nature Reserve, described as 'probably the finest example of upland birchwood in Britain. A small type of juniper forms an understorey beneath the birch and areas of treeless scrub. The soils are calcareous and there is a range of rich upland grassland, marsh and flush communities. The whole complex resembles some of the upland birchwoods in Norway.' You will not, however, find the actual birches referred to until you are quite a bit lower down the hill.

The path back down is clearly visible running off north-east from the summit. The descent is a fairly consistent angle, nowhere desperately steep but still quite demanding on the knees and ankles. About a third of the way down, a group of five large cairns (presumably a marker for those making the ascent from this side) provides a good reason to pause. Another good reason is the fine panorama of Braemar below, the whole village clearly spread out.

Braemar is one of the highest settlements of any size in Scotland, being at just over 1000ft

Braemar from Morrone. At just over 1000ft, the village is one of the highest settlements of any size in Scotland. (Photo: Roger Smith)

(305m) elevation. This and its position at the confluence of two major valleys makes it a notorious frost hollow; frost has in fact been recorded here in every month of the year, and Braemar holds the record for Britain's lowest winter temperature of -28°C (-18°F) recorded in January 1982. During that very cold spell a famous photograph appeared in the Scottish press of a mature stag looking longingly into the window of Braemar's butcher's shop!

But Braemar gets plenty of sunshine as well. Local people hope particularly for fine weather on the first weekend in September, when the famous Braemar Gathering takes place on the showground you can see in the centre of the village as you walk down Morrone. The Gathering is traditionally attended by members of the Royal Family, who at this time of year are usually staying at nearby Balmoral.

Lower down the hill the birches start to appear, particularly to the left of the path. Where the path divides, take the left fork to a seat and viewpoint, with a very fine aspect looking out over the valley of the Dee towards the mighty hills beyond.

From this point follow the path down and to the right, through splendid mature birch and past a small pond, the home of quarrelsome ducks, to the back road into Braemar. Although this walk is quite straightforward—a simple ascent of one hill, starting and finishing in a village—I hope you will agree with me that it is very satisfying. It is by no means always necessary to travel long distances to get the most out of the hills, and Morrone is a good example of a quiet and relatively undemanding outing providing a worthwhile and indeed even memorable experience.

LOCH BRANDY AND BEN TIRRAN
by Roger Smith

Loch Wharral. (Photo: Roger Smith)

Distance: 10 miles (16 km).
Ascent: 2300ft (700m).
Start/Finish: Car park at Clova.
Maps: OS 1:50,000 Sheet 44.
Summary: Hill paths and rough ground. Last part of walk on minor road. Long ascent to Green Hill compensated for by equally long descent from Ben Tirran.
Points of Interest: Loch Brandy and Loch Wharral, fine lochs in high hanging corries with cliffs around. Green Hill and Ben Tirran are both excellent viewpoints.

This walk takes in two magnificent hanging corries and a high plateau with stupendous views: not at all a bad mixture. As with so many similar walks in Scotland, a decent expenditure of effort is involved, but the reward repays that effort a thousandfold.

Reaching the start of the walk is rewarding in itself. After leaving Kirriemuir, the birthplace of Peter Pan's creator, J.M. Barrie, you travel the 15 long miles (24km) up Glen Clova, a glen of sublime beauty even among the many wondrous glens Scotland owns. As you get higher up the glen, the hills very gradually begin to close in, but never oppressively, until you reach the small hamlet of Clova, at the joining of the roads serving the communities either side of the River South Esk. The road does continue for another four miles to the youth hostel, but Clova is your parking place, in a pleasantly landscaped area provided by the District Council and equipped with toilets and picnic tables.

Start the walk by taking the path to the right of the Clova Hotel. This hostelry (formerly called the Ogilvy Arms) is renowned for its warmth of welcome. It is especially favoured by walkers and climbers as it offers them bunk house accommodation with the facilities of the hotel available as needed. There are a number of similar places in Scotland's mountainous areas, and life would be much the poorer for the outdoor enthusiast without them.

The path passes through a venerable iron gate graced with one of the Scottish Rights of Way Society's distinctive signposts. The through routes indicated to Glen Lee is little used these days: we must be careful not to lose such routes through neglect. The path is well trodden and a notice warns that uncontrolled dogs seen on the hill are likely to be shot: this is sheep country. Heed the warning.

The splendours high above are invisible at this stage. In summer the rich smell of bracken will fill your nostrils, and in autumn the heather will delight the eye, both the common (ling) and bell (erica) varieties being well represented on these hills. Before long the path divides. It matters little which branch you take, as both arrive eventually at Loch Brandy, the first main objective.

The loch lies at a height of over 2000ft (600m), and a fair pech it is too before you get there. On the way up you will see a number of shooting butts, used in August and September to bag grouse. The grouse population on these hills has suffered great fluctuations in recent years, and substantial research programmes have been started to try to establish the reasons. Whatever one might think of shooting game, it brings in valuable income to estates and the shooting season should be respected by walkers.

Above 1500ft (460m) the slopes start to flatten out and the fine cliffs that ring the loch become visible. Loch Brandy's setting could hardly be finer. High above a glen which is itself very fine, it adds sublimity to that scene with its dramatic surrounds. The water is rarely still, as one would expect at that altitude. This and the substantial cliffs that rear up, especially to the west of the loch, make it an unforgettable place.

If you have taken the left hand path, you will now ascend the ridge known as the Snub: if the right, the slope east of the loch. Either way you will reach Green Hill, but not, I would guess, before pausing many times to soak up the scene around you. On Green Hill, magnificence of one kind gives way to magnificence of another. From immediate surroundings dominating the eye you switch to vast horizons of peak upon peak, with the whole East Grampian massif arrayed before you.

It is all stupendous. North-west the dominant feature is without doubt Meikle Pap of Lochnagar, almost rudely thrust up towards the sky. 'Meikle' means 'big' and big it looks, though its summit is far below the real top of Lochnagar, Cac Carn Mor. Other summits crowd the northern horizon, and north-east, clearly above all its neighbours though in no way as dramatic as the Lochnagar group, is Mount Keen, Scotland's most easterly Munro—and also one of the easiest to climb, with one of the old 'Mounth roads' going over the very summit on its way from Glen Esk to Deeside.

This is one of those areas which abounds in the most delightful names for features: Easter Watery Knowe, Benty Roads, Cairn Lick, and The Witter are all nearby. Our attention and our feet however turn to Ben Tirran, a mile and a half eastwards across a delightful mossy plateau. At first there is a clear path, but be careful not to follow it too far as it bends away downhill to return to Glen Clova without attempting Ben Tirran.

The view down the full length of Glen Clova is quite outstanding. In clear conditions you can actually see the sea from here: a magnet for those, like myself, who have walked coast-to-coast across Scotland. But our more immediate objective is Tirran's summit, frustratingly hidden by the nearer slopes. The way across is indicated by neat small cairns until the final upslope by a lochan, where a compass bearing may be needed as a check. Like all such areas of rounded, smooth hills, one can look very much like another and a careful check on distance and ascent is needed.

This is one of the areas where you may if you are lucky see that elusive bird the dotterel in spring and summer. It breeds on these high plateaux and in very few other places in Britain. More common but still lovely birds such as curlew, ptarmigan and skylarks share the airspace and add to the pleasure of the walk. On the ground you will be unlucky not to see red deer. In summer the most likely grouping is a hind or two with calves. At first there seems to be just one animal. Then you realise there are more, and still more! Their camouflage is really exceptional.

The summit of Ben Tirran presents no problems but like so many such hills is farther than you think from the map. It is marked by an OS triangulation pillar and is blessed with a feeling of space and the same fine view as from Green Hill.

The descent begins by walking south-west for about half a mile on easy almost level ground to Tirran's subsidiary top. From there you have to get down to Loch Wharral, a gem of equal beauty to Loch Brandy though perhaps less visited. The OS map simplifies the situation as regards paths, showing just one. There are many, so the best advice I can give is to ignore them all and hold your course for the outflow of the loch.

If anything, I find Loch Wharral more attractive than Loch Brandy. It is smaller in size and seems somehow to have a friendlier atmosphere about it, notwithstanding the great cliffs that encircle it. My view must have been shared, as I found when I discovered a metal plaque fixed to a small cairn near the outflow. Its inscription reads: 'To the memory of W.A. Forrest, an English lady who so loved Scotland and this glen. Haste ye back'. With feelings like that I doubt if she has ever been away. Ravens croaked the last time I sat here; not an unfriendly sound despite its harshness.

These high lochs support a varied marine life despite their altitude. Pike have been fished here and Brandy is the home of a rare minute water creature called a diatom which is bright orange in colour. This is apparently its only location in Scotland. Sitting up here you can only wonder at the forces which carved out these great hanging corries and the aeons of evolution which then created the flora and fauna found here today. It is easy to feel something of an interloper; I certainly feel it is a considerable privilege to experience and begin to know such beautiful places.

It is also pleasant to reflect that from here the route is virtually all downhill! From the loch outflow, take the path heading down and slightly left. About halfway down it is joined by a more substantial track, doubtless made for stalking purposes, coming in from Rough Crag on the right (as shown on the OS map). The track continues down keeping close to a burn (not originating from Loch Wharral, this one, but from a minor corrie to its east).

Below you will see the trees in the Adielinn Plantation. Just before reaching it, go right to cross the burn, through a gate, and down by the plantation edge. You are quite likely to see roe deer in the trees, and the area abounds with rabbits. Summer birdlife will certainly include lapwings and curlews, and possibly snipe, with grouse on the hill.

At the foot of the hill, a gate gives access to the road. From here it is a pleasant two-mile stroll back to the car park at Clova. Oyster-catchers wheel and call overhead in spring and summer, their bright orange bills unmistakable—as indeed are their calls. They are not the quietest of birds.

For much of the way, especially in the area of Inchdowrie House, the road is fringed with fine birch trees. They are mostly, it would seem, mature or even over-mature and there appears to be little in the way of regeneration. Birch needs a bit of management. I hope the trees will survive and flourish: here as else-where they add greatly to the beauty of the scene, and birch has proved itself useful as timber for wood-burning stoves in some parts of Scotland.

A well-timed circuit of these two fine corrie lochs and the hill behind—just under 3000ft (914m) but no less satisfying for that—will bring you back to the Clova Hotel ready to accept its hospitality. This is a lovely corner of the world and one that never disappoints the walker. Some of its attractions are clear from the glen—indeed the glen itself with its river is very fine—but the best is hidden up above in and around those great bowls scooped out by the ice so many thousands of years ago.

BRAEMAR TO THE COAST (Grampian Region) by Roger Smith

Distance: 68 miles (109km).
Ascent: 9000ft (2750m).
Start/Finish: Start at Braemar. Finish at Dunnottar Castle, Stonehaven.
Maps: OS Sheets 43, 44, 45.
Summary: A fine walk from the heart of the mountains to the coast, including a number of 3000ft hills on the first day. Every type of going underfoot from the rough granite of the

Cairngorms to half a day on minor roads at the end.
Points of Interest: First day in the high East Grampians, with fine hills and interesting bird-life. Second day in hills and glens with associations with Queen Victoria. Third day in lower-lying country ending at a magnificent castle with many historical tales to tell, and then a short walk into a fine coastal town and port.

Above: **The footbridge above Spittal of Glen Muick.** (Photo: Roger Smith)

Facing page

Top: **Sheilin of Mark Bothy.**

Middle: **Glen Dye Bothy.**

Bottom: **Wild goats at Glen Saugh Research Unit.**
(Photos: Roger Smith)

The stretch of country between Braemar and the North Sea coast provides splendid opportunities for a three or four-day walk that encompasses a great variety of scenery and has a superb climax if you choose to end it, as I

suggest, a couple of miles south of the town of Stonehaven. For there, perched on a cliff, are the dramatic ruins of Dunnottar Castle, one of Scotland's finest and a great place to end a walk.

The logistics of the walk are not overly difficult. If you can be taken to Braemar, well and good. If not, the town can be reached by a regular bus service from Aberdeen, and the finish is on the main rail line either back to Aberdeen or going south. There is plenty of accommodation in Braemar, including a youth hostel, and there is another excellent youth hostel at Glen Doll, at the end of the first day's walk. After that you can either camp or take bed and breakfast if you prefer.

The walk is best extended over four days (actually three and a half) but a long third day would see you into Stonehaven if you don't mind a bit of road-bashing at the end. The country graduates downwards from the high hills of the East Grampians to the more rolling cultivated land nearer the coast. The coast itself is very fine.

It is, too, a walk with an almost infinite number of route permutations available, so don't feel obliged to stick to the one I describe here. I can certainly recommend this route but I can also recommend country either side of it! It is not an area in which to be rigidly bound by written descriptions in books: more a place to wander as the spirit moves you, as long as you maintain your general easterly heading.

Day One

Having said that, you actually start out of Braemar by going south! The first objective is to reach Auchallater and pick up the long-established right of way known as Jock's Road. It's either two miles along the A93 or along the back road the other side of the Clunie Water (described in the Morrone walk). Until recently, the latter was not an option, but a footbridge has now been put in place across the burn, and the back road is certainly a more pleasant walk out of the town.

At Auchallater you take the track indicated by the Scottish Rights of Way Society sign-post. This is a very old route used by traders on foot and possibly also with beasts—and almost certainly by whisky smugglers wanting to evade the exciseman. Satisfactory legislation acceptable to the Scots was not introduced until 1823—up to that date there had been a number of attempts to levy punitive taxes imposed from London—and a well-developed trade with its own ways through the hills knew just how to get round this inconvenience.

The 'Jock' of this particular road is not known for certain but untold thousands have followed in his footsteps, and still do, for it is a very popular walk. Its value can be seen by the fact that, if you are fortunate enough to have somebody willing to drop you in Braemar and pick you up in Glen Doll, they will have to cover a good 50 miles (80km) by car as against your 15 on foot!

It is a beautiful walk up Glen Callater, the hills closing in on each side, and you are on a good estate track as far as the loch and its fine old lodge, a distance of about three miles (5km). Here the route choice game starts. Stay on Jock's Road for the straightforward walk over to Glen Doll? Go left and climb Carn an Sagairt Mor (big hill of the priest)? Or, as I suggest, go right to maximise the fact that once you are up on these hills you are on a plateau and can grab a handful of Munros without too much extra effort?

My rightward route recrosses the burn at its outflow from the loch—an ideal spot for a break if you feel like one—and takes the right fork on a track which makes no bones about where it is going. It shoots straight up a stiff ridge, gaining height quickly and effectively. Loch Callater is at nearly 1500ft (450km) but there's that much and more to be done yet before the first summit of the day is bagged.

The serious seeker after Munros can get as many as ten in a long day hereabouts. Five or six is not at all difficult, and if you follow my tracks on this first day out of Braemar, you will have half a dozen under your belt before nightfall.

The first of them is Cairn an Tuirc (hill of the boar), and it is simply enough gained. The track up from the loch very gradually degenerates into a path which continues onto the stony plateau, with the dramatic scoop of Corrie Kander and its loch away down to the left. Cairn an Tuirc's summit is of course right at the far end of the plateau and it can seem quite a long way, though the final slope is very gentle. From the top there is a marvellous view back over Braemar to the Cairngorms beyond, with the tors on Ben Avon standing out very clearly.

From Cairn an Tuirc it is a simple walk across to Cairn of Claise, with little height lost and excellent going underfoot. You can really stride out on these hills. The latter's name means 'hill of the hollow', though it is difficult to see which hollow is referred to. The summit boasts a fine wee stone shelter where you can get out of the wind if need be. I once found a complete copy of *Munro's Tables* jammed in the rocks here—perhaps it was the owner's final summit and he no longer needed the book?

The third Munro in this group is Glas Maol (bare grey hill) but it is a longish diversion and I would not include it—it is very easily climbed from the ski grounds at Cairnwell on the A93. From Cairn of Claise I think it is finally time to turn east, seawards, though the sea still seems a very long way off on this high plateau.

An eastward march of a couple of miles over undistinguished ground leads to Munros numbers 3 and 4, Tolmount and Tom Buidhe, two very easy summits indeed. This high area in one of the few breeding places of the dotterel, which comes in late spring to mate and nest. This beautiful bird with its brown crown to the head, white cheeks and broad white stripe on the breast is still unafraid of man. They are unusual in that the hen does much of the courtship prior to mating.

Dotterel stay above 3000ft (900m) for much of the time, and in all this vast area you are walking over there will probably be only about ten pairs. The breeding success is less than one chick per pair in many years. You may wonder what they find to eat up here: the answer is insects such as flies and beetles and also plants such as the crowberry. The conservation of these lovely birds is of prime importance: do your best not to disturb any you may see.

Talking of feeding, I once met a man eating a lettuce sandwich near the summit of Tolmount. Perhaps I had better explain. I have had the pleasure of being associated with the Ultimate Challenge cross-Scotland walk since its inception in 1980, and have done the walk myself three times. Another regular Challenger is David Thomas from Surrey, a friend of very long standing. Most people on the Challenge (myself included) cut weight to a minimum by for example taking freeze-dried packet foods. Not David: he's a 'real food' man, and is happy to pay the weight penalty that results. Our paths crossed on a fine May day in 1985 just below Tolmount's top. It was good to see him, and I left him happily munching his salad piece at 3000ft.

By leaving a rucksack between them, Tolmount and Tom Buidhe (yellow hill), can be bagged in half an hour. To reach Glen Doll you again have a choice: right over Mayar and Driesh or left by Cairn Bannoch and Broad Cairn. I chose the latter course, which involves crossing the Jock's Road path at just about its highest point, on Crow Craigies, and swinging north to Fafernie before the short scramble up Cairn Bannoch (the name may come from a type of cake or it may just mean peaked hill).

This hill must be one of the smallest Munros in Scotland—its summit cone rises only a hundred feet or so from the plateau, but for all that it is a shapely little top. The walk continues south to Cairn of Gowal and then swings sharply east to reach Broad Cairn, a deceptively big hill with some awkward boulders near the summit. It commands a fine view down Loch Muick (loch of the pigs), part of the royal estate of Balmoral and nowadays a nature reserve with a small visitor centre at its foot.

Invermark Castle, Glen Lee.
(Photo: Roger Smith)

Near the head of the loch is the pinewood surrounding Glas-allt-Shiel, the house built for Queen Victoria in 1868, seven years after Prince Albert had died. She loved all this country and once took an expedition very similar to the one you are following today. It was October 1861, just two months before Albert's early death and it was their last long outing together.

The Queen's diary records:

'Going up Cairn Tuirc we looked down upon Loch Canter, very wild and dark. We proceeded to Cairn Glaishie (Cairn of Claise) at the extreme point of which a cairn has been erected. We got off to take a look at the wonderful panorama which lay stretched out before us. It was beautifully clear, and really it was most interesting to look over such an immense extent of the Highlands.'

The party lunched at Caenlochan and then returned on their hardy ponies to Glenshee.

Our way however is down the rough slopes of Broad Cairn and along the path to the small hut which marks a parting of the ways. A track (known as the Flash of Lightning after its zig zags when seen from below) slants off to the left to go down to Loch Muick. Our path drops sharply down to the right to the lovely pinewood of Bachnagairn. A bridge erected in memory of Roy Tait, a climber who loved these hills, crosses the burn to join a track leading down the glen.

It is a pleasant walk, especially as the end of the day's journey is near. Near the steading of Moulzie the track recrosses the burn, now fairly wide: it is a wading job but there is usually no difficulty, as the ford is shallow enough for vehicle use. There follows a mile or so in a forestry plantation, a sharp right turn and half a mile back to Glen Doll Youth Hostel, a fine old building set in the trees. If you prefer to camp there is a Forestry Commission site nearby.

Glen Doll Youth Hostel is a great place to stop the night on a walk. The others there will almost certainly be walkers, climbers or cyclists and the 'crack' is bound to be good as tales are swapped. You fall asleep listening to the sighing of the wind in the trees and wondering what the morrow holds in store.

Day Two

My suggested second day is a fairly short one, but very enjoyable for all that. It starts by retracing your steps into the plantation towards Moulzie, but leaving the track to take the Capel Mount path up the hill. This is another old way through the hills. It leads to the Spittal of Glen Muick, but we are only using it as a convenient way of gaining height.

The path climbs steeply up through the trees and still more steeply on the open hill above. Once on the flatter ground of the ridge itself, do not continue with the path as it crosses the ridge and starts to descend. Keep up the ridge to the summit of Ferrowie.

The next part of the route needs careful navigation, and in mist can be very tricky, as the hills all look very similar, being heathery lumps rising a couple of hundred feet above small glens which also all look very similar. You begin to see the problem. Accurate compass work and a reasonable judgement of direction are needed.

Walk north from Ferrowie to Watery Hill (about half a mile). You now have to turn east, cross the hill known as Murley and gain the next bump, Knowe of Lee, a total distance of just under two miles (3km). Provided you hold your bearing there should be no real problem, for once off Knowe of Lee the ground starts to slope away eastwards much more steeply into Glen Lee. Even if you miss the path, once you find yourself on a steeper slope you can find it by going north-east instead of east.

This may all sound a bit alarming, but it isn't really: it's as well though to realise that this is fairly featureless country for a short way. To me a navigational problem like this is great fun and adds a lot to the enjoyment of the day. I once hit the beginning of the path on Muckle Cairn, just north of Knowe of Lee, spot on after working across from Glen Muick, and was mighty pleased with myself. Practising compass work is always worthwhile and you can do it anywhere provided you have a map.

Assuming you reach Knowe of Lee in good shape, head north-east off it to pick up the path running down into Glen Lee. The path goes down a steep-sided glen and is clear all the way. Further down it joins the path from Muckle Cairn and becomes a track running down this very lovely glen. You pass a neat bothy and when the track swings round to the right (south) the impressive crags of Craig Maskeldie rise up ahead of you. A side path leads up to the Falls of Unich—very fine after a spell of rain and well worth the short diversion.

A mile or so further on you reach Loch Lee (described by Queen Victoria as 'a wild but not large lake closed in by mountains, with a farmhouse and a few cottages at its edge', which sets the scene very nicely). By the loch is one of the notices erected by the East Grampian Deer Management Group, explaining to the visitor something about stalking and the need to ask people to keep to certain routes during the peak stalking season. These notices are very well done, and are I believe much more effective than some I have seen with much more intimidatory wording, which simply because of that are likely to be ignored.

At Invermark Castle you join the track coming down from Glen Mark, another very old Mounth route crossing Mount Keen, Scotland's most easterly Munro, on its way to Glen Tanar and Aboyne (a great walk for another visit). Our royal traveller came this way too, stopping for a drink at 'a very pure well called the White Well'. It is now called the Queen's Well and has a sort of cupola over it.

There are only a few miles to go now before the day's stretch is done. You are now at the start of Glen Esk: the outflow from Loch Lee has joined with the Water of Mark to become to River North Esk, which makes its way somewhat more directly to the North Sea than we shall do. Our immediate objective is Tarfside: not by the road but by another old hill track which makes a much more pleasant approach.

After passing, on the left, a car park and the lane to Auchronie (which becomes a track describing a vast twelve mile loop into the hills and out again), take the next track slanting off left, to Westbank. Follow this for about a mile, passing the steading on your left, and carry on along a very pleasant grassy path on the north side of the Hill of Rowan. This path, too, is known to have been used as a whisky route in days long gone. On its route you will find a very old stone carved with a cross: its origins and purpose are uncertain.

Nor have I yet been able to discover the reason for the very large monument that crowns the Hill of Rowan. There seems to be no inscription on it, but it is not untypical of many which were erected in Scotland in the nineteenth century, usually to honour somebody who seemed important at the time. On the sides of this hill, ancient field systems have been traced.

The path rejoins the road at a very sharp bend where the Water of Tarf (a name also found in the Atholl lands south-west of Braemar) is bridged: and immediately on your left is the gate to the Parsonage. This haven has been a boon to walkers and stravaigers for a good many years, and is particularly renowned amongst the confraternity of Ultimate Challengers who make their weary way here each May.

The hospitality provided by Mrs Guthrie to Challengers is legendary. It is little wonder that one entry in her visitors' book reads: 'High point of the crossing—seeing a golden eagle. Low point—leaving the Parsonage'. If you stay here I am sure you will feel the same way.

Day Three

After a night at the Parsonage you will emerge in the morning fit and ready for anything. The coast can be reached from here in a day, but it is a long walk—a good 30 miles (48km), a fair amount of it on metalled roads. I prefer to get most of the way done, leaving a pleasant morning's amble to finish off in relaxed style. But the choice is yours, and if your time is limited then the dash for the sea is certainly on—many have done it before you. I once walked in to Montrose from Glen Doll, a distance of 36 miles all on roads, but I wouldn't necessarily recommend it as a day out!

The day from Tarfside starts with an hour or so's road walking, during which you pass the Retreat, an extraordinary folk museum of the area well worth a visit—though I doubt if it will be open at the hour you pass. On your right, the river chuckles its way along, fringed by fine woodlands, and it is noticeable that the hills are getting much lower in altitide as you go further east.

At Fernybank, just past the telephone box if you need to phone your broker urgently, take the farm track on the left. Through Mill of Aucheen take the right fork and start a long steady climb into the hills. This is pleasant walking indeed: clean air, rounded heathery hills and plenty of birdlife, with the lapwings (peezies locally) yelling at you in spring.

It's worth having a look on the map at where you are going. You're heading for Glen Dye, and the route appears to be straightforward. Sure, it isn't difficult, but the path shown connecting your side of the hills and the other side is very easy to miss, and a check bearing is certainly worth taking. The track you are on climbs steadily onto Hill of Turret, and it's then a matter of keeping a north-easterly direction until you cross the watershed and can see Glen Dye ahead of you.

If you are feeling particularly fit, a north-ward diversion of a couple of miles would enable you to bag Mount Battock, Scotland's most easterly 2500ft hill (or Corbett). There's no difficulty involved, and you can regain Glen Dye by walking over Lochnaween Hill and down the track beside the Burn of Baddymicks. Lovely names, aren't they? Just to the south is Bonnyfleeces, which sounds as if it was named by a shepherd who had done particularly well there.

Once into Glen Dye, it's a longish haul with forestry around all the way, but the track is good. I just hope you get a better day than I did in May 1985, when I ended up 'fair drookit' to the extent that I wondered if I would ever dry out. I did, of course.

The path to Cairn an Tuirc from Glen Callater. (Photo: Roger Smith)

Glen Dye too must have been well populated once, but it is now empty save for the trees and the occasional forestry worker. Partway down there is a small bothy for the shelter of which I was grateful that wet May day in 1985.

At Spittal Cottage, where you reach the Cairn o'Mounth road, you have a decision to make. By the most direct route, the coast is about 15 miles (24km) away. If you have made good time so far, you may feel like concentrating your energies into that one last effort and getting there. If you don't feel so inclined—and I suspect most people will fall into this latter category—you have to think about where you

are going to break your journey overnight and how you're going to get there.

This choice of route is not altogether easy. In front of you across the road are hills which may look innocuous on the map but which will give you a couple of hours of real struggle. One of them, a bit to the north, is called Heathery Hill, you will notice. That describes them all, in fact—and deep heather it is too, not easy walking at all and slow going.

If you're looking for overnight accommodation you can find it in Auchenblae and possibly also in Glenbervie or Drumlithie. If you have the means to camp you have a whole forest to choose from—once you've got into it.

The best way forward, especially if the day is fine, is directly up the burn onto Hill of Gothie and into the forest at its highest point. A steep brae leads down to one of the burns that feed Bervie Water, and in a quarter of a mile or so a forestry track crosses this burn.

Keep on the north bank of the burn (i.e. turn *left* along the track)—if you go the other way you are in for a series of tortuous twists and turns as the track contours round a number of hill slopes. The northern arm of the track gives you a pleasant enough walk of about three miles (5km) before leaving the forest at Corsebauld.

The route from here, if you're going directly in, is straightforward—out past Chapelton and turn left on the minor road. If you divert for reasons of accommodation then the best bet is to get back onto this road in the morning. From here in there isn't really a 'route' as such, and it adds to the fun to have to work out the last bit for yourself. It will all be minor road walking—footpaths are very few and far between in this area—but that is not unpleasant for half a day.

You might go through Glenbervie and Drumlithie. The Arbuthnott family have been lairds hereabouts for something like 800 years, and at the village which bears their name, a few miles to the south, is a lovely little church with a thirteenth century chancel. The writer Lewis Grassic Gibbon is buried there. Or you might swing a little further north, along the road already mentioned which makes more directly for Stonehaven, passing through places with delightful names such as Quithel, Elfhill, and Nether Wyndings.

If taking this latter route, you need to turn off the road at Tewel, to cross the Carron Water and go through the three places called Toucks. Now the coast is getting very near and there is a different atmosphere—a tang in the air that draws you on to the sea and the end of your journey. The point you must aim for is Dunnottar Mains on the A92, a couple of miles south of Stonehaven.

Here there is a car park and a track leading to Dunnottar Castle, perched on a crag high above the pounding waves. What a place this is—everybody's idea of what a fortress should look like. Its history does not disappoint either. In the mid-seventeenth century it was beseiged by troops espousing the cause of Cromwell; at the time the crown jewels and other regalia had been sent to Dunnottar for safe keeping. They were smuggled out by hiding some in a lady's clothing and by lowering others down the crag to a waiting boat.

In 1685 a large number of Covenanters were imprisoned here—over 150 people crammed into a tiny space at the height of summer for several weeks. Those that survived this ordeal, and torture as well, were shipped to the Quaker colony of East New Jersey in America. The Covenanters' Stone at the castle records the event, and it was this stone that gave Sir Walter Scott the inspiration for his novel *Old Mortality*.

There are many more stories about Dunnottar which I do not have room for here. Enjoy your visit and note as well as the castle itself the crag on which it stands—a chunk of conglomerate red sandstone in which the strata have been twisted almost into the vertical by the pressures of the Highland Fault on which they sit. This fault can be traced right across Scotland to Dumbarton on the Clyde.

From Dunnottar there is a good footpath along the cliffs to Stonehaven. The birdlife will keep you entertained, with fulmars, cormorants and gulls all present in abundance. Past Downie Point you are in the original part of the town, known as 'Old Steenie'. The area north of the Carron Water was built in the eighteenth century under the direction of Robert Barclay of Ury. It features a fine square where a plaque commemorates Robert Thomson, who invented the pneumatic tyre.

The Barclays have long been a great family hereabouts. One of particular interest to those of us who arrive on foot was Captain Robert Barclay-Allardice, a famous 19th century 'pedestrian', at the time when very large sums of money were wagered on athletic feats. He is most remembered for his feat of walking 1000 miles in 1000 consecutive hours at Newmarket in 1809, dressed in normal clothing including a top hat. For achieving this—and it meant going without normal sleep for 42 days—he won 1000 guineas. I reckon he earned every penny.

Your walk may not have covered 1000 miles but it has covered some very fine country and given you a real impression of the East Grampian area and the Mearns of Kincardineshire which run down to the coast. It's a part of Scotland I never grow tired of.

BEN VRACKIE AND THE PASS OF KILLIE-CRANKIE (Tayside Region) by Roger Smith

Distance: 12 miles (19km).
Ascent: 3000ft (900m).
Start/Finish: Car park in Pitlochry.
Map: OS 1:50,000 Sheets 52 and 43.
Transport: Pitlochry is on the Glasgow/Edinburgh-Inverness rail line.
Summary: Ascent of Ben Vrackie on good hill path; Central part of walk on rough hill ground; Latter part on good riverside paths.
Points of Interest: Ben Vrackie (fine view point); Killiecrankie (battle site, NTS Visitor Centre, dramatic gorge scenery); Loch Faskally (power station, nature trail).

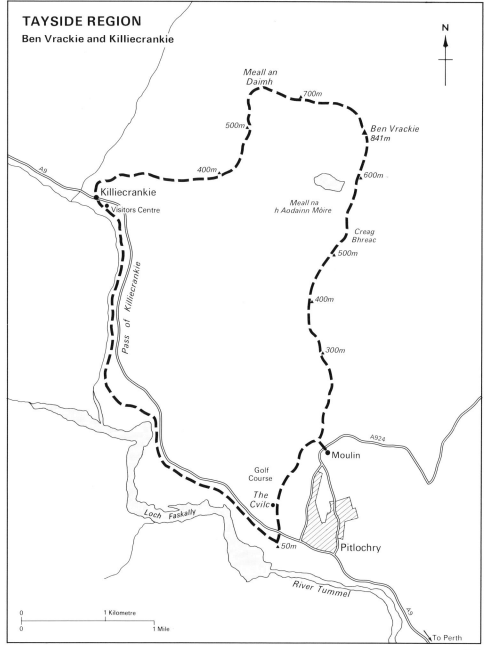

TAYSIDE REGION
Ben Vrackie and Killiecrankie

Meall an Daimh
700m
500m
400m
Ben Vrackie 841m
600m
Killiecrankie
Visitors Centre
Meall na h Aodainn Môire
Creag Bhreac
500m
400m
Pass of Killiecrankie
300m
A9
A924
Moulin
Golf Course
The Cuilc
Loch Faskally
50m
Pitlochry
River Tummel
A9
To Perth

0   1 Kilometre
0   1 Mile

Map showing the 12-mile walk up Ben Vrackie and through the Pass of Killiecrankie. The ascent is on a good hill path, the central part of the walk is on rough ground but the latter part is on good riverside paths.

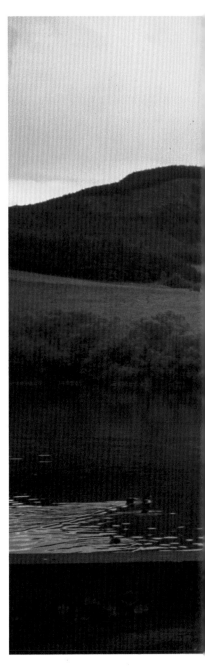

Left: **Killiecrankie.** (Photo: Roger Smith)

Above: **Ben Vrackie seen from the Cuilc.** (Photo: Roger Smith)

This walk links one of Perthshire's most famous hill viewpoints and a gorge steeped in both beauty and history. It provides a varied and absorbing day at any time of the year, though the autumn colouring on the trees in Killiecrankie is particularly fine.

The walk starts in Pitlochry, a busy tourist town in summer even though it has now been bypassed by the A9 Inverness road. Pitlochry is one of those places that grew as a result of the coming of the railway 100 years ago: before that the more important place was Moulin, which we pass on the walk.

Start the walk by going up Larchwood Road (signposted to the Cuilc and Golf Course). The road winds steeply uphill and before long becomes Golf Course Road. The Cuilc is a pleasant small loch at a bend in the road. The resident waterfowl will be disappointed if you have not brought some scraps of food for them. Immediately beyond the Cuilc is a fine little lily pond and then the open slopes of the golf course are reached.

Continue up the road—now a narrow lane—towards Moulin, with Ben Vrackie clearly seen ahead and above. The wooded hill to the left is Craigower, also a fine viewpoint. It is a 'beacon hill' used for signalling at times of national crisis or triumph, and has been owned by the National Trust for Scotland since 1947.

Moulin appears now to be just an outlier of Pitlochry but this was formerly the staging post for travellers, and the Moulin Inn was one of the places where horses were changed on the long and probably wearying coach run from Inverness to Edinburgh. At a T-junction turn left (sign for Ben Vrackie) and note the three houses on the right named successively Craigview, Benview and Hillview!

After a quarter of a mile take the signposted path on the right beside the burn. The rhododendrons here are splendid in spring, as is the gorse, and the trees are a blaze of colour in autumn. In summer fine birches provided welcome shade. Summer is something we have not enjoyed too much of in Scotland in recent years, and it is worth noting that this part of the walk can be rather muddy.

The path emerges from the woods to cross a deer fence by a stile and continues up the hill. This is a very popular and much-loved walk and there is no difficulty in following the path anywhere. Before long a seat is reached. It commands a great view across the Tay Valley and south to the Dunkeld Gap, showing the importance of this route in strategic terms: there is only one way through. The seat is inscribed 'In memort of Terence Toole, RAAF, 1947–1972': a young Australian airman who it would appear was killed in the prime of his youth.

Another fence crossing leads on to Loch a'Choire, a lovely spot at which to pause before the final pull up to Ben Vrackie itself is tackled. The views to the north west up Glen Garry are now opening out. You are at a height of nearly 1700ft (500m) but you still have a hard 1000ft (300m) to climb! There is no difficulty at all in following the path up to the summit of Ben Vrackie but its popularity inevitably means it is worn in places, so some care is needed. But there is no need to hurry and every pause will give you a fresh aspect to enjoy.

The path veers a little to the right and then doubles back for the last pull to the summit cairn and OS triangulation pillar. Whenever I visit one of these pillars I think of the labour involved in carrying the material up there and erecting it. Nowadays helicopters are often used but previously it was all humped up by men (occasionally ponies if the hill was manageable). The cairn beside the pillar carries a view indicator.

It is a view of some splendour. To the north-west the magnificent Beinn a Ghlo group crouch, dominating Glen Tilt. To the west the eye travels far down past Loch Tummel and Loch Rannoch towards the western hills across Rannoch Moor. South

again Schiehallion, the fairy peak, thrusts unmistakably clear. The northern horizon is mountain after mountain, swinging eastwards from the rounded humps of the Monadhliath to the great high mass of the central Cairngorms and on to Ben Avon, whose distinctive rock tors can be picked out even at this distance. It is, I am sure you will agree, worth every bead of sweat expended on the climb.

I have been here in June with swifts flying around me at the very summit. And at the same time as I sat enjoying sunshine on Vrackie, Beinn a Ghlo disappeared in a dark pall of rain. It could easily have been the other way round of course: at no time of year can you take chances with the Scottish hills.

The walk now continues north-west along the clear ridge to Ben Vrackie's outlier Meall an Daimh. If by chance you have done enough you have the simple option of returning to Pitlochry by the outward path: I hope you won't, as the rest of the walk has much to offer and the climbing is nearly all done. It is a delightful walk across to Meall an Daimh, the more so because very few of the many folk who climb Ben Vrackie continue this way. The noise of traffic on the ever busy A9 does disturb the peace, but only marginally.

A short, easy climb leads to the small cairn marking the summit of Meall an Daimh. The views are of course very similar to those from Ben Vrackie but the better for having them to yourself. I don't think that is a selfish attitude. I enjoy company but I also greatly enjoy being in the hills by myself and I have found over the years that even a small diversion from a popular route, such as this one, gives you that solitude if you want it. It's a matter of exercising choice and we are very fortunate in Scotland to have so much choice.

From the summit of Meall an Daimh retrace your steps to the flat col below the top and head south-west to pick up a clear track on the flank of the hill (not marked on the OS map). You are heading for the two small reservoirs clearly visible further down the hill: there are several ways down and no detailed instructions are needed. If it is summer you will very likely have curlews for company.

At the reservoirs turn right onto the rough-surfaced track, used by the Water Board for access, and follow it down to the lane. Turn left and walk down to, and under, the A9, noting the fine pair of stone eagles on the gateposts of Old Faskally House. The lane joins the old A9 by the National Trust for Scotland Visitor Centre, which is well worth a stop. It tells the history of the area and also has useful facilities such as toilets and a teashop which are very

The summit memorial on Ben Vrackie. (Photo: Roger Smith)

welcome at this stage of a walk! The Visitor Centre is open from early April to late October every day.

The walk continues by taking the signposted path from the north end of the visitor centre down to the River Garry and the pass. Killiecrankie is not just a beautiful place but a historically important one. Within a very small compass here are river, path, road and railway and the close confines of the gorge make it an obvious place for an ambush. In 1689 there was just such a battle, during the turbulent period when the Jacobites tried to keep the Stuart line on the throne against the powerful forces supporting William of Orange.

On 27 July 1689 a Jacobite army led by John Graham of Claverhouse, Viscount Dundee, routed a Williamite band under Major-General Mackay here. Victory was hard-won: 'Bonny Dundee' as he was known was killed in the fight and his men, now under Colonel Cannon, were themselves put to the sword at Dunkeld a month later. The Stuart rebellion continued until the disaster of Colloden in 1746: the Killiecrankie part of the story is well told in the visitor centre and it is worth remembering the history of the place as you walk through it.

A beautiful walk it is too back to Pitlochry, along a riverside path which is, in its early stages, by no means flat! Shortly after you join it you pass a splendid railway viaduct designed by Joseph Mitchell and completed in 1863 at a cost of £5,730: a considerable sum in those days. It looks easily ready to stand for another century, and I have to say that it intrudes on the natural beauty of the scene hardly at all, in stark contrast to the massive new road viaduct higher up the hill, which, fine engineering feat though it may be, I find perfectly hideous and totally out of keeping with the small and intimate scale of the pass.

Before long the path reaches Loch Faskally. All along this stretch the combination of trees and water delight the eye and the loch appears a natural extension of the river. In fact it is not, being of quite recent construction as part of a major scheme supplying electricity through hydro power. Clunie power station itself is soon visible across the loch.

The path then rounds Loch Dunmore, where a nature trail makes a pleasant short diversion, and faces you with a choice: left up the road and directly back into the town, or right across the Clunie footbridge to the south side of the loch and river. The ladder is perhaps the more pleasant way.

After passing under the A9 bypass you reach another bridge where you can visit the dam and fish ladder. An excellent exhibition here tells the story of the hydro-electric system in this area—a fascinating topic in itself—and the life of the salmon which if you are lucky can be seen passing up the latter constructed specially for them.

A short stroll from the dam takes you back into the centre of Pitlochry, where, as you would expect in a town orientated very much towards the visitor, you will find plenty of places to refresh yourself and reflect on the walk you have just finished. I hope you will agree that either of its two very distinct parts, and certainly the combination of the two, make it one of the best.

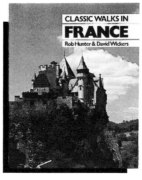

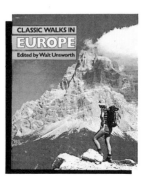

OXFORD ILLUSTRATED PRESS

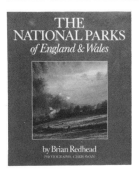

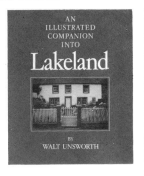

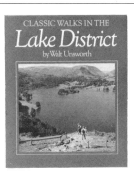

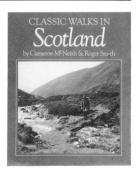

The National Parks of England and Wales
by Brian Redhead
This is a celebration of our 10 National Parks through the words of Brian Redhead and the stunning colour photography of Chris Swan.
A beautiful book that will be given full media promotion.
*Approx 160pp 250 x 205mm colour throughout
ISBN 0 946609 82 9
£14.95*

An Illustrated Companion Into Lakeland
by Walt Unsworth
Beginning with Kendal, this book describes in leisurely fashion all the valleys and well-known villages of this most popular area of England. Illustrated in colour, it is the ideal companion for the thousands of tourists who visit each year.
*Approx 120pp 250 x 205mm plus 48pp colour
ISBN 0 946609 67 5
£14.95*

Classic Walks in The Lake District
by Walt Unsworth
Most of the forty walks are in the wilds of The National Park, but coverage has been extended to include some neglected areas to give the walker an unusually wide scope: from the high central fells to the coast at Silverdale and the gentle river Eden.
*Approx 144pp 250 x 205mm incl 72pp colour
ISBN 0 946609 50 0
£14.95*

Classic Walks in Scotland
by Cameron McNeish and Roger Smith
Forty walks that take you into the most beautiful parts of Scotland – the Highlands, Grampians, Borders, Tayside, The Isle of Skye and Strathclyde. Illustrated throughout.
*Approx 144pp 250 x 205mm incl 72pp colour, maps
ISBN 0 946609 51 9
£14.95*

THE GREAT OUTDOORS

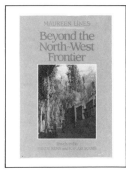

The Hill Walker's Manual
by Bill Birkett
Over a 3-year period the mountain rescue services had to deal with 2,799 casualties and 316 fatalities in mainland Britain. This book, which covers all walkers need to know about understanding the hills, equipment, clothing, navigation, techniques, survival and photography is essential reading for anyone contemplating walking in the hills.
*Approx 140pp 250 x 205mm b&w photos, maps, diagrams, 32pp colour
ISBN 0 946609 55 1
£14.95*

Nanda Devi: The Tragic Expedition
by John Roskelley
This is a story of strong emotion – of conflicting ambitions, of death and victory, of desire and regret. It is the story of top mountaineer Willi Unsoeld who took his daughter, Nanda Devi Unsoeld, to the mountain after which she was named, and of her heart-breaking death on that mountain. This is an unusual book by an outspoken and honest writer.
*240pp 230 x 150mm plus 32pp b&w photos
ISBN 0 946609 72 1
£9.95*

Beyond The North-West Frontier: Travels in The Hindu Kush and Karakorams
by Maureen Lines
This is the culmination of the author's many years of travel in the remote and romantic lands of Pakistan and of her visits to the Kalash valleys where she now lives for several months of the year. A remarkable story by a remarkable woman.
*Approx. 180pp 240 x 172mm b&w and colour photos, maps
ISBN 0 946609 68 3
£12.95*

Oxford Illustrated Press

BOOKS FOR THE GREAT OUTDOORS

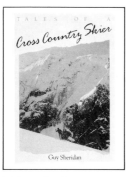

Tales of a Cross-Country Skier
by Guy Sheridan
As an Olympic competitor in this sport and with 16 winters' experience in the Mountain and Arctic Warfare Cadre of the Royal Marines, Guy writes with authority about some of his most physically demanding and enjoyable trips in Iran, the Western Himalayas, Iceland, Britain, America and the Yukon.
185pp 240 x 172mm
8pp colour, line illusts, maps, diagrams
ISBN 0 946609 47 0
£9.95

Tales of a Coarse Angler
by David Plummer
David Plummer is masterly at describing the many different rivers and their settings where he has pursued pike, barbel, tench, roach, rudd, perch and tope. From his own experience he imparts invaluable kowledge on how to read stillwater and flowing rivers; how to interpret fish movement and behaviour and how to understand the various techniques to outwit them.
132pp 240 x 172mm
plus 32pp colour, line illusts
ISBN 0 946609 53 5
£14.95

The Graeme Pullen Guide to Freshwater Fishing Baits
In this useful book are detailed over 20 baits that have been successful for the author together with tips on how to store and present them and which fish you are likely to catch with each. In addition are two in-depth chapters on maggot farming and the production of boilies.
80pp 240 x 172mm
plus 32pp colour
ISBN 0 946609 73 X
£9.95

The Graeme Pullen Guide to Sea Fishing Baits
This practical book tells you where to find the baits, how to catch, store and present them, and which fish you are likely to catch with them. An invaluable and easy-to-read guide for both beginner and experienced angler alike.
92pp 240 x 172mm
plus 32pp colour
ISBN 0 946609 74 8
£9.95

CYCLING

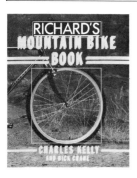

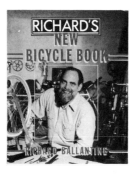

Richard's Mountainbike Book
by Charles Kelly and Nicholas Crane
This heralds the beginning of a new series of cycling books of which Richard Ballantine is the editor. Now that mountainbikes are becoming popular, this complete history, technical guide and riding manual will be essential reading to enthusiasts.
192pp 250 x 205mm
plus 32pp colour, diagrams, line illusts
ISBN 0 946609 78 0
£12.95

Richard's NEW Bicycle Book
by Richard Ballantine
The first edition of this publishing phenomenon sold over 250,000 copies in Britain alone. Now, at last, this guru of all cyclists has completely revised and updated the book and added new material. It is being published for the first time in hardback and with colour.
350pp 250 x 205mm
plus 32pp colour, line illusts, diagrams
ISBN 0 946609 77 2
£14.95

For further details of these and other outdoor books, please request our catalogue from The Oxford Illustrated Press, Sparkford, Yeovil, Somerset BA22 7JJ.

Oxford Illustrated Press